BF
311
.P51913

Piaget, Jean,
1896-

Success and
understanding

DATE			
AUG 19'82			
MAR 1 6 1988	OCT 0 4 2006		
AUG 0 6 2014			

SUCCESS AND UNDERSTANDING

COLLABORATORS

M. AMANN, C. L. BONNET, M. F. GRAVEN,
A. HENRIQUES, M. LABARTHE, R. MAIER,
A. MOREAU, C. OTHENIN-GIRARD,
C. STRATZ, S. UZAN, T. VERGOPOULO

Success and Understanding

JEAN PIAGET

Translated by
ARNOLD J. POMERANS

HARVARD UNIVERSITY PRESS
CAMBRIDGE, MASSACHUSETTS
1978

Copyright © 1978 by Routledge & Kegan Paul Ltd
Second printing, 1978
Printed in the United States of America
Originally published in French as *Réussir et comprendre*
(Paris: Presses Universitaires de France)
© 1974 Presses Universitaires de France

Library of Congress Cataloging in Publication Data

Piaget, Jean, 1896–
  Success and understanding.

  Translation of Réussir et comprendre.
  Includes bibliographical references and index.
  1. Cognition. I. Title.
BF311.P51913   153.4   78–16435
ISBN 0–674–85387–3

Preface

In his rather neglected but interesting *Les Formes inférieures de l'explication* (1927), D. Essertier has devoted a few pages, written with obvious reserve, to the relationship of skill (technique) and knowledge (science): '*Homo faber* will . . . long remain a mechanic who ignores mechanics' (p. 23), for it must be recognized that 'the manufacture of artificial tools was not necessarily *the* primitive form of intelligence and that this form could not, in any case, have been the only original one, from which all the others were derived' (pp. 31–2). Nevertheless, 'the first form of knowledge was, indeed, a form of doing, though it should not be forgotten that the source of the evolution of thought does not lie here, and that this first "physics" appeared relatively late in the day' (p. 34). 'Knowledge is contained in tools. But if we look more closely, it is not from tools that it is deduced, but from the intelligence as such' (p. 35). In short, 'the persistent illusion of continuity masks the very problem of evolution' (p. 36).

It seemed expedient to quote these comments because they show that the combined lights of history, prehistory and ethnography do not suffice to solve the important problem of the relationship between action and thought, and that their findings must be complemented with a psychogenetic analysis of the data. Essertier is quite right to make a qualitative distinction between 'doing' and 'knowing', and also to stress the time lag between them, but these are not sufficient grounds for questioning their filiation. However to reconcile the affiliation of 'knowing' to 'doing' with their qualitative differences, we must lay hold of the underlying transformative mechanism, and this is precisely what psychogenetic studies can help us to do, whereas history or anthropology can only throw light on the succession of, or differences in, level.

v

The first step of our analysis was taken in our preliminary *The Grasp of Consciousness*, in which we drew attention to precociously successful actions, complex enough to suggest all the characteristics of knowledge, or rather of 'know-how'; and argued that the progression from this practical form of knowledge to thought was effected with the help of cognizance, which in no way reduces to a sudden illumination but involves a true conceptualization, that is, a transformation of action schemata into concepts and operations. Now this fundamental transformation is wrought many years after the achievement of practical success because cognizance is delayed by a host of deformations, including the most spectacular 'repressions', as a result of which the subject fails to 'see' easily observable features ensuring the success of his actions.

In the present work, we shall first try to determine whether the autonomy and cognitive character of action are maintained, prior to cognizance, even when the action is not precociously successful but is effected by stages and by means of increasingly complex co-ordinations. Next, we shall look at the gradual reversal of that situation as soon as conceptualization catches up with action, to outstrip it at about the age of 11–12 years, when it begins to direct action and to programme it in advance. Our main purpose is to define the similarities of, and differences between, 'success' as the legitimization of 'know-how', and 'understanding' as a characteristic of conceptualization, regardless of whether it succeeds action or precedes and guides it. With the help of the data gathered in this way, we shall finally try to verify the laws governing the progression of cognizance from the periphery to the centre, and the interdependence of the movements of interiorization (in the direction of logico-mathematical structures) and of externalization (in the physical direction), and also make some preliminary remarks on the relationship between affirmations (or positive elements of conceptualization) and negations, a relationship which constitutes an important aspect of the processes leading from the periphery to the centre.

The topics covered in this book are thus wide enough to justify the publication of a separate work, the more so, I should like to repeat, as the solution of the problems examined is likely to throw fresh light on the fundamental epistemological question of the relationship between technical skill and knowledge.

J. P.

Contents

SUCCESS AND UNDERSTANDING

CHAPTER ONE

Houses of Cards[1]

Constructing a house or a roof of cards, or merely leaning one card against another to form a T-shaped figure, raises all sorts of special problems. In particular, the relative weightlessness and thinness of the cards make it difficult to apply such common physical concepts as thrust, support, resistance, etc. As a result, these delicate constructions throw a most interesting light on the practical action of leaning[2] one object against, or resting it on, another (*cf.* chapter 4), no less than on our subjects' conscious grasp (cognizance) and conceptualization of that action.

In fact, two distinct cognitive aspects must be co-ordinated before such actions can be interpreted. The first of these is logical and intervenes in all comparisons of the leaning card with the one on which it presses down. Next there is a geometrical aspect, bearing essentially on the positions of the cards (parallel, perpendicular, etc.) by which their equilibrium is ensured. Finally there is a dynamic aspect which depends on whether a card is thought to rest on another or to immobilize it by means of an effect halfway between pressure and thrust (9–11 year olds sometimes speak of the weight of the cards).

The child is presented with a pile of playing cards and asked to construct a 'house' (the demonstrator having first established whether or not the child has done this before). In case of difficulty, the child is asked to begin with a 'roof' of two cards and is then encouraged to proceed to various other constructions (including a T-shaped figure with a vertical and an oblique card). Having allowed the child to proceed with the minimum of interference, the

---

[1] In collaboration with R. Maier.

[2] The French verb *appuyer* means variously 'to lean', 'to support', 'to press' and 'to prop up'. (Trans.)

demonstrator goes on to ask various questions about the equilibrium, for instance enquiring what will happen if a given card is removed, and so forth.

Level IA

Examples

PAS (5,4) tries to build a house by placing two cards vertically on the table, one with each hand, transferring both to one hand and placing a third on top with the (now) free hand. He makes several attempts. How about a roof with two cards? (Numerous attempts, then success.) How do they manage to keep up? *They're firmest at the bottom.* And on top? *They hold by the edges.* Does one card hold up the other? *That one, because it's the king.* Can you put up two cards like that (one vertical and the other at 120°)? *No.* Try all the same. (He succeeds after several trials and then adds two symmetrically placed cards (house of four cards).) Does one card hold up the others? *This one* (sloping) *holds this one and that one.* And what about the third? *This one holds that one and that one holds these.* If I remove this one will some of the cards fall down? *Everything will fall down* (false). He predicts that the cards will fall outwards.

CAL (6,6) tries to build a house by holding one card in each hand, setting them up vertically and at right angles to each other, and then resting a third on top of them. Failure. What about a small roof? (Success.) Does that hold? *Yes.* Why? *I've held that one* (1) *and I've put this one* (2) *on top.* Does one hold up the other? *Yes, this one* (1). Why?... Can you add another one? (Puts up a third card at a slant, and rights it gradually.) Could you set them up like this (in a triangle)? (He succeeds by leaning 1 against 2 and 3 against the other side of 2 but leaving a very slight gap between 3 and 1. Does this one 3 stand up all by itself? *Yes it does* (3 does not touch 1). How does 1 stay up? *With 2.* Can you remove one but leave the rest standing? (He removes 1.) Why does it stand up?... What will happen if you remove two? Will both of them fall down, or just this one (3)? *Just that one* (3).

JUL (6,3): Can you make two cards stand up on edge? (He holds up just one then tries to build a kind of roof, but at first without adjusting the edges of the two cards. Finally success.) How does it keep up? *Because it touches.* How so?... Does one hold up the

2

other? *Yes. This one; no, that one.* And what about this one? *It holds it up as well.* Can you put these cards up differently? (He tries to arrange them in a straight line. He fails to build a house even with three cards.) Can you do this (T-shaped figure)? (He makes them touch at the bottom.) (He is shown the T and the roof.) Is that the same thing? *No.* In this one (T), are the cards straight or bent? *Straight* (clearly fails to appreciate that one of the cards is at a slant). And here (roof)? *Bent.* In this one (T), which holds up which? *This one* (vertical) *holds up that one. If it weren't there the other one would fall down.*

Level IB

At Level IB, the subjects grasp that some of the cards must be at an angle.

Examples

MON (5,4) tries first to construct a roof with two cards but at too obtuse an angle, and then a house with two parallel, vertical cards carrying a third card across the top (collapse). She tries another roof and succeeds. Why does that one stay up? *Because I've made it tighter.* How do they keep together? *Because they are together.* Where do they hold? *By the corners.* Does one hold up the other? . . . What if I removed one? *The other will fall down.* Why? *Because they won't be together any longer.* Can you put them up like that (three cards; 1 and 2 at 30° and 2 and 3 at 70°)? (She produces a correct copy.) How does that one keep up? *By the two sides* (1 and 3). Does it stand up better or worse than before? *The same.* Can you make one like this (a vertical card touched by another three-quarters of the way up at an angle of 120°)? She holds them up vertically, then gradually changes the inclination and succeeds. Why does it suddenly hold up? *Because I've made it lean over a bit.* Does one of these cards hold up better than the other? *They're the same.* Do they stand up the same way? *No.* What's the difference? . . . Is it the same as that one (roof)? *No, because that one stands up and this one doesn't* (false). Can you build a wall like that (— —)? (She tries.) Why doesn't it stand up? . . . And can you make a single card stand up? *No* (hesitation, then tries again).

GIL (6,11) succeeds straightaway in building a roof with two lateral cards supporting two further cards (house of four cards).

3

How do they stand up? *Here* (top) *they touch and there* (bottom) *they're held up by the small hairs of the carpet.* Do they hold by the top or by the bottom? *By the bottom . . . by the hairs.* If I remove one (from the roof) will the other ones stay up? *No, we need a second card to hold it up.* Why? *Because they prop each other up in the middle. One pushes against the other and so they stay up.* Can you build walls along the side of this house? *If everything is straight* (vertical) *I can't; they must prop each other up.* I'd like you to make me a corner of a house. (He leans one card against another, vertical, card: T). Which card keeps up which? *That one* (the vertical) *is stuck between the hairs, that props it all up, it's that one* (the vertical) *which does it.* Why? *It holds the other one up, but perhaps the other one does the same.* But does one do more holding up than the other? *It's the first one* (the vertical card) *because it holds better. The other leans. But not this one, so it* (the vertical card) *has a better hold than the other one.* Will it stand up by itself? *No. There must always be two, and they must touch.* Is it the same thing here (roof) as there (T)? *Over there* (roof) *it's the two that hold each other up. But one is not so steep and so it holds better. You can never say which one is the higher one, and it's the highest one which holds it all up.* But is there one that's higher here (roof)? *Here it's the same thing, it's the hairs. Over there, one* (the vertical card of the T) *stays up better, so the other one* (the leaning card) *can rest on it.*

COR (7,7) after numerous trials, constructs a tent (roof) surrounded by a square covered with two horizontal cards (8 cards in all); two cards of the square lean against the edges of the tent and the other two are held up by the first two. What did you do? *I put two cards like this, two like that,* etc. (points to the angles but proffers no further explanation). A vertical card held up by a leaning one: What if I remove that one (the leaning one)? *It won't hold the other one up. I think this one* (the vertical card) *holds up that one.*

It is characteristic of subjects at level IA that, despite some successes (all of these subjects manage to construct a roof with two cards and many follow on with a construction of four cards) they do not mention or consider the fact that some of the cards are set up at a slant. This fact must, however, dawn on some if only for brief moments, since they make practical use of it. Thus JUL, in reply to a question, pointed to the sloping cards of the roof (but not that of the figure T). However, since they do not appreciate the causal role of the inclination, they tend to ignore it. Another remarkable reaction is their failure to distinguish between propping up and pressing down, let alone to appreciate the reciprocal nature of these two effects. Thus, when it came to the construction of the T-shaped figure, JUL assumed that the vertical card alone keeps the structure up, because the other card is 'bent' and tends to fall down for that very reason. This explains why JUL started out by trying, first, to stand a single card on edge and then to put up two vertical cards in a straight line. Similarly, MON at level IB tried to stabilize two parallel verticals by putting a third card across them, or even to make a perpendicular card stand up by itself. In brief, these children seem to assign a privileged role to the vertical card, which is not surprising when we consider that we must stand up if we are to keep our balance.

As for the relationship between two leaning cards that hold each other up (roof), these subjects do not appreciate that both play an equally important role. Thus PAS asserted that the King was the most important element of his structure, and CAL attributed the greater importance to the card he had put down first. JUL vacillated between the two cards, though he admitted in the end that each one of the two cards propped up the other (a fact he forgot in his construction of the T). This explains why all these subjects find it so difficult to predict which card will fall and which will remain in place when a particular card is removed.

Subjects at level IB have made progress in two respects. To begin with, they grasp that some of the cards must be put up at an angle. This advance goes hand in hand with an understanding of the causal role of the slant. Thus MON said that her three cards eventually stood up *because I've made it lean over a bit*, and GIL remarked *if everything is straight I can't* (build the walls); *they must prop each other up*. This advance thus involves a tendency to grasp the mutually supporting effects of the cards. MON said the cards held each other up *because they are together* (but the experimenter had used this word in his question). GIL went further and, for a moment, almost attained level IIA when he explained that *they prop each other up in the middle*. But in the same way that MON still demonstrated her continuing faith in the greater stability of verticals, so GIL specified that despite the need for mutual support, it was the *highest* card, that is the least inclined, which *holds better* than the other, and so also paid tacit tribute to the privileged role of the vertical. COR did

5

so quite explicitly when, his gestures notwithstanding, he explained that an inclined card cannot keep a vertical one in position: *It won't hold the other one up. I think this one* (the vertical card) *holds up that one.*

Level IIA

At this level, which brings a general grasp of reversibility, our subjects assume that once two cards are placed symmetrically, they will have reciprocal effects on each other.

Examples

TIE (7,0) constructs a roof. Why does it stay up? *Because the cards hold each other up.* Which one holds up which? *The two hold each other up.* In the same way? *Yes.* He is shown a T-shaped figure, which he copies: How does that one keep up? *This card is skew and so it holds up* (the other), *the other one stands up as well; they keep each other up, both of them.* Is it the same with the roof? *No. This one* (T) *has one at a slant and a straight one and that one* (roof) *has two at a slant.* How does this one (T) stay up? *The straight card holds up the skew one and the skew one holds up the straight. But that one* (the straight card) *holds up more. It pushes a bit to keep that one up.*

FLA (7,3) stands up a vertical card (2) between two inclined cards (1 and 3), then props a fourth one (against 3). Why does 1 stand up? *Because 2 holds it up.* And 3? *Also* (!). And 2? *Because of 1 and 3.* And 4? *Also.* Roof: *They cling together.*

ALA (7,10) tries first of all to set up two vertical cards with one horizontal card across them. The structure will not stand up *because it's very thin* (not sturdy enough). Next he constructs three contiguous roofs. What holds them up? *One holds the next and that one jams against the ground.* Which holds up which? *This one* (1) *holds that one* (2) *and that one* (2) *holds this one* (1), etc. He leans one card (2) against a vertical (1), and another (3) against the bottom edge of 2, and finally places 4 against 1 and 3: *2 holds up 1, 3 holds up 2* (which is, in fact, held up by 1) *and 4 holds up 3* (another misconception). What if I remove 3? *4 and 2* (contiguous) *will fall, down and then 1.* (Tries.) Why didn't they fall down? . . . And what if I remove 4? *1 will fall because it's straight and then 2 will drop away from it.*

6

FRA (8,4) constructs an angle and places a third card on top. Does it do anything? *It holds up 1 and 2.* He next holds up a vertical card (2) with two inclined cards (1 and 3) on either side of it. What makes 3 stand up? *Because it leans on 2.* And 1? *Also.* And 2?... Does it keep up all by itself? *No.* So?...

SCA (8,4). Roof: *They stand up because they touch each other.* And this one (T)? *Because one of them* (the leaning card) *is propped up against the other one.* And how does the other one keep up?... All by itself? *No.* How then? *Don't know.*

STI (8,7). Roof: *Because they hold each other up.* Does one of them do more holding up than the other? *No. It's the same.* In the T-shaped figure, the vertical card does the holding up *because it's right on top. The other one touches it and the two balance.* Is it the same as with the roof? *No. Here* (roof) *they balance by leaning and there* (T) *they balance because one is on top and the other one does the leaning.*

SCO (8,8): *This one* (vertical) *keeps it up.* How?... And the other one?... Does this one stay up just like that one (T)? *Yes.*

BEA (9,6): *This one* (the vertical card) *holds up the other one.* How? *It's like a wall, and the other one just leans against it.* But how? *That one* (vertical) *stands up and so it can't fall and stops the other one from falling too.* But how is it kept up? *It's got an edge, so it can't slip because the other edge touches the other edge and stops it from slipping.* BEA thus believes that the T is balanced in the same way as the roof.

GAB (9,6). Roof: *The two hold each other up.* With four cards, she constructs *two straight ones* (1 and 3) *and two leaning ones,* first propping 2 against 1, then 3 against 1, and finally leaning 4 against 2. How does it stand up? *1 and 4 keep up 2* (1 or 4 suffice). What if I take one away? *The whole thing will collapse because it has to be propped up from both sides.*

We see first of all that, with the roof, all these subjects affirm the reciprocity of the supporting effects, and when asked, the equality of the actions. When it comes to the T-shaped figure, however, though some subjects do state that the leaning card helps to prop up the vertical, they nevertheless continue to believe that the vertical card plays a more important role. Unlike subjects at stage I, they no longer tend to think that the vertical card could stay up by itself; far from it, many of them will insist that with the T-shaped figure no

7

less than with the roof, both cards are needed to keep each other up. But they do not judge their respective contributions to be equivalent because the composition of forces involved is asymmetrical. In fact, they believe that a force ceases to act under static conditions, so much so that, for these subjects, the inclined card does not so much prop up, as is being propped up by, the vertical (FRA, SCA, BEA). Now this is quite in keeping with the explanations these subjects proffer for the roof: they do not argue that the two cards prop each other up but that they 'cling together' (FLA). In the case of the T-shaped figure, the vertical card plays a more effective role because it does not lean so much on the other (*it's like a wall*, BEA said).

A second notable difference between these subjects and those at level IIB goes hand in hand with the failure to distinguish between 'leaning' and 'holding up': the belief that any two touching cards also support each other. Thus ALA, having placed one inclined card against a vertical one and having added another inclined card, etc., attributed the same role to the superfluous cards as to the necessary ones and concluded that if any one were removed all the others would collapse; when they failed to do so he was quite unable to explain why. FRA thought that a horizontal card placed on top of two cards forming an angle will *hold them up*, and GAB having propped up the vertical with an inclined card insisted on adding another *because it has to be propped up from both sides*. These superfluous measures recall the behaviour of subjects at the same level in dealing with counterweights: when the end of a plank kept in place by a counter-weight supports the end of another plank (in the construction of a bridge), subjects at level IIA tend to add another counterweight as if the first no longer sufficed. Such behaviour, in the case of cards no less than of the bridge, probably reflects a failure to construct models of mediate transmission. From the logical point of view, it might seem as if these subjects had taken a first step towards transitivity, which generally appears at level IIA, together with reversibility through reciprocity. In fact, what we have here is rather a confusion of precise physical concepts coupled to the difficulty of composing static forces.

Level IIB and stage III

At about the age of 9–10 years (and in some precocious cases, at the age of 8 years), the card-construction problem is solved.

Examples

ERM (8,2). Roof: *They hold each other up.* T-shaped figure: *One stands on end and the other one holds it up.* Which holds up which? *That one* (the leaning card). And the other one? *It rests on top. The other one holds it up.* He ends up with four (leaning) walls: *Some support each other at the corners: 1 holds 2, 2 holds 3, 3 holds 4, and 4 holds 1.*

HIL (8,7). Roof: Why does it stand up? *Because they support each other on top.* In the same way as the others? *Yes.* Can you arrange them differently? (He constructs a T.) How does this one (the inclined card) stay up? *It's propped against that one, and that one* (the vertical card) *holds it up.* And how does the other one stay up? *Because this one* (the inclined card) *has dropped on top of it and it* (the vertical card) *can't budge because this one lies on top of the other one, and the other one can't fall down.*

CIP (8,8) constructs a T (but at 60°) after he has first built a roof. How does this one (the leaning card) stay up? *It's this one* (the vertical card) *which keeps it up.* And how does that one stay up? *Because the other one leans against its top.* But how does that hold it up? *By lying on top of it.*

CEL (9,0). T: *This one is skew and the other one holds it up.* And how does the other one stay up? *Because the skew one makes it stay up.* Does this one (the inclined card) lean on that one? *Yes.* And that one on this one? *No.*

VIR (9,3) begins by setting up a vertical card between two packs, then proceeds to set up two cards at right angles, followed by three (two leaning, one vertical) and four (same principle). He is asked to compare a T-shaped figure with a roof: *In this one, one of the cards leans against the other one and keeps the two of them up.* Which one does the leaning? *That one.* And the other one? *It keeps this one up.* And the first one (the leaning one)? *It keeps the other one up.* How? *It puts its weight against the other one.*

DOQ (9,11) constructs a square of two vertical cards and two inclined cards (3 and 4). How does 3 stay up? *It is held up by 1 and 2.* And what does 3 do to 1? *It holds it up.* And how does 2 stay up? *It is held up by 3 and 4.*

LIC (10,5). T-shaped figure: *It* (the vertical) *has the other one propped against it and that stops it from slipping.*

There is a marked difference between these reactions and the preceding ones. The inclined card has come to exert pressure thanks

9

to its very position: *It puts its weight against the other one* (VIR); *it has dropped on top of it* (and the vertical card) *can't budge* (HIL); *it stops it from slipping* (LIC); etc. As for the vertical card, it has assumed a purely retaining function: *It stands on end and the other holds it up* (ERN); and unlike the leaning card it is not held up (CEL). As a result the more complex compositions show a clear and transitive conceptualization of the connections.

At stage III, at which hypotheses are first handled and subjects become capable of co-ordinating inversions and reciprocities and hence of understanding actions and reactions, there sometimes arise curious complications, no doubt due to this very need to introduce reciprocity into physical reactions.

Examples

INI (11,3). T: *That one* (the leaning card) *forces it to stay up*. And does this one (the vertical card) lean against the other one? *Yes . . . The two of them keep each other up by leaning against each other.* Do they do the same thing? *The straight one keeps the leaning one up.* And the other one? *If we took it away, the straight one would fall down, so it keeps it up as well; the two of them do almost the same thing . . . As they have the same weight they hold* (each other up). *If we put them up like a roof they would touch over a large area, but here it is only over a small one.*

    FRE (12,0). T: *The skew card leans against the other one, but the two of them hold each other up*. Does this one (the vertical card) hold up the other one? *Yes. If it wasn't there the other one would fall down.* And why doesn't the vertical card fall down? *Because it's kept up by this one*. How? *It holds it up by leaning against it on top.*

It is plain that these subjects' grasp of detail is the same as at level IIB: the inclined card *forces* the other card to stay up; it holds it up *by leaning against it on top*, etc. But because the vertical card also acts as a support, albeit in a contrary sense, and since moreover the two cards *have the same weight* and must therefore act with equal force, these subjects refuse to accept the idea of a privileged action and insist, on logical grounds, that the two cards *do almost the same thing*, and that the vertical card leans on the inclined one (IMI) just as much as the inclined card leans on the vertical, all the while

10

realizing that the 'leaning' is not the same in both cases. With greater physical knowledge, this insistence on reciprocity would lead to dramatic insights, and it is interesting to note the appearance of such scruples at this level.

Conclusions

In respect of the actions involved, the development we have just examined poses no problems: as always our subjects advance step by step after trial and error and at first without any overall plan. In due course, they learn to anticipate more effectively and hence succeed with more complex combinations. As it is, at level IA, our subjects already succeed in building a roof with two cards and become increasingly adept at constructing the T-shaped figure, which means that, in these two cases, they have become capable of using inclinations to stabilize their constructions.

As for the cognizance and conceptualization of the actions thus performed, however, the part played by the inclinations faces them with a long series of difficult problems. First of all, subjects at level IA try, time and again, to put up vertical structures (PAS and CAL by standing two cards up on end and covering them with a horizontal card; JUL by trying to make a single card stay up and then two in a straight line). Though practice soon teaches them the futility of these attempts, not one of them mentions, let alone insists on, the fact that the only viable solutions are those in which one or more of the cards are inclined. At level IB, by contrast, the inclination is remarked upon and used as an explanation, but the subjects still cannot specify how they have arrived at the idea of reciprocity or equilibration in the case of symmetrical structures (roof). In other words, much as subjects at this level believe that counterweights push down or pull up depending on their position, so, in the present case, they believe that inclined cards lean on the vertical cards, which do most of the supporting.

At level IIA, the idea of reciprocity is grasped in the symmetrical structures, but reactions to the T-shaped figure show that the causal significance of the inclination is not yet truly appreciated even though the subjects see clearly (and often state) that the inclined card can only fall forward while the vertical card might equally well fall to the right as to the left. Now it may well be this very connection between the inclination of the leaning card and the direction of its

11

fall, which persuades the subject that the inclined card 'leans' on the vertical much more strongly than the vertical leans on it. In other words, the equivocal meaning of 'leaning' or 'supporting' which tends to be mastered at this level when applied to balance and counterweight, persists much longer in the case of card constructions in which this physical effect is so much more complex. Even so, subjects at this level succeed remarkably well in constructing T-shaped figures, though they still fail to rationalize their actions. To do that, they must first proceed to an inferential co-ordination, and that is precisely what they manage to do at level IIB: by then they have come to appreciate that when the oblique card leans on the vertical, it is not only held up but also immobilizes the vertical by its own weight, by 'dropping on it' or 'lying on top of it'. Although subjects at state III try unsuccessfully to improve upon this explanation by looking for the common elements of roof and T-shaped figure in the direction of a wider reciprocity, the model produced at stage IIB shows most convincingly that in order to co-ordinate the data yielded by his own actions the child must appeal to inobservable, deductive relations which transcend his actions. In this particular case, he must correlate the relative thrusts of the cards (with transitive transmission in the case of several cards) paying due attention to their positions and directions. In other words, the ultimate grasp of the effects, including that of the inclined card, depends on the co-ordination of the weight with the spatial factors, a co-ordination that generally begins at level IIB (conservation of weight despite changes of shape, vertical descent of falling objects, horizontality of water tables due to the weight of the water, early intuition of 'moment', etc.) and develops further at stage III (vector compositions, density, pressure, moment, work).

CHAPTER TWO

Dominoes[1]

When a row of dominoes is stood on end at suitable intervals, the fall of the first leads to that of all the rest, because its narrow upper edge will bear down on the face of its successor. Here we have a simple model of an elementary physical process, and one that can teach us a great deal about the reactions of our subjects and especially about the way they use it to solve practical problems.

Fifty wooden dominoes measuring 48 by 25 by 7 mm are stood on end. We begin by showing the children two dominoes arranged in one of the following ways: | |, / |, | | or | | (which has too wide a gap). They are asked what will happen if the first domino is pushed over. After checking their predictions, the demonstrator constructs a very long series with two extremes *A* and *B* and asks which particular dominoes will fall down (the answers, as we shall see, vary with the level of development). Judging from their predictions, we could equally well have shown the subjects a series of four elements, or hidden a part of the series behind a screen and asked why the visible elements fall down or do not fall down.

In the second part of the interrogation we ask the subjects to arrange the series *A* to *B* so as to produce a general collapse of all the elements but along paths that pose special problems. The first is a simple diagonal, *A* and *B* being situated at opposite sides of a large virtual rectangle (| |). Next, various obstacles are inserted between *A* and *B*: a 'mountain', or one or two rectangular 'lakes' (15 by 21 cm or 16 by 30 cm), which compel the subjects to construct a sinusoidal path, or an irregular 'pond' which, like the mountain, introduces a curved path. The point of these tests is to discover how, depending on their level, our subjects manage to construct these

---

[1] In collaboration with C. Stratz.

oblique or curved paths and yet keep the intervals between successive dominoes small enough to cause the collapse of the whole series. While young subjects do not anticipate that, if two successive elements are at right angles to each other, the fall of the first will not lead to the fall of the second, more advanced subjects arrange even the series \ / or | | so as to ensure contact along the entire row and it is these anticipations or constructions at the higher levels to which we shall be paying special attention.

Level IA

Examples

ROB (4,9) predicts that the second of two parallel dominoes in close proximity will be knocked down by the first. The dominoes are then placed at about 40°. *They won't fall.* Why not? . . . How should we set them up? (He restores them to the parallel position). *Look* (40° arrangement). *They have gone over!* Why? . . . The demonstrator sets up a series of nine vertical dominoes but with a wide gap before the last two which consequently do not fall over. Why not? . . . What must we do to make all of them fall down? . . . The row is closed up and the whole series collapses. Why? *Because you pushed them.* Construction of the series *A–B*: ROB inserts just two elements, too far apart. What is going to happen? *These will fall over* (points to 2 and 3). And this one (4)? *Also.* (Tries: 2 and 4 do not fall down.) Why not? . . . What must we do to make them fall over? . . . (They are brought closer together and collapse.) Why? *Because when you push them they fall down.* (One is removed.) Is it going to fall? *No, it's a little too far.* (Long series) *That will fall* (points to the whole row). (Verification, then series with several wider gaps.) All of them or just some? *All.* (Partial collapse of row.) Why? . . . Diagonal: (He sets up ten elements at 30–40°.) Will they fall down? *No.* Can you fix it so that they do? (He constructs a parallel row at the edge of the table.)

   PAT (5,1) (having seen one domino of a series of 7 knock down another) predicts the fall of the first five: Why not these (6 and 7)? *They're too many.* What makes them fall over? *They're pushed down.* Why did this one fall down (the fifth)? *Because it was pushed.* What was pushed? *The lot.* Wide gap: All of them are going to fall down (Tries). *No.* Why not? *Because.* What must we do to make all of them

14

fall down? *Push them.* When he reconstructs the row, he closes it up but without comment. He is presented with the series *A–B* but with too few elements, and tries unsuccessfully to bring down the whole series. Why haven't they fallen down?... Can you do something about it? (He closes them up.) Why did you do that? *To make them fall down.*

MIC (5,5). Two parallel dominoes: *They're going to fall over.* Next, he constructs a series but at irregular intervals. Some do not fall down and he reconstructs his series by closing it up: success. He is shown an irregular series: *All of them will fall down.* (Tries.) Why didn't they? *Because they weren't strong enough.* Diagonal: *They're going to stay up.* Can you set them up so that they fall down? (He makes minor corrections but with partial success only.) Why didn't all of them fall down? *I didn't pull hard enough.* Pond: no curvature; four dominoes on one side, seven on the other, all in a straight line. Which ones are going to fall over if you push this one? *Those* (the four). And that one (the last of the seven)? *It'll also fall down.*

SCA (5,4) does not bother about the distance between *A* and *B*: *This one is going to make that one (B) fall down.* But if the distance is increased even further, *it'll stay up because it's too far away.* Even so, he leaves large gaps in his series: Does it matter if there is a gap? *No.* (Tries.) Why didn't it work? *Don't know.* What must we do? *Put them very close together.* (He closes up the dominoes nearest to *A* and leaves a gap in front of *B*.) Why didn't that one (*B*) fall down? *Because this one didn't touch it.* To construct the diagonal row, he starts obliquely from *A* but without aiming for *B*, whence an inadequate curvature. He next constructs a straight row from the level of *A* to the level of *B* and a perpendicular row of two elements: Will they fall down? *I don't know.* After several attempts, he joins the two rows with an oblique element ($\angle$|) and declares that they will all fall down. Then he makes a few corrections, but leaves excessive gaps. Having failed, he constructs a curved trajectory from *A* to *B*, with successive elements at various angles (including 2 at 90°) and declares that the whole row will collapse except perhaps for some dominoes at the very end. He makes no attempt to correct his mistakes.

PEO (5,0) for *A* and *B* at some distance from each other: *They will fall down.* (Tries.) Why didn't they? *Because they were too far apart,* but gives the same answer when voicing doubts about the collapse of the last element of a correctly constructed row.

15

DEN (6,5) having predicted and observed the collapse of two successive dominoes does not anticipate a repetition if they are at an angle. When she is proved wrong, she claims that the second will fall over even if it is shifted further down a line parallel to the first (correct) and, indeed, even if it is shifted so far down as to end up out of reach. Correct series: *All of them will fall down*, even if the series continues right across the room. But thinks the same will happen to a series with excessive gaps. Having been proved wrong, she says: *You have to push harder* (does so). For the lake: two straight segments, then, after prompting, a curve but with successive dominoes no longer parallel to each other: *They're all going to fall down.*

It is not easy to define the characteristic conceptualizations of these subjects. Almost all of them expect that the fall of one of two adjoining dominoes will involve the fall of the other due to 'pushing' (ROB, PAT, DEN) or 'pulling' (MIC). But this does not mean that they think the dominoes will fall down in all circumstances: ROB and DEN hold that they must be parallel, and ROB does not think that they will fall along a diagonal. However, these restrictions are all closely related to the idea of pushing: subjects at level IA are convinced that to bring down a passive object, it must be struck head on and not sideways. On the other hand, none of them anticipates that if the gap between two dominoes is larger than the length of the first, the second will not be knocked over. True, if the gap is too blatantly large, they will say the two are 'too far apart', but in the case of less glaring gaps, they never think of comparing the gap with the height or length of the domino. Thus, after having failed to make the correct predictions, PAT and SCA closed up the elements (while DEN increased the gaps!), but merely to augment the force of the 'push', and PEO believed that the row of collapsing dominoes could not be continued over long distances. Similarly, MIC and DEN attributed the effect of excessive gaps to the insufficient 'push' or 'strength' of the dominoes.

In short, the general characteristic of subjects at this level seems to be that they liken dominoes to balls. They fail to grasp the fact that when an upright domino falls over, it describes an arc that causes it to fall on and topple the next domino, and so on. What is lacking in their conceptualization therefore is the idea that one domino can be tilted to press down upon its neighbour, whence their

16

failure to consider the gaps, the more so as they did not propel the moving body as they would have done with a projectile, and merely gave it a slight flick. It should also be noted that their failure to take cognizance of the successive tilting of the dominoes, and hence their failure to attach due importance to the intervals between successive elements, recalls the failure of subjects at the same level to pay due regard to the inclination of cards (chapter 1). There is this difference, of course, that whereas 'leaning' meant 'propping up' in the earlier series of tests, in the present case it means 'knocking down'.

Level IB

Examples

TOR (5,7) starts with a level IA reaction: *All of them are going to fall down.* When they do not, he closes up the row: *We're going to put them like that.* (The demonstrator restores a gap): Are they going to fall down? *No, because that one doesn't touch the other one.* Diagonal: correct. What if you had to go round yourself? *I'd go this way* (detour). He does the same with the dominoes but does not bother to adjust the intervals.

ALA (5,6) for two dominoes not completely parallel: *They're going to touch* (all the same) *and this one will bring the other one down.* Series of four dominoes: Will the fourth one fall over? *No, it's too far away.* And the third? *Yes, the second one will touch it and all three of them will come down.* (Tries.) Why did all four of them fall down? *They all touched, one behind the other.* Long series: Right across the table? *Yes, they're going to touch each other one behind the other.* Then, ALA, now highly intrigued, makes a spontaneous suggestion: *I want to make them fall all round,* but his 'round' is a rectangle, successive dominoes forming straight rows, whence no fall at the four corners. ALA sees what is wrong and, to remedy it, constructs a circle but with dominoes representing a circumference rather than the termini of a series of radii. When the series fails to collapse, ALA makes the appropriate corrections. For the diagonal he places the first dominoes correctly but sets up the last ones in a straight line. For the lake: correct detour (facilitated by the circle he constructed earlier).

LON (6,2). Too large a gap between the two dominoes: *It'll just touch that one.* (Tries, and finds she was mistaken.) *It's because it*

17

didn't push. Series of eight: *The last one will stay up and the one before it, too.* And this one (4)? *Also.* Then which one will fall down? *These* (the first three) *because they* (the rest) *won't get a push.* (Tries.) Why did all of them fall over? *Because they've pushed all the others.* Longer series: *They'll all fall over because they're going to make the others fall as well* (*idem* for the entire length of the room). Series with various gaps: *This one will fall down.* And that one? *No, it's too far away.* What must we do? *Put them sideways.* Diagonal: failure with two horizontals that fail to make contact. Next places one horizontal element at *A* followed by an oblique element and a perpendicular one at *B*. Seeing that *B* does not collapse, she re-aligns the penultimate element to face *B* then adds a third element side on. Failing to bring the series down, she constructs an arc of circle and succeeds.

TIT (6,6). Two elements: *It's not going to fall over, they're too far apart.* How do you know? *Because they're not side by side.* Series of eight: anticipates collapse up to the third element *because they're side by side,* but no transitivity from the fourth onward; after experiment, exclaims: *They were all side by side!* Longer series: anticipates collapse up to about the middle. After verification, predicts collapse of series as far as the wall. Series with gap (hidden by a screen): *They weren't side by side.* Diagonal: success. Lake: failure.

FON (6,7) after the collapse of two elements is asked to construct a long series: he places the second element at a suitable distance and also the third but then packs some fifteen dominoes so closely together that they cannot fall. He is shown a correct series of four but wants to remove the first element: *I can't* (make all four go over) *without taking that one away, because it's too close.* When the demonstrator stops him from doing so, he flicks the penultimate element: *I'll never do it otherwise, it's too hard.* After demonstration, series of eleven: *This one will make the other one fall over and then perhaps that one and perhaps that one as well* (4). (Experiment.) *Oh, that's great!* Lake: Correct solution, but uncertainty of success. He then constructs a path consisting of two straight rows at 120° and says: *I want to see something.* What? *Whether they fall even when they're apart.* Then he returns to the curve but with a perpendicular element towards the end.

LUC (6,8) when *A* and *B* are moved further apart after an initial attempt: *Now it's too far.* Series of eight: *This lot* (up to about the middle) *will fall down*. And the rest? *They won't because they're too far apart*. (Tries). *They went down because they weren't too far apart after all.* And this lot (right across the table)? *These here will fall over* (points to a third). And the rest? *No, they're too far*. (Tries.) *They weren't too far!* And right across the classroom floor? *They won't all fall down*. Long series with a gap in the middle: *The last ones won't fall down*. Then, without mentioning the gap, closes it up. Diagonal: success after several trials. Lake: a straight line on either side with large gaps: *They'll all fall down because it's not a very long way*. (Experiment.) *No, because the lake is too big.*

KAT (7,8) appreciates the role of the gap between *A* and *B* but believes that, in the series of eight, the last one will not fall *because it's further away than the second*. But why does that stop it from falling? (She picks up a domino and measures the distance.) *There's a gap.* The series is closed up, and she predicts that two thirds will fall down. Why stop there? (She measures again.) *Yes, all of them will fall down because they've been closed up.* Diagonal: arc of circle but with perpendicular elements at the end.

These level IB reactions are somewhat paradoxical: they combine considerable progress with an inability to exploit it. The great progress is the comprehension of the importance of the gap between successive dominoes. True, our subjects do not mention these factors explicitly but when, like TOR, ALA, or LON they assert that, at a certain distance, one domino will not 'touch' its successor, the word 'touch' obviously means that it will not 'lean against' the next one and throw it over, since it goes without saying that before it starts to 'lean' the two do not 'touch'. Appreciating the importance of the gap between the two dominoes therefore implies appreciating the fact that by pressing on the first, it can be made to 'lean' upon the second. Let us note once again the parallel with the construction of the houses of cards in chapter 1: subjects at level IB also discover that one of the cards 'leans' against the other, albeit 'leaning' in that case means 'propping up' rather than 'toppling over'.

And just as, in the case of the playing cards, the subject does not exploit his discovery and fails to grasp the reciprocal relationship of the two cards (attributing a privileged role to one), so in the present situation, the child at level IB, while grasping the mechanism of the fall of the two adjoining dominoes, fails to generalize this discovery by extending it to a long series of successive dominoes: even in a series of four, ALA thought that the fall of the first did not imply that of the fourth because *it's too far away*, as if the intermediate elements did not matter. LON and TIT similarly reserved their explanation for the first three elements because *the rest won't get a push*. FON went so far as to remove the first domino, so as to make the second reach the fourth, and KAT measured the distance between 1 and 4 with a single domino, saying: *There's a gap*, as if dealing with the gap between two successive elements.

Admittedly, after verification, these subjects succeed in generalizing their explicative model, but before seeing for themselves, they fail to grasp that the transitive relation extends beyond the third element. This fact, let us repeat, provides striking corroboration of what we have noted elsewhere[1] about the relationship between the mediate transmission of movements and operational transitivity: for lack of the latter, subjects at level IB treat the former as a chain of immediate transmissions. However, we still needed proof that in elementary physical situations these subjects do not arrive at even quasi-logical transitivity. This proof has been adduced by our present study and what is more in the clearest possible manner.

Stages II and III

At about the age of 7–8 years, a grasp of transitivity and of recurrence emerges but even before it does, there are intermediate cases which help to throw light on the genesis of these new co-ordinations:

Examples (intermediate cases)

CRI (7,4) thinks that *A* is *too far away* from *B* (false). For a series of 12: *The other* (second) *one is going to fall down*. And the last one? *No*. And this one (middle)? *No*. Why not? *These* (the first two) *are too far apart*. What must we do to make them fall down? . . . Which ones will fall over? *These* (the first three). And the fourth? *Also*. And the last? *No*. And the fifth? *Yes*. And the last? *No*. And the sixth? *Yes*, etc. Up to where? *Up to the end*. Right across the table? *Yes*. And in the classroom (on the floor)? *No*. Pond: success after several attempts. Two lakes: failure because of the angles (+90°).

---

[1] See 'La Transmission des mouvements', vol. 27 of *Etudes d'épistémologie génétique* (P.U.F., 1972).

ARI (7,10) appreciates the significance of the gap between *A* and *B*. Series: only the first two will fall down *because they are very close* but not the last ones *because they are too small* (= because the first ones are not tall enough). But when he is asked about each domino in turn, he says that all of them will fall down. Lake: failure (use of perpendicular elements).

TIE (7,6). Series: *That one will bring down several more*, but not all. Then concludes that all of them will fall down *because there is one that pushes in front and the others will fall down with the one that's gone over.*

Examples (level IIA)

OLI (7,7). Series: *All the rest will fall down because if there is one that falls like this, all the others must fall in the same direction.* Interval *AB*: he measures the gap roughly to see if *B* will fall down. Lake: one element is set at 90°. After failure, he says: *When that one turns it can't fall like this* (gesture of perpendicularity). Successful forking.

FLA (7,10). Series: *1 brings down 2, 2 brings down 3.* And then does it stop? *No, 4 brings down 5*, etc. (Experiment.) Why do all of them go down? *Because we pushed the first one.* Long series (across the floor): *They'll all go down.* Gap (hidden by a screen): the last one did not fall down because one of the invisible elements *was too far from the one before.* Diagonal: success. Pond: curve, but linking two rectilinear segments, whence incorrect angles (*ca.* 90°).

VIR (7,11). AB: *We'll have to see about the distance.* Series: *All of them are going to fall over.* Right across the classroom? *Yes.* Diagonal: success. Pond: angle of 90°, then success.

TAU (8,11) carefully constructs a series of twelve dominoes, and then says cautiously: *Perhaps they won't fall down towards the end because there is less force there.* But when the series is extended even further, he says: *They'll all fall over because each time* (with each individual fall) *the next one will get a push.* Pond: still difficulties with the angles; correct curve until just beyond the pond but then perpendicular transition to a rectilinear series leading to the end. He then changes the inclination of the intermediate elements to avoid *too large a gap otherwise they won't touch*, but fails.

RIN (8,6). Series: They will all fall down *in turn*, but uses perpendiculars to round the obstacles.

21

PAU (9,3) also uses perpendiculars to round the obstacles, then corrects the angles but fails to consider the distances. Why didn't it work? *We have to turn them round like this* (|$\searrow$). Will that fall down? *I don't know.*

At level IIB, the angular problem is resolved by correct anticipation or by immediate correction.

Examples

MAT (8,6) for *A* and *B* differing in height: *B* will fall over because *there is a bit that goes with the first one* but if the distance between them is large *it won't fall down because they are apart: there is a space and they will drop into it.* If they are placed at an angle, *B* will not fall down because *it's across.* When he is proved wrong, he explains that both dominoes went over because *they were brought close together.* Diagonal: wrong angle, but immediately corrected. Pond: correct curvature. Are you sure? *Not all that sure* (he indicates a large angle) *because sometimes it goes sideways* (he corrects the series by closing it up and by reducing the parallelism to a minimum).

DAN (9,4) like TAN at level IIA, is not sure whether the last element in a long series will fall down: *Perhaps it'll stay up* because *there isn't enough push left.* Then correct generalization. Lakes, etc.: sometimes parallel arrangements with differences in height and partial impact; sometimes correctly graduated angles. To determine the correct distance, DAN allows one element to drop on to the next by way of experimentation. Successful forking (Y-shaped).

LIP (9,11). Series: All the dominoes will fall down within *a fraction of a second.* With wooden blocks slightly more elongated than dominoes, he allows larger gaps *because they are longer so they can touch all the same.* Lakes, etc.: twists, some of them too great: *I put too much of a bend on it so they didn't fall against each other . . . Before there was only one like that* (oblique), *the big face could strike the little one, but not this time.*

GAB (10,0) closes up the elements for the detours: *If you leave one out at the turns they can fall sideways.*

No further advances are observed at stage III except perhaps for some better anticipations and often a quicker appreciation of the principles involved.

Examples

PED (11,7): *They don't have to be too far apart. At the corners we have to turn them but just a little so that they don't drop off to the side.*

SYL (12,0): *We have to watch the curve . . .* (construction) *but they run the same way in both directions.*

NIC (12,0): *If they were closer together the dominoes would go down more quickly because they wouldn't have the time to slow each other down.* What makes the whole lot of them fall over? *The weight of the first domino.* And if we used dominoes made of plastic? *They would have to be put closer together. Oh no, it's the same thing, from the first to the twentieth, but you can't have some made of plastic and others of lead and of wood.*

This particular transition from levels IIA and IIB provides further analogies with our analysis of playing-card constructions, and this despite the fact that the act of 'leaning' has two opposite effects in the two cases. Thus, subjects at level IIA generalize the results of that act by appealing to reciprocity in one case (houses of cards) and to transitivity in the other (dominoes). Admittedly, some of our present subjects, TAU and DAN amongst them, doubt whether the dominoes will keep falling down right to the end of the series, but no longer, as at level IB or like such intermediate subjects as CRI, ARI and TIE, because they have not grasped the transitive effect of the fall of one element upon the next, but rather for dynamic reasons: the 'force' or 'push' transmitted across the series is believed to die out gradually. (This is a common stage II response, except in cases where the effects are cumulative.) The clearest indication of the difference between level IB and level IIA reactions is that whereas CRI and ARI first deny transitivity but come to accept it after a step-by-step argument, TAU and DAN lose their dynamic doubts the moment the series is extended and they can no longer fix the boundary of a transmission which they previously believed came to a stop at some undefined point.

However, though stage IIA is characterized by a grasp of the transitivity of the 'leaning' action in the case of the dominoes, and of its reciprocity in the case of the cards, a double blank persists at this stage in respect of non-symmetrical or non-linear situations. That blank is caused by the difficulty of defining the directions of the pressure exerted by the leaning elements or the results. In the case of the dominoes, this problem arises with particular force when the trajectory is curved: from OLI to PAU, none of our subjects anticipated that, when they are perpendicular to each other, one domino will not 'lean' on the next, and their trials and errors showed up the deficiencies of their directional representations. Similarly, in the case of perpendicular cards arranged to form a T, in which the inclined card props up the vertical, these subjects attribute the principal role to the latter as if it kept up the one leaning against it, all by itself.

At level IIB these problems disappear in both cases, and at stage III the subjects feel the need for explanations involving weight and similar forces.

Conclusion

In chapter 4, where we shall be looking at actions involving counterweights, we shall be discussing the ambiguous nature of pressure (pulling down on the one hand, and propping up on the other). This ambivalence extends to the concept of weight itself, which in the same situations may be variously treated as a cause of subsidence or support. It is remarkable that this ambiguity should in no way hamper the child's ability to use and develop the idea of pressure; moreover, when we compare the relative levels of development in the domino experiments, where the pressure brings down the successive elements with those we met in the card experiments, where its essential function is to prop up the various structures, we discover a very close correspondence between the two.

Nor is that all. In order to surmount the ambiguities and distortions resulting from the neglect of the inclinations at level IA and to confer a rational status upon the action of leaning or pressing, and the consequent collapse or support of the two types of element, two conditions must be fulfilled simultaneously and jointly: the coordination of the respective actions previously considered in isolation (because here as elsewhere co-ordination is the basis of rationality, while the conceptualization of isolated, particular actions gives rise to all sorts of distortions); and, on the other hand, the fitting of each type of leaning or pressing in each process into a precise spatial context (position and direction), without which the action loses its significance and gives rise to nothing but contradictions.

In the particular cases of our dominoes and cards, these two conditions are met gradually: the transition from level IA to level IB is marked by progress in the grasp of the role of the inclinations (and, with the dominoes, of the role of the corresponding gaps); the transition from level IB to level IIA, by contrast, is characterized by logico-dynamic co-ordinations (transitivities and reciprocities); the transition from IIA to IIB, in its turn, once again involves a spatial elaboration, that of the direction which the leaning element must assume to prop up or bring down. These advances are not fortuitous. The reason why subjects at level IB discover the role of the inclination and of the gap, which children at level IA still ignore, is that they have begun to engage in more active regulations, which forces them to pay greater heed to these two factors, and hence to proceed to new co-ordinations engendering transitivity and reciprocity, because the effects of the two factors make themselves felt throughout the series. But since these effects are, in turn, dependent on position and direction, there ensues a further refinement of the active adjustments and a grasp of these supplementary variables.

Now the general characteristics of this development also apply to the conception of the action of weights and counterweights (chapter 4), and of balances or see-saws (chapter 5) in particular. We shall, in fact, be struck by the presence of the same ambiguities and initial distortions, followed by the same alternations of progress in the spatialization and co-ordination of the actions as we have already remarked upon. At level IA we shall rediscover the same tendency to vacillate between the powers of weights to press down or hold up, our subjects, for instance placing a counterweight on the wrong side of a board, or on the fulcrum, or topping a fragile structure with a heavy object to make it stand up better. These errors go hand in hand with failures of co-ordination: objects are thought to act separately because they are heavy or light and not by virtue of the relation x is heavier than y. When working with a balance, these subjects concern themselves exclusively with one of the sides (or with each of the two pans in turn, but not simultaneously), clearly failing to understand the nature of equilibrium in its quantitive sense.

Starting from this lack of differentiation and co-ordination reminiscent of our present level IA, the advance to level IB will similarly go hand in hand with spatial or logico-geometrical progress: the subject begins to pay heed to the symmetries or asymmetries, which explains his tendency to place a weight in the centre of a balance so as to stabilize its two sides all at once, or to place the end of one plank on that of another in the construction of a bridge, all the while 're-inforcing' the whole with counterweights arranged in accordance with mistaken ideas of symmetry: the relation 'heavier' being equated with assistance by the stronger to the weaker and not yet with the interaction of opposite effects.

At level IIA we shall rediscover a general attempt at co-ordination, this time in the form of general reversibility (equilibrium of quantified weights) and also of reciprocity and transitivity. Finally, at level IIB this progress in co-ordination will lead to the active regulation of new spatial relations: weights will be judged to act according to their position (incipient intuition of 'moment'), and counterweights will be positioned not only in accordance with the location of the weights but also with the direction in which the action is transmitted.

In brief the development of the child's ability to deal with the weight of objects shows a remarkable convergence with the development of his ability to deal with leaning objects in which the weight is thought to play no role (except for some subjects at stage III), e.g. in the recurrent fall of dominoes or with houses of cards.

However, before we proceed to weights and counterweights, we must first examine the problem of transmission, which we have just encountered in the fall of dominoes.

CHAPTER THREE

The Transmission of Movements[1]

The immediate and mediate transmission of movements has been examined at some length in our work on causality,[2] in the course of which the child was shown various forms of transmission and asked to interpret them. In the present work, by contrast, the child is instructed, say, to reach a certain goal and, in order to do so, he must first be sure that there is transmission of movement. Hence it is not his explanation of the latter which we shall be examining here but his discovery of transmission following the free exercise of his practical intelligence, and also his conscious distinction between those of his actions that lead to failure and those that lead to success.

In Part I of this chapter we shall be working with the set of small balls suspended from a horizontal bar we used in our earlier studies with A. Szeminska, but instead of having the impulse conducted by a row of contiguous and immobile balls we shall be using two balls at such a distance from each other that the first cannot set the second in motion unless the child himself introduces intermedia. In Part II we shall be examining a similar but much easier problem: the transmission of movements by building blocks placed on a table.

I THE TRANSMISSION OF MOVEMENT BY SUSPENDED BALLS

We use a horizontal bar with eight hooks, and large pearls or 'balls' on threads that can be looped round the hooks (one small black ball, eight small red balls, one small red ball on a long thread, one

---

[1] In collaboration with C. L. Bonnet.
[2] *Etudes d'épistémologie génétique*, vol. 27 (P.U.F., 1972).

small yellow ball on a short thread, four medium-sized balls on normal threads, a medium-sized ball with a normal thread, a medium-sized ball with a long thread, a large ball and a ruler that can be suspended horizontally from its two ends).

The child is shown the bar with a small red ball and the small black ball attached to its extremities, and asked to move the black ball not by touching it but by using the first red ball and any other of the objects provided. Since young subjects often forget about the first ball, they must be reminded that it plays an essential part in the experiment. Moreover, when they unhook the first ball to bring it nearer to the black, as they tend to do, the demonstrator will immediately return it to the original hook with instructions that it should be left there. Many subjects will now hook up one of the intermedia, for example the ruler, but instead of striking it with the red ball, they will push it against the black.

While they are engaged on the performance of this task, the subjects are asked what they think will happen if they use such and such a ball. After various failures and successes, they are asked to give an account of what they have done, backed up with drawings, and to describe their own actions from the objects' point of view.

If they have been unsuccessful, they can finally be shown the solution: to suspend the balls and to strike the first one. The demonstrator carefully observes their reactions, i.e. whether they use or fail to use the proposed solution when they repeat the whole experiment.

Level IA

Examples

YVE (4,6) tries vainly to reach the black ball with the first. *I'm going to use all these balls* (he hooks them up). Can you make the black one move? *I can't with the first one: it's too far away.* And with all these? *No, I shan't manage* (he knocks the first ball against the ruler and pushes the ruler against the black). Can you explain what you did? *The black one plays with the first one and makes it swing.* Return to the initial situation: YVE strikes the black ball with the tip of his index finger then strikes the red ball: *The red budges and the black budges all by itself.* The demonstrator now hooks up a second red ball and knocks the first against it: *They thump each other.*

YVE takes the ruler and strikes the first two balls simultaneously: the black ball moves. Can you recall what you did before (the demonstrator hooks up all the red balls)? How can we make the black one move? (YVE strikes each ball sideways, including the black one.) *Look* (the first ball is released against the second and the movement is transmitted). *The black one has moved.* How? *Your hand budged the first one and so the black one budged as well* (as if it had done so independently!).

BRU (4,0): Can you think of some way to move the black ball with the red? (She picks up the ruler and strikes each ball in turn.) After she is shown the solution: *I've taken the red* (the first ball) *in my hand, let it go and that knocked against the black. They all knock against the black.* Her drawing shows a row of balls: *I took a red one and hit it and that one hit all the others.*

ROL (4,6): I'd like you to find something with which to move the black ball but without touching it. (He flips the thread of the red ball with his finger.) Did the black one move? *No. It needs more of a hit.* (Attempt and failure.) *What we want is a longer thread* (he replaces the red ball with another on a long thread). *It's moved!* His drawing shows two suspended balls joined by a stroke symbolizing their impact. Return to the initial situation (red ball on a short thread): Can you use something else? (He hooks up another ball and pushes it against the black without bothering about the first: success. Then he hooks up a further ball and strikes it with the second.) Show me how you've done it. (He uses the first ball, ignores the others and tries in vain.) Show me once more. (He uses the second ball and succeeds.) And what did the first one do? *It budged the black* (he uses it again and tries in vain). With which one did you budge the black? *With that one* (the second). I'd like you to use the first. *Then we have to remove all the others. No, we don't.* (He strikes the third ball with the second.) Which one did you use? *That one* (the third). And what if you used the first? (He removes the two others.) Can you use all of them? (He sets them all up.) What have you done? *Learning to count.* Try with the first one. *I can't* (points to the thread). *It's too short.* And if I let the first one go (gesture)? *Perhaps it will make all the other ones swing.* And the black? *It's going to swing with the rest.* Try. (He flips the first ball, but sideways. It describes a curve, sets off the others, and the black begins to move slightly.) Well? *They're all swinging, they've budged the black.*

29

RAP (4,6) tries vainly to reach the black ball with the first. He hooks it up closer: success. The first ball is put back in its place, and he now pushes it with one hand while pushing the black ball towards it with the other: *I can't do it like that* (without touching the black). He now hooks up a second ball and lets it go with the first but without bothering about the direction. The balls gyrate and one slightly touches the thread of the black. What have you done? *The second touched the black and the first one touched the second,* but his gestures suggest a mutual effect and his drawing shows a hand holding the balls together: *My hand made a hook.* And what happened then? *The first one touched the second and the second touched the black.* His conceptualization thus suggests a grasp of transmission that he has failed to use in practice.

OLI (4,10) hooks up the red ball next to the black and in so doing makes them touch by accident. How did you manage that? *Like this.* I'd like you to use something else. (He takes the red ball off the hook without touching the black.) Did it move? *That one doesn't move.* So? (He puts the red ball back on the hook nearest to the black and flicks it.) Try it some other way. (He suspends the ruler so that it touches the red ball (first hook) then unhooks it and moves it hook by hook towards the black, which he flips with his finger): *There you are.* What did you do? *I moved it with my hand.*

PAP (5,0) suspends a ball close to the black one and flicks it. When asked to do better than that, she hooks up all the balls and sets off each in turn, the last hitting the black.

TOC (5,6) having failed with the first ball, interposes a large white ball and hits the black with it: *I've hung up another one and that budged it.* Why? *Because the black knocked the white.* And what did the white do? *It just budged. It didn't do anything. It let itself go. It budged.*

TUN (5,6) after the usual failures, is shown the correct method of hooking up the balls. Can you repeat that? (Succeeds.) What did you do? *Like that* (pushes all of them at once). (All the balls are removed.) Try it some other way. (He hooks up a large ball somewhere in the middle of the rod and then hits the black ball with a ruler.) And what is that one (the large ball) for? (He removes it.)

BIL (5,9). Same situation: *It banged against the others, and then it budged the black; all the balls made the black budge.* All of them knocked against the black? *Yes.*

30

NIC (6,0) despite his age has not gone beyond level IA. He tries vainly to make the first ball hit the black, then hooks up the ruler horizontally and strikes both balls with it. All his other solutions involve suspending various intermedia and flicking them towards the black, even though he was specifically asked to use the first red ball. He reverts to his own method even after a demonstration.

Let us recall first of all that from the last stage of the sensorimotor period (12–18 months) the child is capable of 'instrumental behaviour', for instance of using a stick to reach a distant object. However, it is impossible to say whether the stick constitutes an authentic intermedium or 'mediator' between the active mover (the hand) and the passive mover (the displaced object), or whether its instrumental function is simply to extend the arm and the hand. Now, earlier studies of the mediate transmission of movement have shown the relatively late emergence of mediation, whence the importance we attached to determining its status in the sphere of practical intelligence.

The answers of subjects at level IA seem quite unequivocal in this respect. On the one hand, they try to use every type of immediate transmission (direct contact between the first red ball and the black objective) or some method of extending the manual action: ROL, for instance, replaced the original red ball with one on a longer thread, while YVE and OLI used the ruler but moved it by hand and not by flicking the first red ball against it. Moreover, none of these subjects thought of using the other balls as intermedia, and this is the crux of the difference between mediate and immediate transmission. Thus YVE, who hooked up all the balls after failing with the first one alone, did not use them as intermedia but, having first struck the black ball with the ruler, flicked all the other balls in a parallel direction, and when the demonstrator removed all but one between the two at the ends, he struck the first two simultaneously. PAP used the same method as YVE; ROL added a second ball but failed to use it as an intermedium; subsequently he added a third ball and striking it against the second accidentally achieved mediate transmission; when asked to hook up all the balls he failed to see the point and made the first ball swing sideways. RAP seemed to come close to mediate transmission in his verbal explanation, but in practice he released the first two balls together. In general, when these subjects are shown the correct solution, they fail to grasp the idea of mediate transmission and declare, like BRU, ROL, TUN and BIL that it was the joint impact of all the other balls that moved the black (which is what TUN demonstrated in action).

In respect of the conscious grasp of these actions or the conceptualization of the observed effects two points deserve special mention. While some subjects (e.g. YVE) explain the observed transmission (with all the intermediate balls hooked up) by distorting the data, thus arriving at something like transmission over a distance (*Your hand budged the first one and so the black one budged as well; cf. the red budges and the black budges all by itself*) as if no more than two balls were involved, an idea that agrees with what we know of level IA reactions in general; the majority, by contrast, holds that it is the joint action of all the balls which causes the black to move. The second point worth stressing is the frequency with which these subjects change the order of the impacts, notably when more than two elements are present. Two factors are responsible for these changes. The first is that, when one ball has collided with another, both are set into motion and the subject tends to forget which one started the process. On the other hand it may happen (for instance with RAP) that having failed to reach the black with the first red ball, the subject will push the black with his other hand to bring it closer to the red; in that case, too, the order of succession is distorted. In any event, whatever the precise reasons for these inversions or omissions, we saw that ROL, who struck the third ball with the second, believed that he used the first. TOC who struck the black ball with an intermediate white one, asserted that it was the white one which was struck (*cf.* YVE, who after pushing the red against a ruler and the ruler against the black, thought that he had just watched the opposite effect: *The black one plays with the first one and makes it swing*). This difficulty in registering the correct order of succession explains why, when a subject does seem concerned about it, the impression may arise that he has arrived at the idea of quasi-mediate transmission, but the importance of this reaction must not be exaggerated. Thus when ROL pushed the third ball with the second and achieved success, he did so quite accidentally (which explains his difficulty in copying that solution). Again, when RAP, who hit the black ball by the simultaneous release of two balls (on the second and third hooks), conceptualized his success by saying that *the second touched the black and the first one touched the second*, it is tempting to conclude that in his case the conceptualization was of a higher level (IB) than the action (IA). But though he even produced an excellent drawing of the first two balls being held together, RAP was in fact merely describing the order of succession in which the balls had been hooked up. Nevertheless it is likely that this tendency of paying heed to the order of succession does help to shape the behaviour we encounter at the next level.

Level IB

We are about to rediscover, but in spontaneous actions, the earliest forms of quasi-mediate transmission mentioned in earlier studies of causality: the idea of a chain of immediate transmissions, in other words of a purely 'external' mediate transmissions by successive impulses and not yet the idea of a force traversing a number of moving bodies. In fact, in the present series of tests based on actions performed freely by the child rather than on his observations of a previously organized system of mediate transmissions, level IB marks the transition from the absence of mediate transmission to the actual or imagined discovery of simple chain reactions.

Examples (intermediate cases)

LAT (4,9) tries vainly to reach the black ball with the first red one, then flicks one with each hand and knocks them together (cf. RAP, level IA). Next she hooks up a second red ball at the centre of the bar: *The first one will go there* (to the left), *the second will go like this* (oscillations at right angles to the correct direction) *and the black is going to stay put.* But how can we make it move? LAT replaces the second ball with a larger one and says: *The first will knock against the big one and the big one will knock the black* (propels the first ball too softly, then increases the force and succeeds). After a drawing representing 'the path' by a stroke underneath the aligned balls, the initial situation is restored: LAT inserts two more balls and says: *The first one* (in front of the newly inserted balls) *will touch the black, and the others will go like this* (sideways). Can you hit the black by using just one? (She flicks the penultimate ball against the black.)

PEP (5,6) fails to reach the black ball with the first red, adds another ball close to the first and yet another close to the black and strikes both. Next she hooks up the first ball close to the black and when it is put back in the right place, hooks up all the balls and sets them off in succession. She then strikes the first one of the series and notes the effect on the black. While drawing what she has seen, she explains: *This one budged that one, that one budged this one, and so on. I've set this one going and all the rest moved as well.*

PER (5,6) tries vainly to reach the black ball with the first, then hooks up the rest and pushes all of them simultaneously towards the black: *I've pushed all the red ones.* What did they do? *They made the black one move.* How? (She unhooks the first ball and flicks it against the black; then replaces it with a large ball and flicks it at the others.) *There you are.* Did the big one touch the black? *Yes.* And the others? *They played along.* Can you find something else to do it with? (She suspends the ruler vertically between the first ball and the black: success.) What did you do? *I did it like this* (indicates the movement of the first ball towards the black and *vice versa*!). Tell me in words. *I pushed the red one and then the black one budged* (her drawing shows the ruler between the two balls).

VAL (5,6) after failure with the first ball, suspends the ruler and pushes it directly at the black. Then she substitutes an average-sized ball and hits it towards the black. And the two together? (She flicks the first ball at the second): *I pushed the first one and it pushed the second which touched the black.*

MES (6,4), after various failures, is told to hook up all the balls and sees the point straightaway. *There are all these bits and pieces and one of them is closest to the black, that's why I can do it* (he taps the first ball). *I've hit it and then all the balls started moving and this one knocked against the black one, that's how I was able to do it.*

PER (6,5) after several failures, suspends the ruler vertically and strikes the black ball with it. Then she hooks it up horizontally and strikes the black again. She next substitutes a large white ball and hits the first red one: *I've pushed the red one, it pushed the white and the white one made the black one flap about.*

SCA (6,5) taps the first ball and the black one alternately with the ruler, then proposes to move the first ball three hooks forward. When he is reminded of his assignment, he hooks up a second red ball at the centre of the rod and strikes it: *I hit the first of the red balls with the ruler and it knocked against the second; the second knocked the third.* I'd like you to do it with something other than

34

the ruler. *I can knock it with a ball* (he throws the first ball at the second). His drawing shows the order he followed but he adds: *I've forgotten to make them go from this side* (flicking the black ball at the red).

JAQ (6,11), after failure, inserts a second (larger) red ball and hits the black with it, then strikes both red balls simultaneously and so again hits the black. She then adds a third red ball and hits all three simultaneously. Explain what you've done. *I hung up three balls, and pushed the first one with my hand and made it hit the second. Then the bigger one hit the small one* (the third). Gesture of open palm pushing the first ball.

GRO (7,2) begins by hooking up an intermediate ball on a long and then one on a short thread, and pushes it directly by hand but fails except with the long thread. Next she tries to hook up the black ball closer to the centre, and the first red ball as well, and when she is told that she is not allowed to do so, says: *Let's push the first one against this one so that it touches the black* (success after several fruitless attempts before moving the intermediate ball closer to the black).

NIC (7,2) first strikes the black ball and then the first; he next hooks up two other balls, strikes the last one and then both together. He then changes them about, bringing the larger one closer to the black: *It's bigger so it'll push the black one more easily.* Explain. He touches the hooks as if he were planning a campaign: *One here, one there, another there, and one there. Then I make them swing and if I touch that lot* (the threads) *the black will start swinging.* (Does not use enough force.) *Must do it a bit harder.* Explain. *I've put three balls on the hooks, I'll push them more quickly, that's easy enough.*

DAL (7,3) suspends a ruler between the two balls and hits the black. He is reminded that the first red ball must 'do something'. *So that it moves without touching the ruler?* What do you think? *I push the red, that pushes the ruler, and that pushes the black.* He substitutes a ball for the ruler and says: *I've pushed the red, that's pushed the white which pushed the black.*

GON (7,8) and CAR (7,9). Same procedure but with immediate use of the white ball, which they push by hand and not with the first ball.

All these responses show that children at level IB, who readily

35

interpret the ready-made spectacle of the transmission of movement through a series of contiguous and stationary balls as a chain of immediate transmissions, find it much more difficult to discover this chain through spontaneous actions. This is clear proof that mediate transmission is at first conceived as a chain of immediate transmissions the various links of which it takes time to join together into a whole. This approach heralds, but does not yet amount to, a real grasp of transitivity. The problem is to explain how these subjects arrive at the idea of fitting two immediate transmissions into a single series. Two central concepts seem to intervene here, and it is their synthesis which opens the way for operational transitivity: the order (or direction) of the immediate transmissions and the possible substitution of an external agent for the subject's own action. The order of the transmissions may seem to be self-evident, but we have seen that, at level IA, this is not always the case: quite a few subjects move one of the rear balls closer to the front, mainly because they consider the oscillations so many obstacles to the transmission, and hence try to reduce their amplitude. This was still done by the intermediate subject LAT who, before discovering an episodic type of mediate transmission, struck the black and the red simultaneously, and it was undoubtedly the importance he attached to their oscillations that prevented him from taking advantage of his subsequent discovery. Hence it is clear that, before they can link up a chain of immediate transmissions, our subjects must grasp their order of succession, something several of them drove home to us when they hinted at that order before learning to use it in practice: PEP hooked up all the balls and then tapped each of them in turn; NIC touched all the hooks in the correct order before attaching the balls to them, and so on.

Moreover, these subjects also teach us something about the role of what one might call 'retroactive substitution'. Most of them, in fact, start out by suspending one or several intermediate balls between the first red and the black and move these balls instead of the first. The discovery of mediation is the substitution of the action of the object for that of the subject, that is pushing the median ball with the preceding one rather than directly by hand – in short, using the first ball as a substitute for the impact of the hand on the second. The reader may object that our account is purely tautological, but it should be recalled that at the beginning everything is done by hand: subjects at level IA often start off by striking the black ball (by hand or with the ruler), and the substitution of an intermedium for this direct action is a great advance, even if the subject activates the intermedium directly: the substitution of the action of a third object for that of the hand is part of the long process of delegating individual actions to objects. On the other hand, since mediate transmission is comparable to operational transitivity, as we have stressed elsewhere, it is useful to recall that operational transitivity is based on regular substitutions: to deduce $A < C$, from $A < B$ and $B < C$ is, in fact, tantamount to substituting A for B in the relation $B < C$. It is therefore of some importance to discover the roots of such substitutions in the systematic delegation of manual actions to external objects. We shall be returning to this point in due course.

Stages II and III. Conclusions

The characteristic advance of subjects at stage II is that they appeal directly or almost directly to mediate transmission, though with one qualification: most of them believe that they must use large balls, etc. to augment the force of the impact.

Examples

JOE (7,0) (an unusually interesting case because he went spontaneously beyond his preliminary assignment): Can you find something to move the black ball without touching it? (No reference is made to the red ball, which has not yet been hooked up.) (He selects a large ball, suspends it to the right of the black but immediately hooks up a series of other balls to the left, and striking the large ball against the black produces a transmission of movement in the wrong direction.) *I took this big ball and then it touched the other one and budged it, and then it budged that one* (etc., complete enumeration). Next he demonstrates transmission in the opposite direction. The experiment is now repeated in the usual way: a small red ball and a black ball at either end of the rod. JOE hooks up a ball on a long string and upon discovering that striking the latter with the first is not enough, he inserts two more balls and produces the required transmission. A week later, his drawings from memory begin with a series of balls of decreasing size (large, medium, small), as if a large ball was essential for the transmission of movement.

37

His subsequent drawings still show a series of medium-sized balls and a small final one.

CRI (7,10) starts off by trying to knock the two terminal balls against each other and observes that the distance is too great: he then inserts another ball close to the first, moves it to the middle of the bar, strikes the first ball and succeeds. Could you do it differently? (He replaces the central ball with a larger one.) *The small one pushes the big one and the big one pushes too and the black one starts moving, but you do have to push.*

BOU (8,10) begins, as at level IB, by suspending an intermediate ball on a long thread and pulling it as far as it will go from left to right, possibly so as to gauge the distance, for she succeeds immediately after moving the intermediate ball towards the centre and replacing it with a larger one: *I've put this one on the fourth hook and pushed the first one and the big one has the black, the red one pushed the big one and the big one pushed the black.*

TER (9,7) hooks up a medium-sized ball on a long thread next to the first ball, strikes the latter against the thread of the second which collides with the black: *It isn't all that complicated but it isn't easy either.* Can you do it differently? (She hooks up two and then three intermediate balls including a medium-sized one and one on a long thread.) *I take the red* (first ball), *make it go and then it falls on the others and finally on the black.*

While all these subjects discover the principle of mediate transmission straight away or fairly quickly (which agrees with what we have observed in our study of causality), it should be noted that they apparently feel the need to include large balls or balls on long threads among the intermedia as if a series of balls equal in size to the first was likely to prove less effective. Quite possibly, this idea is connected with the 'semi-internal' *cum* 'semi-external' character of the transmissions, an effect we also observed with immobile intermedia, each of which seemed to our subjects to have shifted ever so slightly to ensure the passage of the movement. This point cannot, of course, be verified in our present series of tests since all the intermedia move in fact, but the deliberate choice of larger balls, as if to encourage the transmission, suggests a failure to grasp the conservation of transmitted motion. In any case, it is a striking fact that, at stage III (11–12 years) the subjects no longer think along such lines.

Examples

THO (10,3) tries with the first ball alone, then hooks up a second ball of the same size: *No, perhaps it won't go right to the top*, and strikes it. *I tapped this one* (the first ball) *so that it should hit the other which budged to hit the black*. She adds a third ball of the same size and indicates by a gesture what she would do with it and then explains: *Otherwise I could have put one on each of the hooks to make quite sure*.

FAS (11,10) immediately suspends a ball of the same size close to the first one, and another close to the black. He strikes the first and exclaims: *It won't play*. He then adds three further balls of the same size and succeeds: *I've pushed the first to make the black one budge without touching it*.

BOI (12,6) hooks up a ball of equal size right next to the first, then moves it towards the middle: *If I raise the ball on the left to an angle of 45°, it will hit the middle one and that one will hit the one on the right*. Is there a different way? (He hooks up two intermedia of equal size.)

The progress from immediate transmission (level IA) to mediate transmission (stage III) raises a greater number of problems than did the ready-made transmission system which we presented to our subjects for the study of causality, and this despite the fact that this system involved immobile intermedia which introduced an extra difficulty. This is because, in the earlier experiments, the grasp of mediate transmission came gradually in the wake of progress in transitivity without our having had to determine how that progress was achieved, while in the present experiments we had to establish the relationship between such progress and the child's own actions.

The sensorimotor, instrumental behaviour which is at the origin of this development seems already to imply such transitivity: the hand pushes the stick, the stick pushes the object, therefore the hand pushes the object. In fact, this is not yet the case, because the stick is at first conceived as a mere extension of the arm and hence of the direct effect of the hand on the object. It would therefore be an oversimplification were we to argue that transitivity is derived directly by reflexive abstraction from such instrumental behaviour. For though this process is undoubtedly involved, its mechanism has to be elucidated in the framework of a series of new constructions.

Now the two most delicate points in that elucidation are the role of these substitutions by delegation of actions to objects (mentioned in the preceding paragraph) and the conceptualization of the actions in these substitutions.

As far as the substitutions are concerned, the general line of development is perfectly clear. At the beginning, the subject instead of making objects act on one another, does everything he possibly can to obtain the desired result by his own exertions: he touches the black ball himself or brings the first ball close up to it to make the two touch directly; if he is instructed to refrain from doing so, he suspends other balls close to the black, forgetting all about the first one; or else he may interpose a ruler between the first ball and the black and himself push the ruler. Some of these subjects even go so far as to leave the ruler – considered as a fictitious intermedium – in its place and push the black ball by inserting a finger between it and the end of the ruler. In brief, whenever possible, these subjects perform all the actions they could delegate to the objects except for the final push which recalls the function of the stick in sensorimotor behaviour: it is an extension of the hand and not an independently activated intermedium. The importance of level IB is therefore that, starting out in the way we have just described, the subject ends up by delegating to objects powers he reserved for his own actions until then: instead of hitting the black ball C (goal) with an intermediate ball B directly activated by himself, the subject (S) strikes B with the first ball A of the series. As a result, the intermediate ball B which, until then was a mere prolongation of the action of S, acquires a role equivalent to that of the ball A, whence we have the two homogeneous relations $A \rightarrow B$ and $B \rightarrow C$: in that case the substitution of A for the subject S allows the substitution of A for B in the second relation, i.e. the conclusion $A \rightarrow C$, which marks the beginning of transitivity. It is therefore no exaggeration to describe the substitution of the object A for the subject S (which is a particular case of the 'attribution' of actions or operations to objects, characteristic of causality) as the motor of this regular substitution of A for B which is the source of all transitivity, that fundamental property of mediate transmissions.

It should be mentioned that the gradual delegation of the subject's own powers to objects was also observed in an earlier study with B. Inhelder of a field in which transitivity also intervenes but without causality, namely spontaneous measurement. Thus when children were asked to compare the heights of two towers at some distance from each other we noticed the following reactions: (1) a simple movement of the eye to compare the towers by direct inspection; (2) a manual movement to make the two towers stand side by side (as in (1), a kind of immediate transmission of magnitudes); (3) a bodily movement consisting of measuring one tower with two hands and trying to transfer this measurement to the other; (4) a beginning of transitivity by construction of a third tower serving as a common measure and lending itself to being moved and applied from one to the other; (5, etc.) the use of sticks, etc., serving as rulers. There is an obvious similarity between this development by successive delegation of one's own actions to the object and by ordered substitutions and the present situation, the only difference being that we have substituted the transport of movements for the transport of magnitudes.

There remains the fundamental problem of the grasp of consciousness, considered as the link between practical behaviour, involving failure and successes, and its consequences, every act of conscious understanding being a conceptualization that leads from actions to explanations.

The first point to stress is that, contrary to what happened in so many of our experiments, the subjects taking the present test had few difficulties in describing what they had done, verbally, by gestures or by drawings (some of which were clumsy, but not because of the inherent problems). It is only at level IA that one encounters difficulties in this respect, due both to pre-notions about the transmission (collective action of balls arranged in a series, etc.) and inversions of the order of succession.

Nor is that all, for it looks very much as if there might sometimes be progress even as the subject passes from action to conceptualization. That is what we suspected when RAP, at level IA, described an order of succession that was absent from his actions. At level IB we discovered the same reactions (e.g. on the part of PEP, PER and JAQ): two or more balls that were released simultaneously were subsequently said to have moved in succession. It would thus seem that the idea of order, which is a fundamental operational concept (and which, in general, is obtained by reflexive abstractions from the order inherent in the co-ordination of actions) is imposed upon conceptualization even when the child fails to make use of this order in his actions. Here we might well have one of the factors, which coupled to the delegations and substitutions we mentioned earlier, encourages the emergence of transitivity, which also consists of regular substitutions.

II THE TRANSMISSION OF MOVEMENT BY BUILDING BLOCKS

Since there seemed to be so wide a gap between instrumental behaviour in which a stick, etc. is treated as a mere extension of the arm, and mediate transmission, we thought it of interest to examine the transmission of movements by building blocks resting on a table, and resembling both the 'instruments' used in sensorimotor behaviour and also such intermedia as the balls examined in Section I. We were particularly anxious to analyse the child's conscious grasp of the actions he had performed, as we felt that this analysis would throw further light on the conclusions we drew from the ball experiments.

The subjects were presented with a number of square or rectangular blocks, a 'doll' (monkey, piglet, etc.) which they had to move, and an elongated block or pusher (P). The instructions were formulated as follows: I'd like you to find some way of moving the doll without touching it by hand. You may only touch this piece (P) and I would like you to use all the blocks set out on the table (three at first and then an increasing number).

There are three distinct situations. In situation I three square blocks in a straight line are placed between the doll and P: if the subject wishes to use them, all he has to do is to push P. Situation II: a large rectangular block is placed halfway between P and the doll but to their right and at right angles to the edge of the table. Situation III: as II but with another block (square) added on the left, opposite the rectangular block.

After performing the experiment, the subjects are asked to describe the movement of the blocks as well as the order in which they used them. They are also asked for drawings of the blocks, the hand, the paths described and if possible of 'how they touched' (point of impact, etc.).

Finally, the demonstrator announces that he is going to perform the experiment himself under precise instructions from the subject.

Levels IA and IAA

If we characterize level IA by the absence of spontaneous recourse to intermedia (*cf.* Section I), then we shall find that this reaction occurs with some 50 per cent of children between the ages of 4 and 5 years. The remaining 50 per cent may be said to be on another level, which we shall call IAA, and which also involves the use of intermedia, but not straightaway. Their reactions are thus appreciably in advance of the level IB reactions described in section I.

Examples (level IA)

FRA (4,9) first moves the doll with her hand. The instructions are repeated, and she now places the doll on one of the blocks and moves that by hand. She is shown how one block can move another, and uses one to push the doll. She is reminded that she must use all the blocks, picks up the pusher, and ignores all the blocks. I'd like the others to do something as well. (She moves a block towards the doll.) And the rest? (She joins up all the blocks.) *I've put everything together and then I've pushed with my hand.* Situation II: same reactions. Situation III: she places two blocks at right angles to the correct path and moves them by hand: *I put down two straight blocks and then I pushed.* She is shown the correct way and copies it. *Me, I pushed P and there was one block that went like that* (across the path). *When I first pushed with that one* (the block) *all of them came together and pushed.* But how did they come to lie like that (the rectangular block alongside P and 3 and 4 alongside 2)? *Me, I pushed P, that pushed this one* (1) *which pushed those* (2–4) *and those pushed this one* (1).

AMA (5,0) begins by thumping the table to move the doll, then pushes it with P, bypassing the blocks between P and it. When the demonstrator makes a gesture of pushing a block with P, she continues and says: *We took the big one and pushed it at the little green one and then we joined them* (all together) *and pushed them at the small monkey and made it move.* Situation II: she describes a curve with P. What were you trying to do? *Not to budge the blue one* (the intermediate block!). But you must use it. (She touches both blocks, but goes on to move the doll with P): *I went for the small green one, came back for the blue and then I went for the little monkey.*

Since there is little point in adding to these examples, we shall simply sum up the chief solutions offered by subjects at level IA. The simplest is to ignore the blocks and to move the doll by hand (FRA) or by thumping the table (AMA). (Thumping, incidentally, is an elementary form of transmission of the type that emerges at the penultimate sensorimotor stage.) The second solution is to use the blocks as vehicles on which the doll can be placed and slid across the table. The third reaction is to push the blocks sporadically and in turn, or to remove them before moving the doll by hand. The fourth boils down to pushing the doll with P or with a single block. The fifth, like the second, is to use the blocks as vehicles, but for P, which is thus brought into contact with the doll. A sixth solution, which is more advanced, is to push P in the direction of the doll and to pull any block in the way along instead of using it as an intermedium. The seventh solution is to concentrate all the blocks (FRA) and to use this collective object as a substitute for P. In situations II and III we are offered the same solutions, but with a tendency to use the lateral blocks as complements to, and possibly as extensions of, P (level IAA).

As for their grasp of the actions they have performed, our subjects focus attention on the end results and tend to neglect or forget the method: when they are asked to copy what the demonstrator has done, they simply move the doll or P without recalling which block they have touched, let alone in what order (cf. the circular explanation of FRA).

In general, the reactions of these subjects are thus very similar to the level IA reactions we described in Section I, but with this difference: it is well before the age of $5\frac{1}{2}$–6 years that they proceed to transmissions with the help of a number of intermedia. Thus by the age of 4–5 years, half of our subjects have begun to use all the blocks placed directly between P and the doll. Hence it would seem that transmission by blocks differs radically from the transitive impact of balls and that it is more akin to the precocious use of sticks as extensions of the arm. If that is so, then the negative reactions at level IA would reflect, not so much incomprehension of instrumental transmission, as a reluctance to follow instructions – after all, it is so much simpler to move the doll by hand or with P and a waste of time to bother about the blocks. But let us first look at the behaviour of subjects at level IAA, contemporaneous with level IA and slightly distinct from level IB.

Examples

BRU (4,3) was at level IA in the ball experiments three months earlier (see Section I). She begins by pushing the doll with *P*: *Well, I put it very close and then I pushed with it.* I'd like you to use all (3) blocks. She places a red block on a blue one, pushes them out of the way and finishes up by moving the doll with *P* alone. But I'd like you to use these. (She sets them up.) *I laid them next to each other, put my stick behind and then it moved.* And the blocks? *They shoved the little pig.* Situation II: she pushes a block with *P* but in all sorts of directions. What have you done? *I put this one* (a block) *against the pig and shoved with my stick* (*P*). Show me the way it went. (She points in the right direction but ignores her successive moves.) Did it go straight? *No, it turned.* When she is handed back all the blocks and presented with situation I, she aligns all the blocks and pushes with *P*. What did you do? *I pushed the blocks to make them touch.* Why did this one budge the pig? *Because I pushed my stick and then it pushed everything.* How is that possible? *Because I pushed with it.*

JOE (4,7) exactly the same reactions, except that his drawing fails to show the direction.

FON (4,6) after similar beginnings: *We must push them all, the others mustn't move too quickly* (they must not be flicked). After succeeding: *I pushed it* (the doll) *from behind* (with the blocks). How? *They're stuck together, they are like one and they pushed the doll and my hands pushed as well.* Situation II: He sets up blocks to form a ∨ between *P* and the doll but at some distance and looks perplexed: *They have to get together so that all of them can do something.* Why not like that? *Because they delign themselves* (a splendid neologism to express the loss of linearity!). He then sets up all the blocks in a straight line.

GRE (5,4): *I've pushed all the blocks with my hand.* And what did they do? *They stayed in front of my long stick.* That's all? *They also pushed.* How? *Because the big block pushed them.*

These reactions show very clearly that the precociously discovered transmissions of these 4 to 5 year olds are of a different type from those introduced at level IB in section I (suspended ball experiments). In fact, to move a doll with the pusher *P*, as almost all of these subjects did initially, is nothing but instrumental behaviour based

45

on the extension of one's own arm. As for pushing the blocks with *P*, it might seem that these subjects were beginning to have an inkling of mediate transmission by the concatenation of immediate transmissions, but it is easy to show that this interpretation would be quite mistaken. Thus when BRU says *I've laid them next to each other* (that is, one in front of the other) and *I put my stick behind*, it is clear that her column of juxtaposed blocks was, in fact, an extension of *P*. In fact, a series of blocks lying side by side suggests the idea of a whole made up of articulated segments, in the same way that the bamboo sticks fitted together by Köhler's chimpanzees constitute the prolongation of the initial stick. *They are stuck together*, said FON; *they are like one and they pushed the doll*, because, as he explained, *I pushed it from behind*. His final *my hands pushed as well* thus suggests the idea of a continuous action. Similarly, in situation II, FON claimed that *unless they stick together so that all of them can do something*, they will become 'deligned'. GRE, for his part, explained that *they stayed in front of my long stick* as if they played no part in moving the doll, then conceded that *they also pushed*, the qualifications of 'staying in front' and 'also' pushing once again suggesting the idea of a simple extension of his own action.

In short, when a ball set in motion by the child sets off others, the subject supplies no more than the initial impulse and then delegates his powers to the balls themselves; hence he must come to accept the idea of the transmission of movement from one element to the next before he can consciously use these elements as intermedia; by contrast, when he pushes a series of juxtaposed blocks, he is pushing them himself all the way and has no need to think of them as intermedia: he could achieve the same effect by pushing just one of them, of which the rest are unnecessary extensions. This explains why level IAA, though of greater complexity than level IA, is contemporaneous with it: subjects classified as IA may simply have refused to bother about useless complications, while those at the level IAA, following the instructions, obliged the demonstrator by extending their initial instrument *P*.

The best proof of the close relationship between subjects at levels IA and IAA respectively, is their conscious grasp of the actions they have performed. If subjects at level IAA know better than subjects at level IA which blocks they have pushed and which have done the pushing, they are no better than the others when it comes to defining the succession and direction of the movements (*cf.* BRU) and all they remember of their actions is the result. Nor can they distinguish between what the blocks have done and their own actions.

Level IB and stages II and III

At the age of $5\frac{1}{2}$–7 years, and sometimes up to 8 years, one observes two advances over the preceding reactions. With situation I, the general behaviour is the same as at level IAA, but the subject now treats the successive actions of the intermedia as a chain of immediate transmissions, and no longer as a simple extension of *P*. This fine distinction, often difficult to establish, is most pronounced in situations II and III, in which *P* is applied straightaway to the intermediate blocks and the latter are pushed against the doll. The second advance is that instead of trying various solutions, these subjects move the blocks straightaway in the direction of the doll.

Examples (level IB)

LAI (5,6) first of all ignores the blocks, then uses them all and guides them towards the doll. Situation II: he places the lateral block parallel to *P* and sweeps it towards the doll in an arc of circle: *I've made it go round a bit, like a letter of a tunnel.* Situation III: pushes *P* against the block on the right and helping out with his hand, pushes both against the left block and then leads all three towards the doll.

GOI (5,4) straightaway pushes all the blocks at the doll. How did you do that? *The biggest one of them pushed them all.* Which one touched the bear? *The last one.* And that one (*P*)? *It pushed these two* (first and second blocks). And that one (the second block)? *It pushed that one* (the third block). Situation II: immediate success by rotation: *The big one pushed that one to push the little bear.* Situation III: *P* is joined to the left block and then to the right block. All three propel the bear but GOI has to correct various deflections by hand. *I pushed the little bear with those two.* Show me how to do it. *You move these two blocks, but you mustn't touch them, only that one (P); you have to put them in front.* (He sets up the blocks at right angles to *P*.)

MAN (6,4) fails in situation II through clumsiness but explains what she intended to do: *We had to put this block here, the other one there, the next one here and then I pushed.* Fresh attempt: she applies

P to the first block, etc. Situation III: she constructs a series but as the blocks are of unequal size and become deflected, she adjusts them by hand.

GAN (6,6) follows a curved trajectory for II and constructs an oblique row for III, but corrects the deflections by hand and ignores them in his verbal account.

DAN (6,7) II: succeeds with *P* but does not recall how he corrected the deflections.

All these subjects display the common level IB characteristics: concatenation of the immediate transmissions and differentiation between curved and rectilinear paths (often exaggerated in their drawings). They have a fair grasp of these characteristics but not of the deflections and consequent corrections, although from this point onwards they distinguish clearly between what their hands do and what the blocks do.

Stage II (7–10 years) brings two innovations: a clear grasp of the directions to be followed and careful selection of the correct point of impact. Simple though their behaviour is, it is remarkable that even with so relatively straightforward a method, our subjects nevertheless see fit to comment on these two aspects of their responses.

Examples (stage II)

AMA (7,4), like several other seven year olds, says of situation II: *I've been trying to make sure that this lot* (the blocks) *does not go beyond* (bypass) *the monkey.* How did you hold *P*? *Like that* (near the middle). Situation II: *I took care not to push the small block too much to the right, in case it slithered across . . . I pushed it slap in the centre to make it go forward.* She then pivots the block, aims it obliquely at the monkey and says: *They have to touch each other like that, or else it won't work.* Can you touch any side you like with *P*? *No.* (She repeats the action and demonstrates where *P* must be applied.) Situation III: *The blocks must not slide across, else we won't be able to get at the others* (she corrects a deflection with *P*); etc.

STU (7,7) demonstrates (situation II) how the block can be pivoted with *P*. *You have to be very careful to get it in the right place.*

OLI (8,0): What did you look out for? *Where to put the rod* (*P*), *so that it doesn't lose touch* (with the block) *and turns properly.*

Subjects at stage III often add causal explanations to these specifications of the direction and point of impact.

Examples

FLA (10,9): *You push a bit on the side; that's almost like adding a bit of extra weight.* As for the transmission, *a bit of power* passes from one moving body to the next, beginning with the hands.

TOM (11,9): *If I take it in the middle it's like a balance* (in equilibrium); *if I take it on the side it's also like a balance* (in disequilibrium), *it'll drop . . . It's as if the wood had an axle in the centre; it pivots.*

The reader might be interested if, by way of a conclusion we compared the development we have just examined with the findings of two other authors. A. Rey[1] presented his subjects with two stationary blocks, each with a slot and a sliding shaft. The two blocks were so far apart that the shaft in the first could not reach the shaft in the second unless one or several strips of variable length were interposed between them. Subjects from $3\frac{1}{2}$–$4\frac{1}{2}$ years were unable to come up with a solution; some squeezed the longest strip between the blocks but not between the shafts. Subjects from the ages of $4\frac{1}{2}$ to $5\frac{1}{2}$ years (comparable to our level IA) still failed to solve the problem until they were shown how to do so with a ruler, whereupon they substituted the shafts. Subjects at level IB ($5\frac{1}{2}$ to $6\frac{1}{2}$ or 7) arrived at an empirical solution after several trials and errors or else after picking up clues from the demonstrator. At level IIA (7–8 years and in one or two precocious cases) success was immediate.

In his *La Structuration de l'instrument chez l'enfant* (1971) T. Mounoud tells us that he asked his subjects to push an object right across a table with the help of one or several of six sticks of various lengths. One of these sticks was straight and the others bent at right angles in different ways. Mounoud recorded three types of reaction: random choice of sticks (but with gradual preference for the longer ones); exclusive use of the straight stick (because it is 'straighter' or even 'longer'); and the choice of longer sticks however bent, the others seeming 'too small'. In general, Mounoud found that 2–4 year olds tend to integrate objects into the action; that 4–5

---

[1] *L'Intelligence practique chez l'enfant*, 1934, chapter IV.

year olds (our level IA) tend to project the action into the object, and that 6–7 year olds (our level IB) tend to accept transmission (which Mounoud calls 'relative') and to pay due regard to the respective powers of the object and of the action. But no matter whether there was complete integration or projection, the basis of Mounoud's elementary transmissions was invariably an instrumental extension (of the hand) due to a failure to distinguish the object from the subject in the case of integration, and the subject from the object in the case of projection which, from our point of view, comes back to the same thing. At our level IB, by contrast, there appears an authentic form of immediate or 'externally mediate' transmission.

The findings of these two authors thus agree largely with our own, even though in Mounoud's experiments there were no intermedia between instrument and object. It is therefore all the more interesting to discover that for Mounoud's subjects, too, the instrument was at first nothing more than an extension of the subject's action or body and that it did not become an intermedium until level IB.

This brings us to the relationship between this development and that of the child's intellectual grasp of the processes involved. Since that grasp is the result of active regulations of his actions, it is absent at level IA, where the only active and conscious regulation (in the case of the blocks) is the combination of the intermedia into a single block which extends the instrument P, or (in the case of the balls) a change of procedure. By contrast, from level IB onwards, there is active regulation and with it a grasp of the order of succession. Such regulation leads sooner or later to anticipatory co-ordination and consequently to the appearance of transitivity at level IIA.

CHAPTER FOUR

Counterweights and Bridges

I THE PROBLEM OF COUNTERWEIGHTS[1]

In this study we tried to find out how young subjects would solve the problem of bridging two 'mountains' (boxes) with a number of metal cubes and short 'planks', across which they could drive a miniature car. Now apart from the easy way out ('driving' the car down the side of one box and up the side of the other or constructing pillars), we discovered the precocious use of counterweights, and interesting conceptualizations of the effect of their pressure.[2] This provided us with an excellent chance of analysing the child's grasp of consciousness in a situation in which the object not only lends itself to simple constructions (e.g. building a road up a hill)[3] but also plays a dynamic role comparable to that of a catapult.

The subjects were handed two boxes of identical dimensions representing mountains separated by a river and asked to move objects of different weight (a figure, a rabbit or a car) from one to the other. To that end they were also provided with 'planks' (wood, metal or cardboard strips) of different lengths, a plastic ruler, copper or aluminium cubes, modelling clay and cork. The cubes were identical in size, though later we added some that were smaller or much larger than the rest.

The boxes were at first laid down flat, which enabled the subjects to construct a pillar with the cubes for a bridge of only two planks. Next the boxes were stood on end vertically, and the cubes no

---

[1] In collaboration with M. F. Graven.

[2] The French verb *appuyer*, as we saw earlier, means *inter alia* 'to press down', and 'to prop up'. (Trans.)

[3] See chapter 5 of *The Grasp of Consciousness*, Routledge & Kegan Paul, 1977.

longer sufficed for that solution. Instead, the subjects were forced to push two planks slightly over the edges of the boxes (which forced them to solve a preliminary balancing problem) and to lay a third on top of their free ends, or else to push them out further over the 'river' and secure them with counterweights before putting down the third plank; or finally to secure one with a counterweight and lay the second on the end of the first. As we shall see, every one of these solutions raises special problems with which we were familiar from our previous studies of causality and the concept of weight, but which we could now examine in the context of the child's free exercise of his practical intelligence, in which case his conceptualizations are the direct reflections of the actions he has just performed.

Level IA

Examples

LAU (4,4): *We must build a plank* (he puts the metal strip on the table between the two boxes, covers it with a wooden strip and a cardboard strip and sets the figure down). But there's water at the bottom. (He juxtaposes four cubes on the planks, then substitutes a single cube plus two superposed cubes, and finally two sets of two cubes.) Have you any other ideas? (He leans a plank against one of the boxes and lays another one across the cubes.) The boxes are stood on end: he increases the height of his pillar by two cubes, puts up another four topped by the cardboard strip: *the little man can stand up there* (on the cardboard). But clearly dissatisfied, LAU goes on to lay two planks (wood and cardboard) across the upper edges of the boxes without adjusting the overhang. Collapse, adjustment, success. He now tries to complete the bridge with a metal strip: collapse. He starts again with one metal and one wooden strip topped with cardboard. How did you make it (stand up)? *I thought we must put down this one and that.* Why? *For it to hold.* And if I remove that one (metal)? (He places the wood and cardboard strips across the edges of the two boxes.) Is that safe? *No, we need that bit of iron back.* Or something else? (Puts a copper cube on the side of the cardboard strip overhanging the 'river'!) He then gives up, and erects four cubes in the middle of the 'river' but not high enough to reach the planks.

BEN (4,11) first puts a cube on the table between the two boxes, then leans two inclined planks, on which the figure can cross the river, against the cube. Next she piles up cubes right to the top of and against one of the boxes, but returns to the system of inclined planks. Can't you build a bridge higher up? *No, it would fall down.* She nevertheless puts one cardboard and one wooden strip over the edges of the two boxes letting a third of each overhang the 'river' and then lays a metal strip across them. When it falls off, she covers the wooden strip with it. Having failed to construct a continuous bridge, she apparently wants to ensure the equilibrium of at least one of the two sides, and to that end she now superposes three planks with a slight overhang. Why did you put the metal there? *Otherwise it won't stay there because there isn't enough to hold it up.* Where? *Here* (in the centre). What shall we do? (She places two cubes on the strips which she has meanwhile placed across the edges of the boxes, thus suggesting that she may be beginning to think in terms of counterweights.) [Do they serve any purpose? *Yes, but I haven't got any more strips to put on and so* . . . (She is handed some more strips.) She superposes two strips on each side (overhang of one quarter) with a cube on top and a third strip on top of the cube!

ISA (4,8) holds one strip in his hand, then holds up two between the boxes (without making contact with their edges) and finally puts them down. He then piles up two cubes on each side of the 'river', connects them with a strip and adds an oblique strip for the descent. Vertical boxes: same behaviour at first, then places a slightly protruding strip on one box (but on one box only).

BUS (4,10) puts down one strip on each of the boxes and joins them by holding them together. Then he constructs a pillar in the centre. When the boxes are stood on end, he tries to join up two strips (wood and cardboard); they collapse and, instead of holding their ends together in his hand, he puts down two counterweights, a copper cube C and an aluminium cube A. What made you do that? *Because they're heavy.* What if we replace A with the cork? *It's going to break* (collapse). *No, it's going to stay up, it's not going to break because it's not heavy.* With cork and aluminium counterweights and the planks in equilibrium he says *it's hard, it presses down, it holds like this* (like his hands did at the beginning). But when he reconstructs the bridge, he places two counterweights on the wooden plank: C on the box and the cork on the other end. The structure collapses *because it's not heavy*, as if a heavier weight placed between the two boxes would provide better support.

MUR (4,9) like LAU and BUS places counterweights between the boxes. He begins (after building pillars for the horizontal boxes) by adjusting the metal and wood planks until they balance, but cannot tell how he did it: *I just knew.* And if you had to explain? *We have to put down this one* (wood) *and then that one* (metal) *and then this one* (cardboard laid over the metal). And if we stick the wood over the edge of the mountain (with inadequate support)? (He puts down a copper counterweight.) *It's firm. I'll put down this one, it'll hold.* Could you use cork instead? *No, it's not very firm. It's not made of iron.* Why does it hold with the copper? . . . He centres the cardboard strip over the metal and the wood and places the aluminium counterweight (*A*) between the two boxes! And if we used the cork (instead of *A*)? *No, that's not very firm.* And this one (Plasticine)? *I don't think so. It's the kind that gives, it's not very solid.*

CLA (4,7) lays the wooden and cardboard strips over the edges of the two boxes and, holding them in her hand, slides them across until they balance. She then lays the metal strip across their middle and seeing the result, exclaims: *It won't do, it's too heavy.* She restores equilibrium and puts the cardboard strip over the middle but cannot explain how she did it. And if we move the wood (the demonstrator moves it a fraction)? *It will rock.* How do you know? *I just do. I found out all by myself.* She is shown several variations with the cardboard strip, which is made to stay up or to fall off. She restores equilibrium: Why doesn't it fall down? *I did it very gently.* CLA next balances the wooden and metal strips: Did you move anything? *No.* Perhaps this one? (Affirmative nod of the head.)

VER (5,0) fills the gap between the boxes with cubes, then places a strip with a slight overhang on one of the boxes and a second one with a considerable overhang on the other: collapse. She adjusts the strips and pushes the cardboard between the ends of the two over-hanging strips: collapse. Why did they fall down? *Because cardboard is not the same as wood.* What do you mean? *This one is grey and the wood is yellow.* She uses one of the wooden strips and the plastic ruler and places a second wooden strip across the middle: success. Why does that hold? *Because the two are the same.* Is it firm? *Not all that firm, because the ruler doesn't hold very well.* Why not? *Because it's made of glass.* Holding up one end of a wooden strip by hand, she adds a small metal strip: *We must put this one here,*

54

because it's a bit heavier. This gives her the idea of using the cubes as counterweights, and she selects the biggest *because they're heavier.* But then, to retain one of the wooden strips she places a heavy cube on the supported part and a lighter cube on the unsupported part, the first for keeping it in place and the second for preventing its fall! *A weight will not make the plank fall off if we put it down gently.*

CAT (4,10 and again at 5,3) first puts down the wooden and cardboard strips and then lays a metal strip across their centres, topped by a slab of Plasticine, perhaps to try its effect. But despite the collapse of her bridge she continues with a copper cube, three cubes, etc. on the metal strip. Next she shifts them all towards the boxes, moves them back towards the middle, and finishes up with an aluminium cube (*fell off because it is too heavy*) and the cork (*that fell off because it's too light*). Suddenly she thinks of putting the cubes on the part of the strips supported by the boxes (counterweights) and succeeds. This time the aluminium cubes and copper cubes stay in place *because they're heavy* and because they are needed to *hold it all up.* And the cork? *No, that's too light, it'll fall off.* She thus seemed to have reached level IB, and when she was seen again at 5,3 that impression was at first confirmed. But when the weight of the car caused the collapse of her bridge, made up of two wooden strips (one of which covered two metal strips), she placed a large counterweight on the single strip and a smaller one on the thicker strip. Will the car get across this time? *No.* She puts a slab of Plasticine on the free end (between the two boxes) of the single wooden strip. Why do you put it in the middle? . . . The bridge collapses and she starts all over again and says: *Because it's better that way.*

ROB (5,10) also places a metal strip and an aluminium cube on the free ends of the correctly placed wood and cardboard strips. When the bridge collapses (*it's too heavy, it won't hold*) he decides to prop it up with pillars. Then he returns to the overhang method. The demonstrator next moves the strips about and asks: What makes them stay up sometimes and fall down at others? *It's too light, because you are getting too close* (to the other box) *and it* (the wooden strip) *is too light.* What about one like that (metal)? *No, because it's thin. If it were thick it would hold.*

GAN (6,8) after various solutions with pillars, etc. puts down two overhanging wooden strips and lays a cardboard strip over them. The strip stays up *because it's lighter than the two strips,* which suggests level IB, but soon afterwards she uses two overhanging metal strips and lays a wooden strip over them saying *that will hold because the wood is heavier than the two irons.* After failure, she rests the end of one wooden strip on the end of another, and puts counterweights on the two opposite ends. Then she 'strengthens' the whole by adding two further counterweights at the junction of the strips, thus preparing the collapse of the bridge.

It is characteristic of these subjects that when they eventually get round to the method of overhanging strips, they are able to balance them by adjusting the length of the overhang. They do not, however, grasp the reason why their manoeuvres are successful and though some of them have begun to consider the weight in certain situations and sometimes even to use counterweights, their actions and, *a fortiori,* their conceptualizations show that they confuse the pull of the weight with its retaining function: they lack a systematic grasp of weight relations.

We must first of all try to justify this method of distinguishing level IA from level IB, where weight relations begin to be applied in action. We might equally well have distinguished the two levels by the respective absence and use of counterweights. But on the one hand, the use of counterweights is too common in subjects from 4 years upwards to suggest a higher level of development, and the case of BEN (among others) shows that there is every possible intermediate stage between the superposition of various strips (*because there isn't enough to hold it up*) or the random piling up of cubes and the use of counterweights proper. Now what matters is not so much the idea of counterweights, which is a simple extension of the manual action of pressing the ends of the strip against the boxes, as the way in which it is interpreted and, in this respect, it is clear that the conceptualizations of subjects at level IA reflect a non-relational conception of weight, and that this is therefore their most characteristic feature.

Before dwelling on this point at greater length, let us first of all look at the positive aspect of these subjects' simplest reactions, once they have discovered that none of the strips can be used to join the two boxes directly. Their first reaction (LAU and BEN) is to place the strips and the cubes on the table between the boxes (forgetting that the bridge is meant to ford an expanse of water) and if necessary to add sloping strips or stairs to allow the figures or cars to climb down from one box and up the next. Their second reaction is to construct a pile of cubes between the two boxes to support the two strips, and to build a horizontal bridge, which is easy enough to do when the boxes lie flat. But when they are stood on end, another solution is needed, and then the real problems begin: the subject must try to balance the strips by careful adjustment of their projection.

Now the main importance of these reactions is that they combine the successful balancing of the overhanging strips with a failure to grasp the reasons for this success. Thus MUR's explanation was *I just knew*, and he thought that equilibrium depends on the material of the strips. Moreover, when the overhang became excessive he placed a counterweight on the wrong end. CLA realized that if the overhang is too large, *it will rock*, but when asked what she did to avoid that, she simply said *I did it very gently* and congratulated herself on having *found out all by myself*. ROB, almost six years old, admittedly invoked the weight but in the wrong sense: if the plank has too great an overhang it will collapse because *it's too light* (wood strip) or *because it's thin, if it were thick it would hold*, (metal strip). In our earlier study of causality we extended a ruler over the edge of a table: 4 to 5 year olds knew that it would fall off when it stuck out by approximately half its length, but their initial explanation was based on symmetry (the overhanging piece *is a bit too long*) and the weight was not invoked before the age of *ca.* 7 years. In the present case, where the objects (the strips) are less elongated than a thin ruler and in which the overhang is not presented as gradually, symmetry is never invoked in the conceptualizations of the action.

Once the two strips are in equilibrium they must still be joined together because they are now too short to form a bridge. The child naturally resorts to all sorts of manipulations before or after balancing the strips: he holds one up between the boxes to find out whether it is too short, or he pushes two strips towards each other and holds them together between two fingers, or (and this is an essential preparation for the use of counterweights) he presses the other ends of the two strips against the boxes. Having finished these explorations, he is left with two solutions, both direct extensions of the manipulations we have just described: he can either join the two balancing strips with a third to complete the bridge, or else he can move the two strips forward and retain them with the help of counterweights (or, of course, combine these two methods).

57

Now this second part of these subjects' bridge-building attempts faces us with a special problem: neither their actions nor their conceptualizations are adequate, and we want to know whether it is the lack of adequate concepts which hampers their action or whether it is the failure to act in an adequate manner, reinforced by awareness of this inadequacy, which explains the inadequacy of their conceptualizations. It is here that the use they make of counter-weights is particularly instructive.

For even the laying of a third strip on the two in equilibrium is highly significant. LAU, for example, placed a metal strip on the wood and cardboard strips. Had he failed to consider the relative weights, or was he simply trying to support the original strips from above? His subsequent behaviour suggests the second alternative, for he later replaced the metal strip with a copper cube over the join of the two lower strips. BEN, CLA and CAT also placed metal strips over two other strips and ROB went so far as to add an aluminium cube with the evident intention of restraining the rest with its weight. After the failure of this attempt, he nevertheless contended that *it's too heavy* (as did CLA), an apparent contradiction we shall examine below.

But first it must be stressed that every one of our subjects at level IA who made use of counterweights, placed them not only on the box ends of the strips but also on their free ends. BEN was the only exception because, for her, the cubes were nothing but substitutes for the strips, her idea (which throws much light on the role she attributed to counterweights) being that the more strips are piled up on the edge of a box, the better they will hold (*cf.* ROB who asked for a 'thicker' metal strip) because heavy objects stay in place regardless of the state of equilibrium. That is precisely why LAU placed a copper cube on the free end of the cardboard strip. BUS, who used the copper and aluminium cubes as true counterweights (*because it's hard it presses down*, etc.), went on to add a cork to the free end of the wooden strip and when his bridge collapsed stated explicitly that it did so *because it's not heavy*. MUR and CAT behaved similarly, and VER ended up with a solution that brought out the equivocal function of counterweights at this level: she placed a heavy weight on the box end of the strip and a lighter weight on the other end in the belief that the first would retain the bridge and the second was light enough to assist the first without bringing the structure down.

How can we explain these surprisingly contradictory actions, this treatment of weight as something that arbitrarily pulls down or retains? To answer that question we must examine the subject's own actions that led to the discovery of these two contrary functions. That weights should cause objects to fall down seems quite obvious to the child who, very early on, learns that by pressing on an object he can push it down. But the fact that weights can also retain objects and prevent their fall is quite a different experience, and the child thinks it paradoxical that both experiences should be based on the same action of pressing, in our case, a strip against the box, first by hand and then with a heavy cube. To the child, this means that this equivocal action can be attributed absolutely to particular objects, and as yet without any relational hypotheses about the interactions of these objects: in fact every one of the child's own actions is born of such false absolutes reflecting his egocentric perspective, and unidirectional motivity. It follows that if his hand has the power of holding a plank up at either end, the counterweight to which this power is delegated will do exactly the same.

If that is true of the schemata governing the actions of the child, it goes without saying that the conscious grasp of these actions will give rise to a conceptualization that, even while reflecting the actions, will accentuate their non-relational character by turning the effects of the weight into the results of a power inherent in the qualities of objects and not of their interactions. This explains why BUS equated 'heavy' with 'hard': *because it's hard it presses down*, while MUR equated it with 'firm': *the cork is not as firm as the iron*, and the Plasticine even less so because *it's the kind that gives, it's not very solid*. VER even went so far as to identify the weight of an object with its general qualities: a wooden plank will retain another because they are *the same*, while cardboard and wood which are *not the same colour*, will not. In these circumstances the subject is clearly unable to proceed to the correlations which would enable him to grasp that a given object acts in one direction because it is heavier than another, and in the opposite direction because it is lighter. For all that, subjects at this level do make certain active correlations, for instance adjusting the relative overhang of a strip so that it balances on the edge of the box, or deploying the thrust of the counterweight successfully. However, appearances to the contrary, these partial successes are in no way accompanied by relational conceptualizations. Thus when ROB said: *It's too heavy, it won't hold* to explain the collapse of his bridge (cardboard and wood, topped by a metal strip and an aluminium cube), it might seem as if he had grasped the function of the weight, but a moment later he blamed another collapse on the lightness of the wooden strip. Similarly BUS thought the bridge would collapse *because it's not heavy.* In other words, these subjects admittedly assume that the pressure of one object can be increased or counteracted by that of another, but as this pressure is ambivalent and has contradictory effects, the resulting relations between the objects cannot possibly seem coherent.

Level IB

The appropriate correlations first appear at level IB.

Examples

PAG (4,4 advanced) places the strips on the boxes straightaway and holds their free ends together. Next he constructs a pillar under their meeting point. With the boxes standing on end, he tries to, and succeeds in, balancing each plank separately. Why does it stay up? *Because before* (when the planks protruded too far) *it wasn't heavy but now it holds. When the wood goes up to here* (right across the box) *it holds very much better.* And if we separated the mountains? (He places the figure as a counterweight on the supported end of a plank): *That holds better.* Why? *Because it's heavier than my hand.* (At this moment a cube falls off the table. PAG picks it up and puts it on the plank.) *That'll work better: it's heavier than the figure.* He then pulls out the planks so that the end of one rests on the end of the other but places the counterweight on the box end of the supported plank and not on the one that does the supporting. After collapse, he places an aluminium cube on the right plank and adds a cork: *We have to put two down here.* Won't the cork work all by itself? *No, it's not heavy enough.* Why does it have to be heavy? *It holds much better when it's heavy; the cork isn't heavy but the iron is heavier than the wood.*

NEU (5,3) begins with pillars, and when he goes on to the over-hanging planks begins with a level IA reaction: he rests the end of one plank on the end of the other and tries to 'consolidate' them by placing a third plank over them. But the collapse of the structure

60

obviously teaches him better, for he piles up small blocks and cubes on the box end of the supporting plank. Subsequently, to allow a rabbit to cross the two (wooden) planks he uses the motor car as a counterweight *because it's heavier than the planks*. And will the little man do as well? *I don't think so, we'd have to add this plate.* He then reverts to level IA behaviour by placing the strip on the meeting point of the two planks, but next adds two strips and the motor car in the correct position: *It's heavier than those thin bits of wood.* When seen fifteen days later, he immediately constructs an over-lapping bridge retained with a copper counterweight *because it's heavier than the plank*. He adds further counterweights for the passage of the motor car.

RAC (5,11) immediately puts down one overhanging plank, and rests the end of the second, retained by a counterweight, on its end. No cubes on the other side? *No, that'll hold by itself.* The rabbit passes successfully, but for the motor cars he adds cubes, and this time on either side. To lend the structure greater strength, she replaces the two wooden planks with metal strips topped with wood. Why didn't it collapse? *Because the wood is over the metal and they are held down by the cubes* (but she adds two small cubes on the ends of the central wooden plank). If we took these two (cubes) away would it still hold? *No, it would collapse.* She thus displays a residue of level IA behaviour. She is next shown two planks (wood and metal) of the same length, the first protruding further than the second: *It* (the wood) *ought to have a heavier* (counter) *weight because it sticks out more.* And like this (equal overhangs)? *The same weights* (experiment: the metal plank collapses). *The weight wasn't heavy enough.* But the wood held, didn't it? *The other cube was heavier* (wrong). (They are changed round: further collapse.) *That's because the metal is not as heavy as the wood.* Is that why it fell off? *Yes* (fresh residue of IA behaviour). Weigh these. *The metal is heavier.* Why doesn't it stay up, then? . . .

NIC (6,2) begins by filling in the bottom between the two boxes then constructs two pillars and can think of nothing else to do. He is then shown a plank with a considerable overhang. Why does it fall off? *Because something is needed to hold it* (and he puts down a counterweight). Is there a way of making the plank stay up all by itself? *More of it must go on the mountain. Right now there is less wood on the box than over the empty bit and that weighs less than the rest.* Why does the cube hold it up? *Because it's iron, it's heavier.*

Heavier than what? *No, but it holds all the same.* Can the rabbit pass? *No, it's heavier than the wood* (that is, heavier than the plank itself and not than the cube that retains it). He reconstructs the bridge with a plank whose free end rests on the other plank but puts counterweights on both boxes and more on the supported plank. Why? *It has to be heavier than the wood.* But when invited to replace these counterweights with cork, he says: *No, because that weighs less and the plank will drop off. Ah, no, this plank is held up by the other one and by that cube* (which means that its counterweights may be removed).

VIE (6,8) uses counterweights straightaway but explains her behaviour as follows: *The plank is not heavy enough to stay up by itself, that's why we have to put down something heavy.*

FAR (6,7) still places a metal strip on two wooden planks without counterweights (level IA response), lays further strips over the box ends, and discovers that the projecting plank *will not fall off because it is close enough to the mountain* and that the counterweights must be *heavier than the planks and the man in the empty bit.* On the other hand, when one of these planks supports the other, she refuses to remove the counterweight from the second. The demonstrator replaces her counterweight with a cork and FAR is surprised: *Perhaps it holds because it has just a tiny bit of force; the wood must be a bit lighter than the cork.*

HER (6,11) has the same reaction: he refuses to replace a metal counterweight on the supported plank with a cork. *That won't hold because the cork is light and the wood is heavier. Look* (experiment). *It didn't fall down because the cork is heavier than the wood.* And if we put the cork in the place of this one and the metal cube here? *That's fine, because that one* (metal) *is heavier than the cork and this one is almost as heavy, but I don't know if it'll hold.* Must one of these two weights be heavier, or can they both be the same? *I don't know, but it's better if we put down these* (metal on both sides) *because they're heavier.*

MOU (6,7) says straightaway that an overhanging plank will fall off *because there isn't enough length to hold it* (on the box). Next she puts down two planks, one of which partly covers the other and, like HER, places heavy counterweights on both sides: Can we remove this one (from the supported plank)? *No, it would tumble down.* Must they be on both sides? *Yes. We can't remove these because those* (on the supporting plank) *cannot hold everything and the rabbit is too heavy.* Look. (Surprised.) Why didn't they collapse? *Because this one* (the supported plank) *is still long enough* (enough of it still rests on the box) *and because the rabbit is very light.* What do we have to think of when we choose a cube? *Of the weight of the bit that helps the plank.* And how can we tell? *We have to see if it holds or not.* Must it be heavier than something? *Heavier than this one* (the lighter cubes) *and heavier than the rabbit.* Identical counterweights are placed on the wooden and metal planks. Will that hold? *No, because this one* (metal) *is too heavy.* So do we have to think of something else? *Yes, of the weight of the plank and of the weight of the cube that is going to help* it because we have to add something.

This transitional stage is characterized, on the plane of action, by the immediate balancing of the projecting planks and by the spontaneous and rapid use of counterweights and, on the plane of conceptualization, by the incipient correlation of the weights. These developments merit our careful consideration.

Thus while there has been a notable advance in the practical solutions proffered, there are still a great many gaps. On the one hand, residues of level IA behaviour are fairly frequent. NEU who had the (increasingly common) idea of placing the end of one plank on that of the other, felt that he could enhance the retaining effect by placing a small metal plank on their junction as if the added weight were some sort of glue (we have nevertheless treated NEU as a subject at level IB because he went on to apply the relation 'heavier than' to the counterweights and the planks they held up). NIC, after balancing two planks with counterweights, added a third plank that did not reach the edges of either box and a counterweight on each of its two ends thus endangering his entire structure. FAR added a metal plank to the two lighter, overhanging planks, etc. We thus gain the impression that, though these subjects manage to correlate weights, they do not initially discard the (level IA) idea that weight simultaneously props up and pulls down and, in particular, that it can retain itself. On the other hand, we now meet the almost general reaction (except for RAC at the beginning and NIC at the end) of placing counterweights on both the supporting and the supported planks, and of thinking that both counterweights are indispensable. For much the same reasons RAC replaced the wooden planks held down by heavy counterweights with two metal strips. Other reactions (doubling the planks on one or on both sides, etc.)

63

also reflect the general tendency to consider that the force of the counterweights must be augmented with that of more weighty planks.

When we pass to the conceptualization of these actions, we note one remarkable advance and a second that leads half the way to the correct correlations. The first is the conscious grasp of what was partly or fully done in practice even at level IA: the balancing of the overhanging planks. PAG, at the age of 4, claimed that a plank *holds much better* when one of its sides covers the entire box; RAC wanted to put down a heavier counterweight when the plank *sticks out more*; NIC said explicitly that the section supported by the box must be longer, since otherwise *these is less wood on the box . . . and that weighs less than the bit in the empty place*; FAR held the same views as RAC; and MOU spoke of the length needed to hold the plank down on the box.

But while this involves a clear correlation of the two parts of a single object and even though that correlation is often expressed in terms of weight, the correlation, by these subjects, of the counterweights with the object they retain represents a much more spectacular advance. Though he was only four years old, PAG already stated that the iron (the counterweight) is heavier than the wood (the retained plank); *it's heavier than the planks*, said NEU; *it's heavier than the wood* (NIC); the counterweights must be *heavier than the planks and the man in the empty bit* (FAR). All these expressions bear witness to a systematic correlation of the weights involved. But what is its significance? Our other studies with weights (see *inter alia* the next chapter) seem to suggest that it is only at about 7–8 years (level IIA characterized by additivity and reversibility) that weights are equalized quantitatively on a balance, each side of which moves in an opposite direction to the other and on which equilibrium is reached when the two weights are equal. Must we then assume that, when it comes to counterweights, there is a much earlier understanding of these quantitative compensations between opposite effects, and that the subject uses an equal or heavier counterweight to retain a plank because he understands that this retaining effect is the converse of the plank's own tendency to fall down? This is indeed what his actions might suggest (except for the level IA residues we have mentioned), and all our previous studies also revealed precocious correlations of this type. But in this particular case, the conceptualizations hold the key to this enigma: from the fact that a heavy object will, depending on its situation, fall down or stay up, the subject concludes that the counterweight not only 'helps' to retain the object but must also be heavier than the latter because, from his own experience, he knows that effective help is normally rendered by those who are bigger than himself.

Two of our subjects were remarkably explicit in this respect: *The plank is not heavy enough to hold by itself*, said VIE, *that's why we have to put down something heavy*; and MOU explained that in selecting the counterweight one has to think *of the weight of the plank and of the cube that is going to help it* (the plank), *because we have to add something*. The two verbs 'help' and 'add' suggest that what these subjects have in mind is a strengthening of the inherent powers of the plank. Hence there is not the least contradiction between the residual (level IA) responses we have mentioned and these nascent correlations: the latter are not yet based on compensation, reversibility, and quantitative composition, but on what we might call the synergy of the actions.

This type of conceptualization recalls two sorts of reactions observed in our studies of causality. When one ball has just struck another and when the experiment is repeated but the weight of the second ball is increased, young subjects think that it will go further, because its greater weight is bound to increase the effect of the active ball. Moreover, when three weights are placed on the pan of a balance and the child is asked to say what happens if one of the weights is changed round etc., subjects below a relatively advanced age will 'compose' the forces by introducing synergetic arguments: this one helps that one, etc.

In short, the early correlations that appear at this level are so many psychomorphic or biomorphic interpretations of the actions of partners who are capable of helping or hindering one another. In this case, the original confusion introduced by the ambiguous nature of pressure (up or down) is in no way diminished by the fact that two or more weights are involved in the experiment: the stronger can 'aid' the weaker to stay up. In other words the weight of the plank acts in the same direction as the counterweight: as VIE put it, *the plank is not heavy enough to stay up by itself*. This explains why, when the end of one plank rests on another secured with a counterweight, the child would rather 'aid' the one that is being supported than rely exclusively on the 'strength' of the supporting plank.

Stage II

If the placing of counterweights on two planks, one of which supports the other, can indeed be reduced to the factors we have just mentioned, then such conduct ought to disappear at level IIA, which is the level of relational actions. But a further factor might well be involved, namely the mediate transmission of the actions of the weight because, while the counterweight secures the plank that supports the other, it also secures the other by the agency of the first. Now, we know that mediate transmission still causes problems at Stage II and if the child should think that this type of transmission is involved here, then he will fail to master the problem at level IIA. Hence the following responses are of particular importance.

Examples

GAV (7,2) straightaway explains the equilibrium or fall of the overhanging planks and goes on to construct a bridge of two planks secured with two metal counterweights and topped with a third plank. He rejects cork counterweights *because they're lighter than wood.* He then rests the end of one plank on that of the other and places a heavier counterweight on the supporting plank. Could you do it with weights on one side alone? (He removes the lighter counterweight and discovers that the bridge holds.) *The block holds this plank and the plank is held by that one.* Does one plank hold the other? *No, it's the block* (after which he nevertheless returns the small counterweight to the supported plank). Could we change these blocks about? *Yes, but then you must place this plank on the other, that'll do the opposite.*

MAN (7,3) begins by putting down two metal counterweights *because the blocks hold the plank; without them it wouldn't hold.* Could we put some modelling clay instead of the block on this one (the supported plank)? *It wouldn't hold.* (Tries.) *Gosh, it holds!* And with cork? *Yes. If we put the copper here* (supporting plank) *it will hold because it* (the plank) *holds up the other plank, so the cork wouldn't change anything.* (The counterweights are changed about.) *No, we'd have to put this one* (the supporting plank) *on top of the other one.* But she continues to maintain that it is essential to place a light counterweight on the supported plank.

KHA (7,9) after the erection of several pillars, puts down two projecting planks secured by counterweights and connected with a third plank. The rabbit passes safely but he adds further counterweights before driving the car across. When it, too, has passed successfully he concludes: *It's the same weight as the car on either side, so that makes twice the weight of the car.* He is asked to construct a bridge with two planks and with counterweights on one side only: he lets the ends of the two planks overlap in the centre, places a counterweight on the supporting plank, but to strengthen the structure places a second counterweight on the other plank. Is there nowhere else you can put it? *Yes, but we have to put the rabbit on this side; on the other side it will fall down.*

DUR (7,0). Same situation: he places a large weight on the correct side and two small ones on the other. He is asked to make a bridge with counterweights on one side only: he piles up counterweights on the supporting plank; then, despite his success, reverts to the original solution.

BUL (8,7). Same reactions, but seems to have a good grasp of the relations: *The metal plank* (supported) *makes the other one* (wood) *fall off; if the one is on top of the other one more weight is needed on the one underneath.* But before he allows the car to pass he places counterweights on both ends of the supported plank. When the bridge collapses, he declares: *I don't understand it at all. The copper* (on the supporting plank) *is heavier than the rabbit and the* (supported) *plank!*

WAS (9,10) after constructing a bridge of three planks, goes on to construct another by laying the end of a cardboard strip on the end of a ruler and placing counterweights on both. Why doesn't the rabbit fall off? *The ruler holds the cardboard up.* And if we replaced the copper with cork? *No, the cork has no weight* (tries). *It holds!* Why? *The metal and the ruler hold the cardboard up.* And with the car? *We must put double the weight on each side.* Is there no way of holding it up with weights on one side only? *No, but a single plank would stay up.*

Here now, for comparison, are some level IIB responses, starting with an intermediate case.

STE (9,0) constructs several bridges with three planks and equal counterweights on the two supporting the third. Can you do it with the cubes on one side only? *I don't think so* (she tries with two projecting planks but with too large an overhang of the one carrying the counterweights: failure). Why did it fall down? *Because this side wasn't held up by blocks.* Is there no way of making it work? *No* (but she retracts the plank and adds a further counterweight: the rabbit stays up. She removes the counterweight she has added and the bridge still does not collapse). Why does it stay up? *Because the weights hold this plank and this plank holds the other one.* She then puts down the rabbit, which falls off, and to restore equilibrium she does nothing to the supported plank but adds a metal cube to the supporting plank, explaining that the weights must be heavier *than the* (two) *planks and the car.*

JOA (9,10) after building several pillars, constructs a bridge with two projecting planks and counterweights on the supporting plank only: *It* (the bridge) *is held up on both sides: one side by the* (supporting) *plank and the other by the weight on the mountain.* To strengthen the bridge for the passage of the motor car, he places a counterweight on the supported plank then removes it, and places four cubes on the supporting plank.

JUR (10,6) constructs several pillars, and as soon as the boxes are stood on end, builds a bridge of two projecting planks with a counterweight on the supporting plank. He then places a counterweight on the other plank but explains: *It's not necessary because there is a weight on this wood and the cardboard is lighter.* What must you look out for? *That the weight is heavier than this plank plus the car plus the other plank.*

When we compare the responses of subjects at level IIA with those at level IB we note the emergence of certain characteristics commonly associated with this first of the operational stages. To begin with, there is an appreciation that for two weights to balance they must act in opposite directions. Thus BUL declared that the supported plank makes the other one *fall off*, whence the need for heavier counterweights on the supporting plank. The counterweights are therefore treated as compensations, as acting in opposition to, and no longer in collaboration with the weight. In the second place, we note the emergence of quantitative preoccupations: KHA, for example, engaging in spurious calculations to prove that the counterweights are twice as heavy as the car. Finally and above all, it is clear that subjects at level IIA have an incipient grasp of mediate transmission, which is a causal form of operational transitivity: GAV said that *it's the block*, not the supporting plank that holds up the other plank; MAN said *the block holds the* (supporting) *plank . . . which holds the other plank*, etc. Each of these subjects was therefore convinced that the counterweight acted on the plank supported by the first and not just on the latter.

Nevertheless a curious but characteristic reaction of subjects at level IIA, is that, though they may not think it essential to place counterweights on the supported plank (*cf.* the level IB response: we must, etc.), they nevertheless believe that such counterweights play a useful part. Now, they would be quite justified in this belief if they said simply that one cannot tell in advance if the counterweight on the supporting plank will ensure the safe passage of the rabbit, car, etc. so that, as a precaution, it is best to secure the other plank as well. But what is so interesting about their reactions is that they do not realize that they could achieve the same security by increasing the number of counterweights on one side. Even BUL, despite his precise explanations, and WAS, who had just seen the facts belie his predictions, felt it was essential to add counterweights to both sides the moment the weight of the passing body was increased. Other subjects prefer to place a heavy counterweight on the supporting plank and a light one on the other.

It would therefore seem that even while assuming mediate transmission, by which the pressure of the weight on the first plank is communicated to the second, these subjects fail to appreciate its full effects. Here we have a situation comparable to the transmission of movement which, at this level, remains semi-internal and semi-external, with each of the intermedia continuing to perform its own movements. In the present case, the subjects believe that the second plank is held up by the first and by its counterweight, but that it can still contribute its share to the transitive action. This response is undoubtedly a final residue of the 'aid' concept so widespread at earlier levels (much as the mediate semi-external transmission of movement springs from the concatenation of immediate transmissions).

Level IIB produces quite different reactions: during the practical work the subjects do not touch the supported plank and, if the bridge should collapse, they simply add more counterweights to the supporting plank. In their explanations they argue that *it's not necessary* to consolidate the supported plank (JUR) because *it's held up on both sides* (JAO); it suffices that the single counterweight should be heavier than the two planks and the car (JUR). The

69

reason why these facts are grasped before the purely internal transmission of movements (stage III) is undoubtedly that, in the present
case, the subject has to cope with a succession of 'retaining' actions,
and not with invisible movements.

Stage III and conclusions

Stage III reactions teach us nothing new, except that the subjects
have begun to conceptualize the conditions of equilibrium more
systematically.

Examples

DAR (12,0): a plank will overbalance if *the big part is on top of the
water and the small part over the mountain, so the weight is not even.*
Counterweights are therefore needed: *The block must be chosen by*
(according to) *the weight of the plank and of the person who passes on
top. If the two planks jut out, two heavy blocks must be put on one side
or a single block on each side . . . If you put a block on just one side it
must be equal in weight to the two blocks* (which would have to be
placed on the two sides), *the two planks and the car*, etc.

As far as the relationship between the conscious grasp of the action
itself and its observable effects is concerned, the responses produced
from level IA upwards are of great complexity and throw a great
deal of light on the understanding of the intereffects of action and
object, on the distortions to which they give rise and on the marked
differences between the effects and co-ordinations of particular
actions.

In respect of the intereffects, it is clear that when they themselves
push, support, or pull down an object, its weight does not strike
these subjects as having a dynamic aspect; on the other hand, they
realize that without objects there would be no action of pushing,
supporting, etc. The grasp of weight is thus clearly born of an
interaction between subject and object. But we saw that from level
IA onwards (and that level was not the most primitive we could
have chosen), this interaction is not wholly beneficial, because
conceptualizations born of a conscious grasp of one's own actions
deform the data in various ways, and because the more stringent
analysis needed to correct the initial conceptualizations is impossible

70

in the absence of correlations, the construction of functions, and of inferential co-ordinations; now before the latter can become objective, the subject must engage increasingly not only in particular actions, but also in the general co-ordination of these actions.

In that respect, level IA is one of maximum deformation and minimum co-ordination. Because of the polyvalence of the action of pressing (up or down), the weight of an object is treated variously as a source of retention or collapse. Now, this is not wrong in itself, but before he can abandon the belief that a weight placed on the free extremity of an overhanging plank will act as a counterweight, the subject must be able to correlate its action with its various points of application, and also with the weights and degrees of liberty or retention of the objects on which the pressure is exerted. In other words, the child must pass on from the idea of an absolute force to that of a system of dependencies. The problem is then to determine whether the correlations leading to the discovery of that system are derived from the objective effects, or whether, before he can interpret these effects correctly, the subject must first be able to co-ordinate them. Now the sequence of levels we have encountered not only proves that necessity but also shows that this co-ordinating activity gradually transcends the individual actions and the observable effects they produce, to culminate in reflexive abstraction.

Let us recall, first of all, that at level IA the subject does not yet say that one object is 'heavier' than another (as he does at level IB) but simply that it is 'too heavy' or 'too light' for a particular purpose. All the same, an early correlation does appear at level IA, but it is not conceptualized and internal to the specific action of balancing a plank on the edge of a box. However, this correlation of the overhanging part of the plank with the end resting on the box involves an internal property of a single object (the plank) and can be explained in terms of the symmetry involved in the balance of one's own body (as we saw elsewhere).

At level IB, the subject begins to construct the relation 'heavier than', subordinated to functional dependencies (the retention of the plank is a function of a counterweight heavier than itself, etc.), and the problem is then to determine the source of this relation. It goes without saying that it is based, first of all, on observations of the behaviour of objects because without experience the child would have no inkling of functional dependencies. But that cannot be the whole explanation, since the same experience is not appealed to at

71

level IA. A function is a relation of variations and hence a relation of relations (a more or less heavy counterweight is needed for a more or less heavy plank), which implies a correlation (application) and a given order (the stability of the plank depends on the counterweight and not the converse). Hence, when these functions appear at level IB they not only help to correlate the data, but also introduce general, logico-mathematical co-ordinations (relations of relations, correspondences and order) which even if they do not yet intervene in inferential co-ordinations nevertheless imply the activity of a subject. The following dialectical process therefore occurs: the observed behaviour of the objects corrects the deformations resulting (at level IA) from the polyvalence of the action of pressing (up or down), but it is the subject's co-ordinations of particular actions that first lends intelligible forms to his observations. At first, however, these co-ordinations do not yet lead to a satisfactory conceptualization, or more precisely to the abandonment of the misconception that a heavier weight 'aids' the lighter.

At level IIA, by contrast, the weights of the cubes and of the planks are understood to act in opposite directions, and it is once again the observable behaviour of the objects which suggests this interpretation and helps to correct the level IB conceptualization. But it goes without saying that the observable effects do not co-ordinate themselves; it is only the operational instruments of quantification, reversibility and transitivity which allow a better interpretation of the data. Now despite these advances due to the general co-ordination of actions, the conceptualization of particular actions remains inadequate and helps to perpetuate the idea that the transmission of the retaining force of the counterweight by the supporting plank to the supported plank is not quite sufficient to ensure the stability of the whole.

At level IIB, finally, the child is certain, thanks to an advance in his powers of deduction, of the full effects of this transmission. What we have here, therefore, is a genuine inferential co-ordination, hand in hand with the more refined experimental checks the subject has learned to make. Equilibrium has finally been reached between the alternating movements of correcting the conceptualization of an action as such under the influence of its observed effects, and the intelligible formulation of these effects under the influence of the co-ordination of actions by the subject. This equilibrium is formulated explicitly at stage III.

72

II THE CONSTRUCTION OF BRIDGES
AND STAIRCASES[1]

Section I was devoted to the construction of a bridge but with particular reference to the use of counterweights. The child was presented with planks of different length and weight, cubes of various weights and asked to erect a bridge between two 'mountains' (boxes) which could support the two ends of the bridge, but were so tall (when placed on end) as to exclude the use of pillars (a common solution when the boxes were laid sideways) and hence tended to encourage the use of counterweights. In the following series of tests the material and other factors are far more homogeneous, so that the child can respond more spontaneously and hence reveal the various types of regulations he employs.

The children are handed a box of wooden blocks in the form of parallelepipeds, with bases measuring 2.2 by 2.2 cm and of five different heights: 2.2, 4.4, 6.6, 15 and 19 cm. (We shall refer to these blocks as 1, 2, 3, 4 and 5.) In addition they are provided with a number of wooden arches 4.4 or 10 cm long and 2.2 or 4.4 cm high (these were rarely used). A river is symbolized by a blue tablecloth folded to the required width (usually 20 cm). The child is asked to construct a bridge that would allow a man to cross the river, and also to construct a staircase leading, for example to a rock on an island.

Our account will be shorter than that given in section I, in which many of the relevant points have already been discussed. Instead, we shall be looking at many fresh points of great interest. They all reflect the new arrangements: with the five types of block, the idea of using counterweights does not occur to children below level IIA, i.e. below the age of 7–8 years, and there is a systematic failure to construct the bridge throughout stage I: these subjects consider either the length of the bridge or else its equilibrium, but fail to correlate the corresponding correlations.

Stage I

Examples (level IA)

MAR (5,0) bridges a narrow river with one vertical 3 on either bank

---

[1] In collaboration with R. Maier.

linked by a horizontal 4. When the river is widened she moves one 3 forward, brings 4 up to it, and finds that it no longer reaches the other 3. She replaces the 4 with a 5 which reaches across, but when the river is widened to 20 cm, she uses a 6 extended by a 3, and discovers that both collapse: *It's too small*, and she gives up. Her staircase is a simple series of horizontal and juxtaposed 1s.

SOP (5,8). 20 cm river: she stands a 5 on end on one bank and a 3 plus a 4 on the other and tries to join them with a horizontal 5. When this proves impossible, she extends the horizontal 5 with a 3 supported on the vertical 4. Do you think it will stay up? *No, we must hold up both blocks* (by hand). She then staggers two horizontal 3s on top of a vertical 4 (staircase with steps) and leans the upper 3 against a horizontal 5: collapse. She next puts down a vertical 5 on each bank and connects them with two horizontal 4s, first juxtaposed and then with their ends superposed: collapse. Presented with the island problem, she (like MAR) builds a high tower with a 5 leaning against it, as a staircase might do.

LUS (6,0) places one vertical 4 on each bank, covers one with a horizontal 4 (overhanging by four-fifths of its length!) and the other with a horizontal 5 (also overhanging by four-fifths of its length) and then tries to hold them in place by laying a horizontal 4 across. When he can feel the fragility of his structure, he reduces the overhangs but fails to prevent a collapse. He nevertheless repeats his original construction. Staircase: stands a 5, a 4, a 3, a 2 and a 1 on end.

PHI (6,1) places an arch on one bank, and tops it with an overhanging 5. On the other bank he places another 5 meant to reach the first and leans a third 5 against it as a prop (sort of counterweight). The structure collapses. After a second attempt along similar lines, he uses the lid of the box of blocks (made of cardboard) and retains it by placing 4s on its two ends.

BRI (6,1) having used too tall a base (a 5) tries to construct a staircase with four horizontal and overhanging 3s or 4s, not realizing that the upper elements will collapse. He then retains them by hand.

LIP (6,5) places the centres of two horizontal 3s on two 2s and joins them with a 5: collapse. He next tops the 3s with a set of overhanging 3s: collapse. He adjusts the blocks until they hold, and builds a staggered flight of 4 steps on one of them: collapse.

74

Next, he extends a 3 with a 4 and lays a 5 across them to hold them up!

CLA (6,5) uses a series of 2s and 3s and ignores the fact that they overhang by more than half their lengths. He tries to link them with a 5 which falls off, then tries to turn them into a staircase, fails to balance the steps, and says: *What if I put some weights on the back*? He uses a 1 as a counterweight, then balances two horizontal 3s on each of the 2s serving as bases, and tries to join them with a 5 which proves to be too heavy.

At level IB there is correct anticipation in the construction of the staircase but the construction of the bridge is still impeded by errors of the type we have just encountered.

Examples (level IB)

CAR (7,0). Staircase: *If one puts them far apart* (too large a gap) *the whole lot will collapse and we shan't be able to go on.* For the bridge, having placed a counterweight (1) on the free end of a horizontal block, she moves the base under the counterweight to prop it up!

RIC (7,1) places a 5 on the overhangs of two horizontal blocks in precarious equilibrium *because now we have some weight* (to hold the bridge up). However, at the beginning of all his initial attempts, he holds the elongated blocks up by hand and especially by pressing down on the base whenever the overhang is too great. This does not, however, persuade him to use counterweights.

If we compare these responses to those of the subjects at the same level we discussed in section I, we notice two differences, both due to the homogeneity of the material which discourages the dissociation of the factors involved.

The first difference is striking: whereas the subjects examined in section I made relatively frequent use of counterweights at the age of 4 to 6 years, that is at level IB and even at level IA, and this without any prompting, the present subjects did not. The explanation seems to be that, with heterogeneous material, the subject readily places the planks on the very much larger supporting boxes. Now, since the planks are in obvious danger of falling off if the overhang is too great, the subject is persuaded to hold them back by pressing one of their ends against the support. This quickly gives him the idea of replacing the pressure of the hand with that of a cube (see the intermediate case of BEN). By contrast, when a horizontal block is placed on top of a vertical one (of the same material and cross section, measuring less than 5 cm^2) both its ends will overhang so that all a counterweight on one end does is to balance the weight of the other end. Now this balancing act cannot be performed by subjects at this stage, to whom the chief function of a counterweight is retention, and this even if it is placed on the free end of a plank (as we saw in section I). In this respect the behaviour of CAR (even at level IB) is highly significant: having placed a counterweight on the overhanging part of a horizontal element, she moved the base (vertical element) under the counterweight to reinforce its effect, leaving much too large an overhang on the other side. Similarly PHI, who was coming close to the idea of using counterweights, tried to strengthen a horizontal element by leaning another element against it.

In short, the infrequent use of counterweights in the present test (CLA at 6,5 and CAR at 7,0 were the only two out of our sixteen stage I subjects to use them) and their frequent use by subjects in the earlier test is highly instructive and fully confirms our view that the two distinct functions of weights, namely of retaining and pulling down, are not yet differentiated or co-ordinated at stage I, when the child has not yet conceived of the possibility of balancing forces that act in opposite directions. (The successful construction of staircases at level IB reflects a grasp of the conditions governing the overhang of partly superposed objects and not the realization that two weights can balance each other.)

This lack of co-ordination marks a second difference between the present stage I subjects and those discussed in section I: whereas the latter are constantly reminded by the various materials both of the span of the bridge and also of the conditions of equilibrium, the former, working with elements of the same material, think either of the length of the bridge or of the downward pull of the weights and hence fail to co-ordinate the two: whence their excessive overhangs or their placing of excessively heavy elements on the ends of the horizontals, etc., and more generally their failure to construct bridges even after numerous corrections. It is only at stage II that double anticipation will gradually lead to the necessary co-ordinations and to relatively successful constructions.

76

Stage II

Subjects at stage IIA construct firm bridges with the help of counter-weights but only after many trials and errors.

Examples

TIZ (7,6) begins with the two bases of 1 + 1 + 2 each and then of 2 + 1 + 3 each and, finding that no horizontal piece is long enough to join them, she carefully moves the two vertical 3s forward so that they overhang very slightly and constructs a firm bridge with a 5. When asked for a different construction, she lays the two 3s horizontally across the 2 + 1 bases and then adds the 5: general collapse. She next replaces the horizontal 3 with 2s topped with 1s and adds a 5: collapse. She then places a 1 on the two ends by way of counter-weights. *I've put down a square and that's added more weight.* Can we make it firmer? *Yes* (adds further counterweights). *This makes more weight there than here* (points to the two ends of the 2s, one end of which supports the 5).

GIL (8,0) despite his age begins with a typical stage I reaction: he lays the centre of two horizontal 3s on the base and connects them with a 3 bearing a counterweight of 1 on each side. When the bridge collapses though his general approach was correct, he loads the connecting 3 with more weights to make it stand up better. After the ensuing collapse he replaces the supporting 3 with a 5 carrying heavier counterweights (3s). Next he places a 2 on each of their inner ends which would have provided a firm structure had he not made the typical stage I response (see above) of adding a counter-weight 1 to each of the other ends. After this failure, he changes his tactics completely and retains the horizontal elements by leaning 5s against their ends: success.

ERM (8,5) constructs three vertical pillars (5s) on each bank and discovers that a horizontal 5 is not long enough to link them. He then places a horizontal 5 on each of these triple bases and joins the whole with a 5, having examined the size of the overhang which he reduces correctly. Next he adds a counterweight 2 to each end so as to *keep better balance.*

PAS (8,8) after many trials and errors during which he tries to slant the lateral segments against the central ones, ends up with horizontal elements and counterweights: *Since I've put some weights here* (the two ends) *it's going to hold this* (the middle) *up.* Yes, but how? *It can bring equilibrium.* What is that? *So that the bridge doesn't collapse, to hold it up when someone passes.*

Level IIB is characterized by a decrease in the number of trials and errors, that is, by better anticipation of the possible effects of each manoeuvre.

Examples

TIA (9,1) first explains how a bridge is built and says: *it is held at the edges by the two flat ends. But it must not be moved forward too much or else the bridge will collapse in the middle: it may be curved but should be flat for cars to pass.* After several trials and errors his final construction consists of two 4s retained with counterweights and joined by a 5.

CIP (10,2) is the first subject to construct a staircase, no longer by excessive overhangs, but by a system of steps with a vertical edge: he puts down a 5 horizontally then tops it with a 4, and 3, a 2 and a 1.

At level III (11–12 years) there are no practical advances, but the subjects often volunteer commentaries on the distribution of the weight.

Examples

TOP (11,0): *I put down this one* (counterweight) *so that it doesn't wobble on both sides* (either end). *This one goes here so that it doesn't go down over there ... The weight is distributed like this, first here then there,* etc.

As usual, level IIA sees the beginning of co-ordinations. But they are of two kinds. The first bear on objects (with the help of logico-mathematical connections): the correlation of two weights acting in different positions, one of which helps to pull down the other if it is heavier or retains it if they are equal, hence differentiation and co-ordination between pulling down and retaining by reference to quantifiable actions in opposite directions; and above all trans-mission of the action of one of the weights on the other over a dist-ance (*cf.* PAS's telling: *It can bring equilibrium*), etc. The second set of co-ordinations bears on the actions of subjects: they allow them to plan their actions and to anticipate the overall result by thinking simultaneously of the length of the bridge and of the conditions of equilibrium or of the relative weights. Now, one notices that this co-ordination of the subject's own actions involves the same two dimensions as the logico-mathematical and physical co-ordination of weights or, more precisely, that when he considers the length of the bridge as well as the effect of the weights, the subject is led to the discovery that weights do not simply act in a vertical line but produce interactions between the two ends of a balancing platform.

Conclusions

We are thus brought back to a general problem: is it the co-ordination of the subject's actions that leads him to logico-mathematical and physical connexions, or is it the latter, in the form of a logicization and quantification of weights, conceived as acting in opposite directions, that leads to the co-ordination of the subject's actions? Needless to say, what we have here is a two-way process, but it should be recalled that to co-ordinate his actions and to consolidate his regulations, the subject must have recourse to relations of order, to symmetries and reciprocities, to correspondences and functions, etc., so that every co-ordination of his actions has a logical aspect, opposing or complementing the essentially physical content of the particular actions. Since, however, a co-ordination of actions is tantamount to the simultaneous fusion of a set, not only of actions, but also of corrections and regulations previously effected by stages, we can see how this co-ordination has developed out of the behaviour characteristic of previous levels. It is therefore not in the abstract that regulations, once they lend themselves to anticipations, become operations; this invariably happens in the context of a specific problem demanding the co-ordination of actions in a specific field. But since such problems and such fields are never isolated, and since the subject's activities are complex and lend themselves to projections and generalizations, it remains a fact that the operations appearing at a certain level may be the results of such convergent entities and thus rapidly acquire a more or less general form (the reason why some subjects lag behind the general norm poses a special problem).

In the present series of experiments, a number of factors mark this gradual passage from regulations of the subject's own actions to operational co-ordinations of the objects. Let us recall the distinction between automatic or sensorimotor regulations, which are determined from the outside by the results of actions, and active adjustment which involve intentional choices. The level IA approach to the overhang of the planks belongs to the first of these two categories: the subject is able to regulate their length but by purely manual adjustments and without any conscious grasp of the reasons why he succeeds. As for the active adjustment of the weights, they also begin at level IA but in their simplest form: they are applied to one object at a time (much as, in his construction of the bridge, the subject starts out by thinking only of its length or only of its equilibrium but not of the two simultaneously). At level IB, by contrast, the active adjustments take the form of specific choices and of functional correlations leading to the construction of the relation 'heavier than' and the understanding of the effects of the overhang. However, in the use of counterweights, there is a persistent ambivalence in respect of the action of 'pressing'. The passage from these functions to operational co-ordinations at stage II can therefore be explained by the correlation (due, in its turn, to differentiations of the various active adjustments) of the weights, positions, and lengths, that is of the spatial factors: whence the recognition, followed by the understanding, of the fact that a particular weight may retain the plank, etc. in certain positions, and pull it down in others, and that these effects can be transmitted (the case of PAS) and entail interactions that maintain or disturb equilibrium.

Hence it seems evident that there is a close relationship between progress in the regulations of the subject's own actions and progress in co-ordination and cognizance, the first being primarily determined by the observable data, and the second appealing to endogenous operational structures, which are extensions, by way of increasingly complex regulations, of the subject's own activities.

CHAPTER FIVE

The See-saw[1]

We have already written a great deal on the child's conception of weights and the use of balances, but in a work on practical success and on understanding it was difficult not to revert to the subject. In particular we had to establish to what extent the child's successive conceptualizations depend on or control, his actions. It is clear, in particular, that at about the age of 4 or 5 years, the subject confines his attention to one side of the balance at a time and that it takes a great deal of co-ordination before he comes to consider both simultaneously. We must therefore try to establish whether this co-ordination of the actions is the source of the transitivities and transmissions at work in the subsequent notion that weight must needs interact, or whether it is, on the contrary, an operational (mental) advance which determines the co-ordination of the actions.

The subjects are presented with a balance or see-saw consisting of a 15 cm plank resting on a support or shaft S that can be attached to the centre of the plank or be shifted laterally. The plank has slots for a number of balls serving as weights, all of the same shape but in four different sizes: $A > B > C > D$. Four situations were studied.

I. The plank is presented in a horizontal position, with a small car at its centre. All the subject has to do is to drive the car down a 'road' (paper strip at the bottom of one of the ends of the see-saw) with the help of the weights. To do so, he need merely consider the action of the weight on one side of the improvised balance.

II. The balance is presented with S at the centre, but in a sloping position (which is possible with this rudimentary arrangement) and the subject is asked to straighten it with the help of weights. As

---

[1] In collaboration with M. Amman.

with the last arrangement, he is asked immediately what he has done or intends to do, etc. Next, a number of variations are suggested: the possible addition of balls to each of the two sides; combinations of small and large balls, etc. In particular, the subject is asked to make two piles of weights such that their sums are equal even though their elements differ (nA $n'B$, etc.). He is then asked whether, if these piles were placed on the balance, they would or would not ensure equilibrium.

III. The subject is presented with an inclined plank, with the shaft S fixed under one of its sides, so that one of its arms is appreciably longer than the other. The subject is asked to restore equilibrium with the balls, i.e. by placing a heavier weight on the shorter arm. As in the two previous situations, should the child fail to come up with any kind of satisfactory solution, the demonstrator makes a number of positive suggestions and asks the subject for an interpretation.

IV. Some subjects were presented with a more complex situation: a smaller, 25 cm balance was affixed to one of the holes of the larger balance, and the subject was asked to bring both into equilibrium. This problem proved rather unfruitful, its only interesting feature being that it threw some light on the order of succession of the various attempts (when the subject begins with the large plank, the small one adopts a horizontal position automatically, whereas if he begins with the small plank, its equilibrium will be upset by the balancing of the large plank).

Level IA

Examples

CUR (4,8) tries to bring down the car by placing one of the weights on the 'road' and then waits. As he can think of nothing better, the demonstrator suggests placing one of the weights on the plank but CUR does not react. Could we put it on one end of the plank? *Yes.* Why? *That'll balance.* Can you do it? (He pushes the car with one hand). But with the balls? (He puts down a ball on the 'road', then moves it up on to the plank and the car descends.) What have you done? *I drove it.* And the ball? *I put it here* (on the road) *and then the car was there.* But how did it start off? *I put it* (the ball) *here* (on the end of the plank) *and it started.* Now make it go down over here

82

(on the other side). *I've got an idea. If I make it go click it will slide down* (he presses the plank). What about using the ball? (He does it.) And if we put the ball in the car itself would it start? *Yes. That bit of lead is heavy, it'll make it slide down* (tries). *No, it didn't.* Why not? *Because I don't know.* Part II: He puts a ball in the centre then slightly to one side and as the plank pivots he adds several more: *They fall down.*

SIM (4,7) first places a weight in the car, then on the plank. Part II: He holds the whole balance in his hand. What about using the balls? (He places one to the right.) *No. Or perhaps here* (in the centre). And what if you put one there (bottom) and I put one there at the same time? *Perhaps, I don't know.* (He is shown.) *Yes, because we've used two of them.* What did they do? *They straightened the see-saw.* Do it yourself. (He places one ball one side and as soon as the plank has gone down, moves it to the other side, etc.). When advised to put the two balls down together, and to use heavier weights, he says: *They're quite heavy. If I put these two down at the same time, it's going to tip over.* When this does not happen, he adds one weight to each side, followed by two at the centre. How many can you use? *Eight.* Why? *Because afterwards it's going to tilt.*

CHO (4,9) puts the balls into the car. Did it start? *No.* Why not? *I'm going to put them over the wheels.* Did it start? *No.* You can put them on the plank, you know! (Puts one on one end.) *It went.* How did you do it? *I pressed these to make it go.* Part II: I'd like you to straighten it with these balls. (Presses the balls down on the plank by hand.)

GER (4,8). Situation III: tilted balance with longer arm to the left than to the right: adjusts by hand then puts down three weights on the right and two on the left, no doubt in order to bring the shorter side down, moves the three weights to the left, which makes five against zero, and says that to balance the plank, the largest number of weights must be put *in the middle.* He starts all over again putting more weight on the right side *because that's going to keep it straight.* He is shown a solution: Why does it stay up now? *Because you've put down two big ones.* What will happen if I remove one? *I don't know* (tries). *It tilts to one side.* Why? *Don't know.*

SAN (4,6). Situation III: proposes to place the weights on the short and raised side *to make it keep straight, because the other side has slid down; it's lower,* but goes on to put two large weights on each side. The demonstrator removes the two on the long side, and

SAN explains that the plank balances *because there are only two.* And why on this side and not on the other? *Because over here it would come down.* And if I remove these two (on the short side)? *It's going to hold.* It's going to do what? *Come down here* (the short side!). (Tries.) *No. It's on the other side.* Why? *Because before it was on this side.* Situation II: SAN notices that the sides are *the same.* Nevertheless to keep them in balance he puts the weight down on the left as in III *because before it was on this side.* Are you sure? *Yes.*

COR (5,6) Car: *We'll have to let it down* (by hand). What about the weights? (Puts one on the wrong side, whence failure, then on the right side.) How did you do it? *Pressed.* Situation II: *We'll have to put a weight on this side and one there* (success). *Yes, because there were two weights.* And if we add one here (3:2) will the balance stay up? *Yes.* He tries, then corrects with 2:2, 1:3, 2:2 and 3:3 (first at different and then at equal intervals). Can you put them down just anywhere? *Yes* (displaces one slightly and tilts the plank). *No, we must put them all very close.*

HOR (5,6). Situation I: like COR. Situation II: He tries to prop up the plank with the weights. The demonstrator suggests putting one ball on each end: *That'll stay up* (tries) *because they hold it.* And if we put one more on each side? *It'll come down.* (Tries.) *It comes down because they are too close.* Couldn't you spread them out? *It'll go down* (tries; the plank balances). Why did you think it would go down? *Because I put one there before and it dropped.* Why did it stay up now? *I don't know.* What do the weights do? *They're heavy.*

BEA (5,5). Car: *I push it down with the weight* (using the ball like a stick). Next, she puts down a weight just in front of the car, whence a slight tilt: *The weight made it move* (as if the weight pulled the car). She moves the weight forward slightly but not to the end: *This will make it go down because the weight was heavy.* So? *I've put down a weight, so that it will make it go down.* Situation II: BEA first puts a weight on the uptilted end, another in the middle and thinks that a third on the other end will make the plank tilt that way: *It's going to drop.* Why? *Because there is* (I am going to place) *more weight on the other side.* Then: *It tilts because I've used two weights.*

NEL (5,8) having placed a weight on the wrong side, thinks that if he puts another one on the other side (but without removing the first) he will make the car go down that end because the weight *makes it slope down.* Situation II: *it slopes because it's too heavy.*

In situation III he adds the weight to the left side: *It's not heavy enough.* He adds two more to each side.

YVO (5,6). Situation II: can think of no other solution than to support the plank from underneath, first on one side, then on both. What about doing it from the top? (He tries, but does not put down the weights on each side simultaneously): *That doesn't work, it slopes any which way. First one side went down, and then the other.* And how about that (weights placed simultaneously)? *It's stayed straight.* And if I add one here? *The balance will budge a bit because there is more weight on this side.* And if I take that one off, will both sides be the same weight? *Yes.* Does that matter? *No.* And if I add one on each side will it (the plank) stay straight? *No.* Why not? *Because there was more weight* (than before). Does the weight make a difference? *Yes. Sometimes it makes it tilt.* (Tries.) And why did it remain straight? *It's the air. It passes below and holds it up like that.* And if I add more weights (one on each side) will the plank remain straight? *No, there'll be too much weight.* The same on both sides? *Yes.* And the balance won't keep straight? *No, it won't.* (Tries.) *It stays up.* Why? *There is some air passing underneath.*

RUO (5,6). Situation III: How are the sides? *One is smaller, one is bigger.* I'd like you to make them straight. (She adjusts the plank by hand and distributes weights over its entire length.) (Failure.) Why doesn't it work? *Because I mixed them* (big and small ones). What must we do to make it less heavy here (the long side) and more heavy there? *Put the big ones here* (short side) *and nothing on the other side.* Will that straighten it? *Don't know.* (Tries: success.) Situation II: RUO immediately puts five weights on one side and nothing on the other.

ARS (5,10). Situation II: ARS puts a small weight on each side. *The small one is all right because there's no weight there, the others have too much weight.* Does it matter whether it's the same on both sides? *Don't know.* He is asked to make two piles of the same weight: he constructs each with three small balls and one medium ball. And if we put them on the plank? *It won't keep it straight because when we mix a medium one up with the small ones, the medium one is going to make it tilt.* When he is proved wrong, he claims that the plank balances because he has held it in his hand and that equilibrium has been preserved in spite of the weights. Situation IV: ARS, like all the other young subjects whom we presented with this situation, tries to balance the smaller before balancing the larger, as if the latter could then be righted without disturbing the equilibrium of the former.

KEN (5,2). Situation II: She places a series of four mixed elements on one side and as the plank begins to tilt does the same on the other side adding a further element: *Both are the same on either side.* Why did it go down there? *Because we put in a bit more.* What must we do to straighten it? *Remove that big one and put in this middle one* (she puts down the big one from the other side). *Ah, it's gone back down here.* Then she changes the arrangement, ignoring her own principle of symmetry. She is shown the correct solution: *It doesn't budge because it's the same on both sides.*

LUC (6,7). Situation I: She pushes the car by hand, then with a weight held in her hand. Can't we put it down here (opposite side)? *No, it won't go.* Then where? *I want to put it somewhere else but I don't know where.* Situation II: can think of no solution. What if we put one here (correct side)? *It's going to tilt.* And on the other side? *Also.* And on both? *It's going to tilt on both sides* (alternately). (Tries.) *It keeps straight!* And if we add some more? (She puts two weights on the left and one on the right.) *We can only put down two,* etc.

BIN (6,9) traces the path of the car with his finger then concludes that one must *build small stairs right down to the bottom.* Next, he presses the plank down by hand. Finally he picks up a weight and presses it against the end of the plank. Situation II: can find no solution other than propping the plank up with weights from below. When asked to put the weights on top, he places three round the centre of the plank.

The introductory problem of the descending car tells us a little about these subjects' conception of weight, because, in this test, they do not immediately resort to the balls except as extensions of their own hands, either to push the car, or to tilt the plank (BIN). Their next step is to delegate these actions to the weight itself by letting go of it, but the various reactions we have observed show that what is being delegated at first is an undifferentiated power of bringing the car down or forward; it is only later that experience teaches these subjects how and where to apply that power to best effect. Thus NEL (like COR) placed the weight on the wrong side, and then simply added another weight on the right side but without removing the first, as if the second could act independently. CUR placed a weight on the 'road' before moving it to the end of the plank and, in his verbal account suggested that these two positions derived their effects from each other. BEA placed a weight right in front of the car as if to pull it down (*The weight made it move*), and then slightly closer to the end of the plank (*This will make it go down*). SIM and CHO placed the weights inside the car and when it failed to move CHO moved them *over the wheels*, as if they were an engine. In short, before arriving at the correct position (and often after receiving help) these subjects endow weight with a kind of force acting in all directions, and it is only their subsequent observations which suggest to them the right direction and conditions of descent, thus confining the powers of weights to the action of 'pressing' down (CHO and COR).

When we come to the problem of righting the tilted plank (situation II), it goes without saying that the two chief negative characteristics of subjects at level IA are a failure to quantify the pressures exerted or to account for the interaction of separate weights (notably on two sides of the balance); in other words the positive belief that each weight acts independently of the rest.

As far as quantification is concerned, these subjects certainly grasp the fact that it is possible to press down more or less strongly, and that two weights will have a more powerful action than a single one (SIM, NEL, *et al.*), but what we have here is qualitative synergy and not quantitative additivity. Thus COR and HOR claimed that weights have a stronger effect when they are 'close' together, that is when they can support one another. And, what is still totally missing at this stage is the notion that the sum of the weights on one side must be correlated quantitatively (equality or inequality) with the sum of the weights on the other side. Thus when BEA said *Because I've used two weights* (to balance a ball on the other end and one in the middle), all she was concerned with was the total number of balls on one side and not the weight of the other.

This failure to consider the interaction of the balls, and the belief that each ball plays an autonomous role, were clearly reflected in a number of responses. First of all these subjects generally argue that removing one weight in no way affects the action of the others (*cf.* NEL). In the second place, they think that the action of a weight depends solely on its own value and not on its relation with the rest: ARS placed weights symmetrically on each side but explained that they had to be light since if they had *too much weight* they would make the plank tilt. He went on to say that he did not know whether the two sides must weigh the same. Finally, when asked to build two piles of identical weight, he refused to mix medium-sized balls with small on the plank because *the medium one is going to make it tilt*. RUO, who distributed weights all over the plank, blamed her failure on her having *mixed them up*. In the third place, nearly all these subjects are reluctant to add equal weights to each side, once they have established equilibrium with less: *if I put these two down at the same time, it's going to tip over* (SIM). In the fourth place, once a particular result has been reached, it is believed to prevail regardless of any changes that have occurred. Thus ARS attributed his success to the fact that he had straightened the balance by hand, and HOR did not wish to place a weight in a place where another had previously tilted the plank.

This failure to consider interactions explains why our subjects ignore the fact that weights must be added or removed simultaneously – SIM, who was shown how to balance the plank with a weight at each end, tried to repeat the demonstration, but placed the first ball down on one side and, as the plank tilted, moved the same ball to the other side, quite certain that if he put two balls down simultaneously *it's going to tip over*. LUC also said *it's going to tilt on both sides* and YVO remarked *that it slopes any which way*. Hence it is not in the least surprising that when asked to balance the small plank attached to the large, these subjects, quite unable to correlate the weights, should also ignore the temporal order. In situation III, the inequality of the two sides encourages correlation, and explains the tendency (but no more) to weigh down the small side: only in cases of success is this solution applied to situation II if one returns to it straightaway (see RUO).

Apart from situation III, the only active attempts to deal with both sides of the balance at once, were based on symmetrical considerations. This was clearly demonstrated by KEN and also explains the (badly exploited) solutions of COR and ARS. All these subjects were still a very long way from the equalization of weights: COR agreed to add one ball to one side (whence 3:2) and believed the plank would remain level and KEN forgot his own method.

All in all, the behaviour of these subjects is thus a far cry from even an exclusively practical grasp of equilibrium based on the equalization of weights. Instead, they engage in a disordered series of local manoeuvres to raise the lower side of the plank regardless of the state of the other. Having said this, we can point out that the chief importance of this series of tests, in which the child is as free and active as he likes, is to demonstrate that, in the absence of sensori-motor adaptations and practical successes, there is no tendency to look for causal explanations or interpretations of the observed phenomena. Of the four situations examined, the first is the only one in which partial successes were obtained. In this case, the action, first of all manual (pushing the car and then pressing the plank down by hand), next with the help of weights (pushing with one of the balls but without letting go: BIN), and finally by delega-tion to the weights, led to an explanation based on the direct correla-tion of the data: the car descends because the plank is inclined by pressure on one of its ends. The same is true of situation II, but interestingly enough, our subjects did not look for an explanation, not even when asked about the 'straight' position, i.e. about equilibrium. *I don't know* is all children at this level can say.

Instead, many of these subjects content themselves with three local solutions. The first comes naturally but is quite inadequate: the weights to prop up the plank from underneath. The second involves the subject's own action: *I held it up, then I put down the bits of lead and I kept holding it a little before letting go*, said one of our 5 year olds. The third which alone leads to useful developments but remains episodic at level IA is based on symmetry: *Because there were two weights* said COR, placing one on each end; or *It's the same on both sides* (KEN). But, as we saw, this is still a very long way from the idea of the quantitive equalization of weights.

Level IB

Examples

DER (6,0). To right the plank (situation II), he first props it up on weights. And if I asked you to put them on the balance? *I would put one in the middle.* Why? *To straighten it up.* And if you didn't put it in the middle? *It would go like this* (tilt). And if you put down two? (He puts them down straightaway on the two ends.) Why? *To see if it holds.* Why should it hold? *Because it can't fall on both sides.* And if I did it, could you tell me where to put the balls? *One in the middle.* Then he advises a completely symmetrical arrangement: one in the middle, one at each end and one each between the middle and the ends. And if I brought them closer together (to the end)? *No, that's too heavy; they're not together on the other side.* At the end of the examination, the demonstrator asks: What is the most important thing we must do to straighten the plank? *Put one in the middle.* Situation III: *That one* (the right side) *is longer than this.* Well, have a go. *This side* (the left) *is too heavy.* So? He puts two weights on each side and says: *More there* (on the left) and puts down more weights on the right.

DAV (6,6) manages straightaway to bring the car down. In situation II, he puts down two weights simultaneously: *One on each end to keep it straight.* Can you put down more? *No.* Two on each side perhaps? *No.* Three? *No.* Why not?... *We must have just one on each side.* Situation IV: he starts with the smaller plank.

CAT (6,3) same reactions. Can we add balls on either side? *No, it's going to make the balance go down.* He is handed heavy, medium and light balls and asked to make two piles of the same weight: *You can't do it because these* (A) *are heavier than those* (B) *and those* (C) *are heavier than these* (D). The demonstrator makes the piles, and CAT now grants that they are the *same weight.* And if we put them on the balance? *We can, but not like this* (mixture of C and D equal to A and B). And like that (1A + 2B on either side)? *I don't know. They're heavier than the small ones, so it won't hold up.*

BER (6,6) also refuses to add further balls. *Gosh! It holds!* But no further balls must be added once *there are more than enough.*

SAU (6,4) tries to balance the plank by putting three weights in the centre. Experiment: *I thought that was going to make weight but it didn't.* As he can think of nothing else to do, the demonstrator suggests balls at each end. Will that work? *I'm not so sure.* (Tries.) *Yes.* Can we add more weights? *On both sides perhaps, I don't know, it will certainly make a bit too much weight.* Then he suddenly changes his mind: *We must add balls that are at least as heavy* (as those already placed). He makes several attempts to produce two mixed piles of the same weight and says: *No, I don't know how to do it.*

REB (6,8). Situation II: puts three balls over the centre but not symmetrically: failure. Next he puts four balls over the centre. Could you put them at the end? (Astonished.) *Like that* (one at the centre, one at each end).

SOM (6,10). Situation III: *One side is longer and one is shorter.* Can you straighten it? *By putting some there* (short side: 6 small balls, failure). So? *Don't know.* (She covers the entire plank with weights.) Is it straight? *No, because one side is heavier.* So? *We must put one here* (a large ball at the end of the longer side). Where must we put the heaviest? *Here* (short side). So? *Add more weights.*

MON (6,3). Situation III: *We could put a big one in the middle.* What good would that do? *It would hold the balance straight* (places the weights over the pivot which is not in the centre: failure). *We ought to add small ones* (failure). *We must put more big ones in the middle; if we put them like this* (two in the centre) *it ought to keep straight.* Why? *I can show you but I don't know why.* Look. *Gosh, if there is a lot of weight here* (middle) *it starts to budge!* What must we do then? *Put them here* (short side). *Yes, the weight can make it go up or down.*

FRI (7,0). Situation II: he distributes balls over the entire plank: *One here, one here, one over there . . . we need only put a big one in the middle, it'll make the bar go straight* (attempt: failure). *We must put another one there* (centre). Next, he makes various re-arrangements of the balls and finally succeeds: What if we remove that one in the middle? *It's going to tilt.* Try. *It holds. They are too light* (the three balls on either side). (They are replaced with one heavy ball.) *It's because they are heavy, and heavy weights make the balance stay up.* Equal piles: he constructs $A + B + C + D$ and $B + C + D$. If you put these two piles on the two sides of the balance will it keep straight? *Yes. But we have to take the big one* (A) *away and these two* (B) *as well, and put them in the middle.* And the rest? *We leave them on the sides.*

In general, these reactions boil down to the utilization of the idea of symmetry which emerged at level IA but in an episodic way and with a failure to draw the correct conclusions about the actions of the weights. Now when these are drawn, they force the subject to pay heed to both sides of the balance at once, and hence to consider the interaction of the weights, and they also lead him to the idea that a weight can retain as well as press down.[1]

These two aspects of symmetry are reflected in the most common solution adopted at level IB: placing the weight (or the weights) on

[1] The retaining force of weights was appreciated precociously in the counterweight tests (see chapter 4).

the centre of the plank. Now the centre is first of all what divides the whole into two equal parts: whence the idea that if the weight is placed over the centre, it will have a symmetrical effect on both sides. Moreover, a weight placed over the centre, far from producing a tilt of the plank, is thought to retain or 'hold' it level by pressing on the only point that never tilts. Thus SAU placed three balls over the centre because *I thought that was going to make weight*, evidently believing that the greater weight was bound to retain the plank. When it was suggested that he put two weights on the two ends, he was at first afraid of tilting the plank, but then changed his mind: *We must add balls at least as heavy* (as those already placed). MON said squarely that a big ball over the centre would *hold* the balance straight, then added: *The weight can make it go up or down*, i.e. restore the plank to the horizontal position. FRI said quite un-equivocally: *Heavy weights make the balance stay up.*

When the subject eventually hits upon the idea of placing a weight on each end, this symmetry leads, in its turn, to the formula-tion of a vague notion of compensation, implicit in the earlier solution. Thus DER said: *It can't fall on both sides* – an amusing way of explaining that the inclinations cancel out. But that is as far as it goes; the conception of symmetry characteristic of this level is not yet such as to entail the quantitative equalization of weights, only the qualitative suppression of the causes of the tilts. This is proved by the fact that every one of these subjects was reluctant to add equal weights to the two balls presented in the first place: DAB refused to do so without explanation, but SAU stated that *it will certainly make too much weight*, which is a return to (or a residue of) the idea of absolute weight characteristic of level IA. The residual nature of this approach is more obvious still when the subject is presented with heterogeneous elements. Thus CAT first claimed that it was impossible to build two piles of balls of equal weight by mixing large ones with small ones, then bowed to the experimental evidence but went on to argue that they would behave differently when placed on the plank because the big ones *are heavier than the small ones.*

In short, though subjects at this level have come to accept that a weight is needed on each side to ensure equilibrium, they have done so by relying on symmetry and not on the equalization of weights for which they still lack the appropriate operational instruments: quantification and additivity.

Levels IIA and IIB. Conclusions

These instruments are acquired at the age of 7–8 years (level IIA) and lead to the correct interpretation of the nature of equilibrium, as we have so often pointed out elsewhere. We can therefore be brief.

Examples (level IIA)

NIC (6,7), like the next subject, is at level IIA, despite his age. Situation I: he immediately places the weight on the end of the plank and justifies this procedure in terms of an interaction, though only between that weight and that of the plank: *I thought the ball was heavier than the balance.* And if you put the weight here (centre)? *No, that wouldn't do because it's in the middle: it can't go down.* Situation II: he places one weight on each end: *We need two of the same size.* And what about a heavier one on each side? *Fine.* And can we add some more? *Yes.* On request, he constructs two equal piles with different elements: Would the plank stay level if we put them on? *Yes, because they are the same weight.*

VAL (6,8). Situation III: *I'll put the two big balls on this side because it's higher than the other.* She puts down two small balls then replaces them with two large ones: success. Reason: *it acts the same on both sides.* As there is no ball on the long side, she is clearly thinking of the weight of the two balls she has put down.

CUR (7,4). Situation II: places a small ball on the uptilted side and, when that side drops down, adds a small one to each side. Can you add some more? *Yes* (two and two). And still more? *No, that's too heavy, that would tilt. . . . No, it won't tilt if it's the same on both sides* (puts down six different balls on each side at symmetrical distances and in the correct order).

HEN (7,5). Situation II: agrees to 2:2 after having put down 1:1. *It's as if there were only one.* But she still believes that it makes no difference where the weights are placed.

PAT (7,7) goes so far as to put down 7:7, but not symmetrically.

HER (7,3). Situation III: more are needed on the short side, or else *the balance will tilt on the other side because it's bigger* (and heavier).

GAI (8,0). Situation III: *This bit is longer, it has more weight than the short one, so we must add some balls to make them the same weight.* Situation II (presented immediately afterwards): for

93

equilibrium, *the two sides must weigh the same and the balls must be the same distance.* Is one more important than the other? *They are both as important as each other.* Moreover, a ball at the centre *wouldn't make any weight on the one side or the other.*

Since the distance factor is not based on symmetries but is correlated with the weight, it does not generally intervene before level IIB; to GAI its importance was undoubtedly driven home by situation III.

Let us now look at level IIB.

Examples (level IIB)

BOU (10,2). Situation II: *I've balanced the two ends.* Can we add some more weights? *Yes, but always the same ones and at the two ends.* Why? *If we put one closer and closer to the centre, the other one will win.*

TON (10,7): *The nearer we go to the end, the more it will drop.* He goes on to balance a small ball against a larger one closer to the centre.

This development, with the final stages of which we were familiar from earlier studies, was clarified a good deal further by the spontaneous conduct of these subjects. In particular, we were struck by the fact that they had such difficulties in balancing weights on a 50 cm plank when they realized at level IA that a weight can 'press' on a plank or 'make it slope down' (situation I) and when the car problem is resolved so easily at level IB. Not that there are two big differences between situations I and II: in I the car is set into motion by a simple action (pressure) on one side of the plank, whereas in II it is essential to act on both sides at once; moreover in I the transmissions are simple extensions of the subject's own actions, whereas II involves the transmission of the several actions of the weights by the plank. This poses a problem concerning the relationship between the practical intelligence, including the conceptualizations to which it gives rise, and the general concepts of operational transitivity and causal transmission: does progress in the former entail the formation of the latter, or is it the latter that mould and guide the practical intelligence, thus reflecting a distinct origin which we shall have to determine?

94

In respect of situation I we saw how subjects at level IA pass on from direct action (pushing the car by hand) first to instrumental action (pressing on the plank to tilt it) and then to the use of weights (pressing the plank with a weight held by hand and later released), which does not involve other than immediate modes of transmission or extensions of the instrumental action. The possible role of the weight having been discovered in this way, the solution is almost immediately at level IB.

But how does the subject pass on from these 'one-sided' actions to action on both sides? The reactions of subjects at level IB throw a great deal of light on this question. On the one hand, the importance of the other side is increasingly brought home by a symmetrical factor, both perceptive (good visual forms) and sensorimotor (symmetrical movements) in character, but not yet involving any transmissions: when like weights have been placed on both sides, the result is a qualitative equivalence and not equality between quantities acting in opposite directions. What we have here, therefore, is not compensation by an interaction involving a transmission, but two independent effects. This is what DER put so well when he said *it can't fall on both sides*. On the other hand, if the plank remains 'straight' instead of wobbling from side to side, each of the two weights must of necessity influence the other, which raises the problem of transmission. The main solution proffered at level IB is to minimize it by reducing it to a form very much like immediate transmission: the weight is placed over the centre because, from there, it can 'hold' up both sides simultaneously and directly, so that there is no need for a weight placed at one end to transmit its action right across the plank to a weight at the other end. This 'central' solution shows that, in respect of his practical intelligence, the subject does indeed consider both sides at once (whence his concern with symmetry), but that, in respect of his causal or operational notions in general, he does not yet grasp the idea of the interaction of two weights and hence of mediate transmissions across the plank. In addition, subjects at this level are still undecided about the precise effect of weights, which variously retain or pull downward, whence their peculiar attitude to counterweights (chapter 4): to secure an overhanging plank subjects at sub-stage IB, much like subjects at level IA, sometimes place the counterweights on the free end of the plank (above the 'river') as well as on the other end, as if this supplementary weight would 'help' to retain the plank. Now whereas weights used for 'retaining' have a relationship of mutual aid or synergy, those pulling downwards do not balance unless they are equal and act in opposite senses, with reciprocal transmission of their several actions: whence the temptation of placing the weights over the centre and thus suppressing the entire problem of transmissions and of actions in opposite directions.

Must we therefore conclude that it is progress in practical intelligence, i.e. the co-ordination of actions on two sides (and no longer on one side *or* the other), which explains the formation of mediate transmissions and of opposite directions at level IIA (the weights on one side acting on those of the other through the medium of the plank)? Let us recall that the latter presuppose operational transitivity ($W1$ acts on the plank which acts on $W2$, whence $W1$ acts on $W2$), and in this particular case, also reversibility ($W2$ acts similarly on $W1$) and the cancellation of the opposite directions by compensation (if $W1 = W2$). Are all these innovations engendered by the simple fact that, having neglected the other side of the balance throughout level IA, the practical conduct of subjects at level IB involves attention to both sides simultaneously?

The answer must be yes and no. Yes, because it is clear that unless he acted on both sides of the plank at once, the subject would not be led to assume the mutual influence of the opposite directions involved in the transmissions. But there is a gap of a whole level from the beginning of these practical advances (level IB), to their comprehension (stage II), and something must have happened between the two. Moreover, it is essential to distinguish, within practical intelligence, between the particular actions of placing a weight, removing a weight, selecting positions, etc. and the gradual co-ordinations permitting the incorporation of these different actions into a more effective system. Now these co-ordinations are not derived from the particular actions because the actions themselves were performed at an earlier stage. What we have here is what we have called 'general co-ordinations of actions' (combination, ordination and correspondence) with much deeper (biological) roots and used by the practical intelligence for gradual corrections and regulations. If we are right, then the practical intelligence can indeed be the motor force in the solution of such problems as we are currently examining. However, the discovery of transmissions, transitivities, etc. to which it leads, also involves a reflexive abstraction based on these general co-ordinations, and hence a return to the sources on which the practical intelligence can draw. This analysis may seem complicated, but it is greatly simplified when we remember the specific characteristics of particular actions and general co-ordinations: whereas the former bear on objects and hence have a physical aspect, the latter bear on the actions themselves and, being co-ordinations, have a logico-mathematical character. This is tantamount to saying that the co-ordination of physical actions presupposes recourse to logico-mathematical instruments, however elementary (correspondences, reversibility, transitivity, etc.). Admittedly, since the co-ordinations involved here are applied to a physical problem, we must also consider the process by which the operations involved, though basically logico-mathematical, are attributed to the objects themselves and hence turned into causal factors. This explains the transition from logical transitivity to transmission or from the cancellation of inverse operations $(+ W - W = 0)$ to the compensation of physical actions (weights) in opposite directions, etc. But this continuous (dialectical) exchange between subject and object does not belie the fact that what we have here are two poles, which though fairly undifferentiated in the elementary phases of the understanding become more and more differentiated with the growth of scientific thought.

It should also be pointed out that there is a marked difference between the conscious grasp and conceptualization of particular actions (on one side of the balance only) and their co-ordinations (a fact we have stressed in chapter 4). For lack of adequate co-ordinations, the understanding must remain distorted and in-complete, which explains why the relation 'heavier' does not appear at level IA (only such relations as 'too heavy', 'not heavy enough', 'a little heavy', etc.) and why, if it is used at all at level IB, it is used in a qualitative or ordinal rather than a quantitative sense (due to a residual failure to distinguish between 'pulling down' and 'retain-ing'). By contrast, since the gradual co-ordinations based on the corrections and regulations of the action are themselves the results of reflexive abstractions, they allow of further regulations by which successive actions can be combined into a representative whole. The result is an adequate conceptualization reflected in the emergence of the first concrete operations: reversibility involving the interaction or the compensatory effects of weights acting in opposite directions; transitivity involving the mediate transmission of these actions; additivity allowing of compositions; etc. The difference between particular actions, which have a physical content, and co-ordinations which are logico-mathematical in essence or causal in their attributions to objects, is thus clearly reflected in the conceptualizations to which they give rise.

CHAPTER SIX

Levers[1]

The present study is based on a series of graduated tests: the easiest involves the manipulation of simple bars; next comes an arrangement of two bars at right angles (inverted L); then a bar with a central pivot (screw). The more complex tests involve connected or pivoting arrangements of two, three, four, six or eight bars. These increasingly difficult arrangements are then presented to the child, who does not have to invent but make them work by inserting or moving the screws to various holes. Since these manipulations are of increasing difficulty, they may be considered a kind of training programme during which the child learns to step up the ratio between his successes and failures and also to grasp the reasons for them.

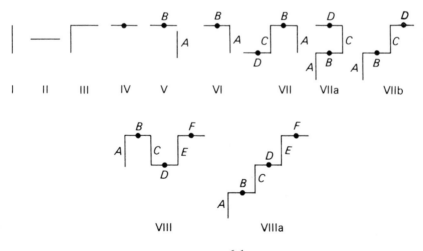

FIGURE 6.1

---

[1] In collaboration with C. Othenin-Girard.

This study therefore reveals a gradual transformation of the relationship between action and conceptualization: whereas the simplest tests provide further examples of a common situation, that of actions preceding comprehension, the more complex tests call for conceptualizations that can precede and guide actions, accompany them or succeed them. In what follows, we shall look at all these various situations and try to determine the respective share of sensorimotor regulations and of actual planning in them.

In all these tests, the subjects are asked to raise or lower a lump of sugar (or matchbox) by means of one or several bars, either free or screwed together (tightly to provide a rigid system of bars or loosely to provide movable sections). The precise arrangements used (to which we shall refer by their Roman figures – see Figure 6.1) are: (I) A vertical bar with which the lump of sugar, placed near its distal end, can be moved up or down. (II) A horizontal bar with the sugar above or below one of its ends, the child being asked to use the other end. (III) A rigid 'crank' with the sugar placed above or below the free end of the horizontal element. (IV) A horizontal bar with a central pivot in the form of a screw which we shall call $H5$. The sugar is first placed above or below one of the ends, with which it can be 'raised' or 'lowered' depending on whether the child pulls or pushes the other end. The pivot screw can be moved into holes ranging from $H1$ (below or above the sugar) to $H9$ (at the other end), and the sugar itself can be moved through various distances for an analysis of radius of action of the bar. (V) The same bar which we shall call B accompanied by a free bar A with which the subject is asked to activate B and hence to raise or lower the sugar; the bar A thus plays exactly the same role as the child's hand plays in IV and he will sometimes say so explicitly. (VI) The bars A and B are similar to those in V but articulated; the sugar is placed above or below the free end of B and the screws can be moved for an analysis of the radius of action of the bar. (VII, VIIa, VIIb, etc.): a system of four bars, two of which are horizontal and two of which are vertical. In this test, as in the preceding one, the child is first asked to adjust the screws so that, when he pulls or pushes A, he will move the sugar with the free end of D. He will have to learn (by trial and error or by inference) that he must pull A to lower the end of D and not to push A as he did in VI. (VIII or VIIIa, etc.): two more bars are added each time, making a total of six, eight in IX or ten bars in X. The subject himself inserts the screws (explaining why the simultaneous insertion of screws in both the vertical and the horizontal elements causes the levers to lock) and must learn that in VIII as in VI he must pull *A* to raise the sugar on *B* or *F* (or the converse with the eight bars of IX, etc.). The solution thus involves the discovery of an alternation law (pulling in order to raise the sugar with one, three or five horizontal screws or pivots, i.e. with two, six or ten bars, and pulling to lower the sugar with two, four or six screws, i.e. with four, eight or twelve bars), that law reflecting the non-commutativity of the rotations and translations.

Level IA

Examples

JER (4,10) is asked to raise a matchbox with a horizontal bar but does so by hand. What about the bar? (He pushes the box with one hand and the bar with the other.) What about pushing the box with the bar? (He moves the bar up to the box, stops and pushes the box by hand.) Is the bar pushing the box? *No.* (He withdraws his hand from the box and uses the bar.) Could you do it by holding the bar at this end (opposite to the box)? (He pushes the whole bar straight up instead of rotating it.) Can you raise it with that (IV; single bar with pivot)? *No. This bit* (the screw) *won't budge.* (Demonstration.) And will it also move the box down? *Yes* (he places the matchbox under one of the ends of the bar and pushes the other end). How did you do that? (He mimes correctly.) *Like that.* What did your finger do? *Brought the matches down.* But where did your finger go? *Down.* A week later he is again presented with IV and a lump of sugar on top of one of its ends: What did we do last time? *Like that* (he correctly pulls the other end down and raises the sugar). (The sugar is placed underneath the bar.) What would happen if we pushed? *We would bring the sugar down.* Can you show me? (He pushes the bar up and lowers the sugar.) Where must your finger go? *Underneath.* (The sugar is hidden under a piece of paper.) Where must your finger go now (demonstrator points to the visible end of the bar)? *Down.* Show me. (He pushes.) *Like that.* Can you say it in words, or must you do it with your thumb? *I don't know.* Tell me where I must put my finger. *Underneath.* The sugar is placed on top of one end of the pivoting bar: How can we make the sugar go up? *It won't go, there's that screw.* What must we do? *Take off the screw.*

(The demonstrator swivels the bar with the screw in *H*.) What if we put it there (*H7*)? *It's too short.* And in the middle? *Yes* (tries). *No.* Look, does it work when I move it? *Yes.* Why? *Because the screw is there.*

MUR (4,6) first pushes the lump of sugar with the bar held vertically and then does as she was asked to do (holds the bar horizontally). What did your finger do? *I moved it up.* How? *Like that* (mimes). Can you explain it better? *I go up and the bar goes straight.* The demonstrator now swivels the bar past the sugar by pressing his finger against one end. Try to do the same. (She does so.) What's the difference? *The bar was all straight, but now it's no longer all straight.* Why? . . . Did you do the same thing with your fingers both times? *No.* Do it once more. (She does so.) Now do it the wrong way. (She does so.) What's the difference? *Now the bar goes up but the sugar doesn't, before the sugar went up.* She is handed the 'crank' but instead of pushing the sugar with its horizontal arm she turns the crank round and pushes its vertical end up. With IV she claims that it is impossible to raise the sugar *because you have put that* (the central screw) *in, and it goes like this* (she tries to demonstrate that the screw immobilizes the bar and when she finds that it swivels, exclaims in obvious amazement: *It budges and turns!* Can you make it go up? *No.* (She pushes and then pulls): *It's gone up!* Where did your finger go? (Gestures a push towards the centre, that is against the screw.) *There.* Why? *Because the bar goes up.* How does it go? (She traces a line that runs from one end of the bar to the centre and then dips underneath the screw.) And the sugar? (Symmetrical path along the other end of the bar as far as the centre and upwards from the screw.) With VI (horizontal bar *B* with a fixed screw and vertical bar *A*) she pushes the vertical bar and brings the sugar down. *That bar* (*B*) *went down.* Where to? *There* (to the left). (The sugar is placed above the end of *B*.) Can you make it go up like that? (She pushes instead of pulling, and fails to shift the sugar. Next, she moves *A* from side to side.)

ANA (5,0) pushes the sugar with the end of I then holds the bar sideways (II) in both hands and pushes the sugar up with the centre of the bar. In situation III, she does use the horizontal side, but prefers to push the sugar with one of the free ends. At 5,3 (second session) she expects nothing will happen with the swivelling bar (IV) but succeeds nevertheless. *It goes up a little bit all the same.* How? *I turn the bar and the bar pushes it.* But the alleged path of her finger is significant: it follows the bar to a point between the screw and the sugar and then raises obliquely (because of confusion with the path of the sugar). By contrast, she retraces the path of the sugar correctly. When asked to do something with the screw to raise the sugar, she simply removes the screw. What would happen if we put it here (*H*2, close to the sugar)?... Try. (She does so.) Does it go up just as before? *Yes*. As high, or higher, or less high? *As high as before* (although the sugar has hardly moved). And like that (*H*8, close to her finger)?... Try. (She does so.) *The sugar goes up the same* (although it was raised much higher).

The double importance of these primitive responses is that they reflect a gravely restricted power of action coupled to cognitive deformations. In respect of their power of action, these subjects have great difficulty in allowing for the rotation of the swivelling bar (IV), even after the event (e.g. MUR). Their cognitive powers reflect this practical impotence, for even when these subjects manage to swivel the bar by imitation, they fail to appreciate that their finger at one end of the bar moves in a direction opposite to that of the sugar at the other end. It is almost as if these children do not understand what is expected of them, for though JER said that his finger *brought the sugar down* when he was asked to say what precisely his finger did, or when the sugar was covered with paper, or even when the demonstrator asked him to show him how to move his finger, he continued to say 'down', even while miming an upward movement. Similarly MUR said of IV (single bar with screw) that *it budges and turns* but thought her finger had followed the bar as far as the screw (cause of these movements) and that the sugar had done likewise before moving up. ANA said that *I turn the bar* (IV) *and the bar pushes it*, and thought that her finger had moved along the bar and then turned towards the sugar. In short, the rotation is conceptualized no better than it is applied in practice, and the lack of active adjustment is such that the automatic or sensorimotor regulations, which occur soon afterwards, do not suffice to correct the conceptual distortions.

The inability to master situation IV is clearly due to a failure to grasp the role of the rotations and perhaps also to the fact that the vertical transmission of a thrust by a horizontal agent confuses subjects at level IA. In effect, whenever they succeed in moving the sugar with the horizontal bar (II), they cannot explain how they have done it (MUR). As for situation III ('crank'), they generally prefer to push the sugar with the end of the vertical bar (MUR and, to some extent, ANA as well). In both cases, they have a clear preference for the vertical and if they succeed with the horizontal bar, it is due to automatic regulations without the least conceptualization of the transmission. It goes without saying that, in these circumstances, they are utterly unable to predict the effects of a change in the position of the screw. This is clear from the reactions of JER and especially of ANA who went so far as to claim that the sugar *goes up the same* with the screw placed in $A8$, $A2$ or $A5$, though she must have noticed the obvious differences.

Level IB

Subjects at this level have an adequate grasp of the movements of their finger in situation IV, anticipating or quickly understanding the effects of the rotation, but still fail to appreciate the effects of screw displacements and cannot cope with situation VI.

Examples

COR (5,9) having first pushed the sugar with the vertical bar (I) moves the horizontal bar (II) straight up with two fingers. With the swivelling bar (IV), she immediately presses one end down to raise the sugar with the other end. What gave you that idea? *Because it can turn.* And if the sugar is here (underneath, but no screw)? (She presses the centre of the bar with one finger as if to replace the screw and pushes the free end with another finger, thus swivelling the bar.) Did you move both fingers? *Just this one.* And what good did the other one do?... (The screw is put in, but she continues to press down the centre of the bar.) What did you do before? *I pressed with both fingers. It's easier with two fingers because then the bar doesn't slip.* The sugar is placed close to the screw which must therefore be shifted; COR does so but on the wrong side, so that one arm of the bar is much too short. She succeeds after several trials and errors but when presented with the double bar (VI), she puts the screw in the vertical arm. At a second session (a week later) she does the same but changes the position of the screw on A with no positive effect. When the demonstrator places the screw in B, COR pushes A up but fails to pull it down and hence to raise the sugar. In situation

VII, she puts her finger directly on the bar beneath the sugar and pushes it up that way.

MAR (5,4). Situation IV (single bar with screw): *We shan't be able to do a thing*. Then he discovers that *it moves crookedly and turns*. What did your finger do? *It moved the bar*. And where did the sugar go? *Up*. And your finger? *Down, on the other side of the bar*. Then he shifts the screw and notices the difference. He is handed an additional bar *A* (V) which he uses with obvious reluctance and without proper understanding. He screws it down on the support near the junction of *A* and *B* and immobilizes the system.

PIE (6,8) like MAR, pushes the horizontal bar straight up, but immediately declares that the swivelling bar will move *like that* (gesture of rotation). *It'll circulate*. Where will these two sides go? *Here and there* (correct). And your finger? *It pulls and ends up here* (correct). When asked to move the screw, he seems to understand what will happen if it is shifted to one side but not to the other, and at the second session (situation V) inserts the screw near the top of *A*, which impedes its vertical movement. Next he moves the screw to *B*8 but thinks that, if he pulls *A*, a small object placed between the screw and the joint will *go up with the bar*. Situation VII (⌐ *A* ↓): he pulls *A* believing that he will raise the sugar on *D*, then, instead of pushing, adds a screw in *C* to the one already in *B*, whence immobilization. Next he inserts screws in two or even three successive elements, etc.

RIC (6,1) immediately places a screw in the centre of IV and rotates the bar. He pulls it down to raise the sugar and correctly demonstrates the movement of his finger. However when shifting the screw from *H*5 (centre) to *H*3, he says *that won't quite go*. He moves it to *H*1 and then to *H*2, and swings the bar up to reach the sugar under the other end. Same conduct with VI: *That's like a clock* (rotation of *A* from six o'clock to three o'clock). Situation VII: two screws (in *A* and in *B*), whence failure.

FIL (7,4) succeeds straightaway in situation IV (single bar with screw) and describes the movements correctly. With V, by contrast, he first pushes the sugar with the independent bar *A*, then uses that bar to press down *B* as if he was using his finger. Situation VI: pushes instead of pulling, and fails to budge the sugar. At the second session, when asked to change the screw in IV he first inserts two screws, whence immobilization, then a single one and concludes: *No, it won't work beyond this one* (*A*4).

105

These subjects grasp the action of the horizontal bar (II) straight-away and also anticipate or realize from the outset that the swivelling bar (IV) will 'turn' (COR). Moreover, they appreciate that their finger must move one side of the bar in the opposite direction to the other end with the sugar. COR (5,9), even swivelled the bar by pressing it down with one of her fingers and pushing one end with another finger. But this early reliance on rotations (which, as we saw, also appears at this level in a different context)[1] does not mean that these subjects have begun to think in terms of circular motion round a pivot; indeed their failure to do so explains their total inability to grasp the effects of displacements of the screw or of its precise function. Thus FIL at 7,4 still put two screws on the single bar (IV). Hence it goes without saying, that these subjects will be at a loss with situation VI (two articulated bars), often immobilizing bar *A* as if the screws had some mysterious power of producing all sorts of rotations and other movements.

At level IB, therefore, our subjects have come to appreciate the effects of the rotation of a bar (IV) but not the causal role of the pivot. To make quite sure that these two factors are independent of each other we asked some of our subjects to raise the sugar in situation II by other means than by moving the whole bar straight up. We accordingly placed an obstacle over its free end, so that, to move the sugar, the subject was forced willy-nilly to rotate the bar in the opposite direction. We found that this problem could not be solved before level IB and that subjects at level IA are at a complete loss when faced with it.

Level IIA

Level IIA brings a grasp of the effects of moving the screw in situations IV and V, coupled to failure in situation VI and beyond.

Examples

VAL (7,5). Swivelling bar (IV): *We can do it like that* (pushes the end of the bar under the sugar). What about the other end? (She pulls it down straight away.) What did you do then? *I made it rise, I pulled my finger back a little bit. It's that* (the screw) *which made it*

---

[1] See Volume 28 of *Etudes d'épistémologie génétique* (P.U.F., 1973).

rise. And if the sugar is there (a little higher)? *It won't work . . . We could also push that bit* (part of the bar underneath the sugar) *but it would have to be a bit longer*. She is handed a slightly longer bar, inserts the screw in *H*1 and swivels the bar. *I made it go up*. And if we put the screw elsewhere? *It would work up to here* (*H*4) *but not beyond* (because the right side of the bar would be too short). Would it go up like this (*H*7)? *A little bit*. And further along? *A bit less*. And here (still further along)? (Tries.) *It doesn't work, it's too short*. Correct prediction also for shifts of the screw in the opposite direction. Situation V: she raises and lowers the sugar on request: *It's just like doing it with my finger*. Situation III: she pushes the sugar up by using the horizontal bar as a vertical rod, then restores it to the original position. With VI, she first of all inserts the screw in *A* which can only be turned sideways as a result, then in *B*, but continues to move *A* sideways. Hence no correlation with V, but part correlation with III.

ISA (7,8) immediately inserts the screw in the centre of bar IV, makes the sugar go up and down, and describes its movements correctly: *The sugar goes up when I go down*, etc. With a lump of sugar placed out of reach she first proposes swivelling the bar in the opposite direction. Can't we change something else? *The screw. We can move it to another hole* (she moves it to *H*7 and, without trying the effect, moves it on to *H*3 and succeeds). Why not here (*H*7)? *Because I can't get there* (reach the sugar). Hence good evaluation of the radii of action. In situation VI, by contrast, she only manages to raise, not to lower, a lump of sugar directly above *B*, and fails to insert the screws in the appropriate holes.

DAM (7,10). IV: correct rotation and description. Sugar placed higher up: *We've only to go a little bit further* (he moves the screw from *H*5 to *H*4 and then to *H*1). *Here* (*H*4) *it'll go up higher than over there* (*H*1). Same grasp of the opposite movement. *Here* (*H*8) *it won't go down any more*. Situation V: same reactions as with IV. By contrast, with VI he does not know where to place the screws (he begins by inserting them in *A* as well as in *B*), and when the demonstrator puts one in *B* only, he does not pull *A* but folds it back against *B*. He also makes various attempts to tighten the joint, etc., then discovers the right way by chance and uses it immediately. Situation VII: a mixture of rare, chance successes and numerous mistakes, including the idea that by pulling *A* *we'll pull down all the bars*. Next, he locks the system by placing screws in *A*, *B*, *C* and *D*.

FRA (8,8) has no difficulty in passing from IV to V: he first swivels *B* by lateral taps with *A* and then by a series of vertical pushes. However he fails to cope with VI, and simply tries to turn the bars upside down.

MIO (8,5) correctly inserts a screw in IV: *If you push you can bring it down and make it* (the other side and the sugar) *go up*. With V, he starts off by pushing instead of pulling when the sugar is above the end of *B*, but quickly corrects himself. With VI, he folds *A* against *B*. The demonstrator then suggests a screw in *B*, and MIO says: *I don't think that'll work*. He looks most surprised when it does. Why did it go up? *Because of the screw*. Can you think of a better explanation? *I've got it in my head but I can't really explain it*. By contrast, he correctly anticipates the effects of moving the screw from *H2* to *H7*: *It'll go a bit further each time*. With VII (four bars) he inserts a screw in the vertical bar and says: *I wonder why it doesn't budge*, as if any screw at all ought to produce some movement. Then he inserts a screw in *C* (vertical) and another in *D* (horizontal): *That doesn't budge, either*, and so on until the end.

RIE (8,8) passes easily from IV to V but thinks that a screw in the horizontal arm *B* of VI *won't work because it can't be budged*. He has clearly failed to appreciate the connection with V. While trying to remove the screw he moves *B* by chance and says: *I've got it!* and pretends to have acted as follows: *You push it up until it locks and then you pull hard to get up some push*. Having observed the result of the push (*if you move your finger up the bar goes down by itself*) he is presented with VII (four bars) with screws already inserted in *B* and *C*. He asks for more screws: *I'm going to put them in all the holes. If it's screwed together everywhere* (if the system is rigid) *it'll go up like that* (in one). To make it less rigid he moves the screw from *B* to *C* (vertical arm) and adds a third screw in *C*; then he removes all three. At the second session he fumbles about for a long time before discovering that it is only the screws on the horizontal bars that will serve his purpose. Having learned this (but *it's hard to explain*) he applies the same rule to VIIb (staircase): *I can tell beforehand that we must put them there* (*B* and *D*) and offers the correct explanation: *All of them go up and down but not in order. When we push, this one* (*A*) *goes up, that one* (*B*) *goes down, this one* (*C*) *goes down and that one* (*D*) *goes up, and the other way round when we pull* (which brings him close to level IIB). With six bars he is lost, and does not understand why the first bar must be pulled if the sugar is to be raised by the last: *I don't know. You'll have to ask the Shah of Persia!*

What is so interesting about these responses is that they combine a partial understanding of the effects of moving the screw in IV or V (changing the radius of action of the free end of the swivelling bar) with a failure to grasp the apparently obvious relationship between situations V (in which the swivelling bar is activated by the free bar *A*) and VI (as V, but with the two bars articulated).

There are two reasons for this reaction. In the first place, when the subject moves the screw himself, he tends to evaluate the new radius of action in terms of lengths: *We've only to go a bit further*, said DAM when moving the screw from *H*5 to *H*4 or *H*1 thus increasing the length of the arm between the screw and the sugar; or *it'll go a bit further* (MIO). But what is involved is a rotation (a process to which subjects from level IB onwards refer as 'turning') i.e. a change from a horizontal to an oblique position, and this is easy to understand with the free bars (IV and V) but much harder with the articulated bars (VI), since the horizontal bar *A* strikes these subjects as being firmly attached to the vertical bar *B* at an angle of 90°.

In the second place, when the child passes on from situation IV to situation V, he is simply substituting a free bar for his finger: *It's just like doing it with my finger*, said VAL. Now the child has no reason to consider the precise path of his finger, since all he did with it was to push the end of the swivelling bar IV up or down. Similarly when he uses the bar *A* instead of his finger he will often begin, as at level IB, to apply it to *B* sideways or obliquely before finally applying it perpendicularly.[1] In situation VI, by contrast, the bar *A*, already joined to *B*, has to be raised or lowered to produce a rotation, albeit that rotation is still considered to be of negligible importance. Hence there is a much greater kinematic heterogeneity between the movement required of *A* and the displacement anticipated for *B*: when they are joined together, the two bars adopt different positions and execute different movements, whereas a bar pushed with a finger or with a bar held by hand, seems to have dynamic and kinematic continuity with the agent. In short, in situation V, the

---

[1] The original assignment for situation V is, in fact, fairly open: Raise the sugar by using *A* and without touching *B* directly – the restriction (hold the bar vertically) is introduced gradually so as to prepare the subject for situation VI.

free bar *A* is wielded as an instrument treated by the subject as an extension of his own attempts to rotate *B*, whereas in situation VI the bar *A* is joined to *B* in such a way that it must experience a translation before it can produce a rotation. Now this heterogeneity constitutes a new, and at first insurmountable, difficulty, whence the common tendency to fold *A* back against *B* (DAM, MIO) or else to tighten the joint, which again helps to move the whole system as one (DAM, FRA). Some subjects even wanted to dispense with the screw in *B* so that *B* could follow the upward movement of *A*. Moreover, when *B* does swivel, these subjects have great difficulty in grasping the displacement of the two ends, something they do easily with the single bar (IV), and this once again because they are unable to co-ordinate the translation of *A* with the rotation of *B*.

As for situations VII, etc., they fail *a fortiori*, because here the co-ordination of heterogeneous rotations and translations which eludes them in situation VI goes hand in hand with an alternation resulting from the non-commutativity of the translations and rotations, as we shall see below.

Level IIB

At level IIB, success in situation VI goes hand in hand with failure in situation VII or with partial success after numerous trials and errors.

Examples

ERI (9,3) swivels the bar (IV), and when handed the loose bar (V) holds it perpendicular to the end of the first bar and lowers the sugar by pushing that end up and raises it by pushing the end down. *It's always the other way round.* Can we make a simpler arrangement? (He inserts a screw at the junction of *A* and *B* but does not pierce the board.) Why did you do that? *To hold the two bars* (which gives VI). How does it move? *The screw makes it go up.* The whole bar? *No, not this bit* (between the screw and the joint); *that goes down and the other one goes up.* (The sugar is placed underneath the bar.) Can you make it go down? *Yes by pushing (A).* By contrast, in situation VII he first inserts screws in the centres of *B*, *C* and *D*. What next? *Pull, but that won't work. This one (C5) holds it back. It's the screws on the horizontal bars that make it swivel, the screws on the vertical bars hold it back* (= lock it). And if we push (*A*) sideways? *It's this one that would hold it back* (horizontal bar). He inserts the screws correctly, but anticipates that if *A* is pushed *everything after this* (*B*5) will go down. Are you sure? *No, that part* (of *D*) *to the left will go down* (correct). However, with the six bars of VIII he no longer argues step by step and hence ignores the alternation, and fails to anticipate the movements of the successive elements.

CLA (9,8) moves the loose bar in V as he did his fingers in IV: sideways and up. In situation VI, he again begins by pushing *A* from the side and then folds it back against *B* to move the sugar. What will happen if we put this one there (screw in *B*5)? *It won't budge. No, I'm wrong, it'll work.* But he still pushes *A* from the side and then pulls: *If I pull, this one* (*A*) *goes down and that one* (*B*) *goes up.* And this bit of paper (placed between the screw and the articulation)? *It'll go up with the bar* (wrong). And to bring the sugar down? *I'll bring this one* (*A*) *up.* A week later, he remembers this principle and inserts the screw in *B*8 and then in *B*5. What if you put it there (*B*8)? *It wouldn't go so high because it isn't long enough. We'll have to put it further back* (*B*5). In situation VIIIa (stairs, but with three steps and six bars), he correctly inserts a screw in each of the three horizontal bars. *If you pull this one* (*A*), *that one* (*B*) *will go down* (correct), *it'll bring down that one* (*E*) *and take that one* (*F*) *up.* His predictions for *E* and *F* are thus correct but only by chance, since he does not argue step by step, let alone understand the law of alternation. Thus when asked about the action of each bar on the next, he predicts the behaviour of *A*, *B* and *C* correctly, then adds: *and the rest the same.* He is next presented with situation VII (four bars) and predicts, no doubt by analogy with VI, that *A* must be pulled to raise the sugar on *D*: (*A*) *goes down,* (*B*) *goes down,* (*C*) *turns,* (*D*) *will go up.* (Experiment): *Oh, no* (*A*) *goes up,* (*B*) *goes down,* (*C*) *turns and* (*D*) *goes up because the screw holds it.* And to bring the sugar down? (*A*) *goes down,* (*B*) *turns,* (*C*) *turns but doesn't go up or down, and* (*D*) *goes down.* If (*C*) doesn't go down, can (*D*) go down? *Yes.* CLA obviously does not grasp the causal relationship in situations beyond VI. However, when asked to draw VII, he is forced to proceed step by step and his diagram is correct except for too great an inclination of *C*. He is then asked if there is some way of telling how to raise the sugar in all these situations, and says: *Yes, we must add 2 bars at a time: with two you pull, with four you push, with six you pull, and with eight you push.* Why is that? *Because there* *are always more twists.* He has therefore come close to the alternation law but without adequate causal understanding, as witness the fact that, on returning to VIIIa, he inserts a screw each in *B, C* and *D* and then says: *No, it won't work – ah, yes, it makes no difference if there are two or three screws.*

JOS (10,2) with V: *I pushed one bar against the other and that made it turn.* Which way did the sugar move? *Opposite to where I pushed.* VI: he begins by trying to fold *A* against *B* (with a screw in *A*9) then inserts a screw in *B*9 and says: *That's like a joint, two bones put together with the fat round them.* He finally moves the screw to *B*5 and realizes that there is the same inversion as in V. In situation VII, he begins by putting a single screw in *B*8, then adds one in *D*2, followed by several successive screws in *C* (vertical), the futility of which he quickly appreciates. What about putting them in (*B*4) and (*C*4)? *It wouldn't move when you pull.* He thus ends up with screws in *B* and *D*: *If we pull (A) it makes (B) turn, that pulls (C) up and turns (D) down.* But he has obviously failed to generalize his final interpretation, since in situation VIII, he inserts a screw in *E* (vertical) and two in *F*, *because (D) pulls (E) and makes (F) turn.* After several trials, he says: *It locks over here (C and D). It's all much too tight.* Eventually he hits upon the solution: screws in *B*, *D* and *F*. And in general? *If I had more bars, I'd put a screw in each of the flats but none along the sides.* Why was it that, with four bars, we had to push to make the sugar go up? *There were less bars* (he describes the movements step by step). And with *B*6? *We'd have to pull.* How do you know? *I just happen to.*

DID (10,5). Situation VII: suggests reinforcing the two vertical bars with another horizontal and then says: *Perhaps I ought to tighten that screw* (articulation *AB*). Find something better. (He inserts a screw in *B*5 then moves it to *B*2): *We saw earlier that it will be too long and rise too high.* What must we do to raise the sugar? *Pull that one (A* = correct). And to bring it down? *Push up.* Situation VII (second session): he again suggests tightening all the joints, then inserts screws in *B*5 and *D*5 and makes what seem to be correct anticipations: *I push on top to make it go up and I pull to make it go down.* How do you know? *I have got it from the last one* (VI which worked the other way round) *and then I tried it out.* He makes the same mistake during the third session. What he does understand, however, is that *a vertical bar and a horizontal mustn't be kept back together; that'll stop it from turning.* Situations VII, etc. (stairs, etc.

with four, eight and six bars): correct responses for four and six bars; wrong responses for eight bars, and failure to discover the law, even while proceeding step by step. At the third session, he claims that *A* must be pulled down to raise the sugar on *D*, but justifies this claim with a false step by step argument: *pulling (A) will make this* (the joint *AB*) *go down and raise that one (BC) as well as this bar (C) and that (D)*. Are you sure? *That one (A) pulls (AB) and raises (BC), and that makes this one (CD) go down*. So this corner (*BC*) goes up and that one (*CD*) goes down. Are they made of elastic? . . . *Oh, that's wrong, we have to push*. However, when he is again presented with a staircase of six steps he discovers the alternation law: the vertical *A* goes down, *C* goes up, *E* goes down, and the right end of *F* goes up: *It goes up one time and down another time*. And this one (eight bars)? *It'll go down*. How can you tell so quickly? *Because there are four level bars; if you want to raise the sugar you must push. If the sugar is over an odd bar you have to pull to make it go up*. DID has thus advanced to stage III at the end of the third session.

Clearly these subjects succeed, but only after indirect suggestions, in passing from situation V to situation VI either straightaway (ERI) or more or less quickly after trial and error. As a result they come to understand that *B* rotates or swivels because of the translation (or quasi-translation) in the opposite direction of one of its ends. However this understanding does not extend to situation VII (4 bars). Even though the screws are often inserted in the correct positions and though there are frequent practical successes, the conceptualizations of these subjects show that they fail to grasp the role of the screws in the intermediate bars or the exact reason why the system locks. This is true, *a fortiori*, of situations VIII etc. because the successive effects of *A* on *B*, *B* on *C*, etc. introduce two kinds of inversions. There is first of all the newly discovered effect of the translation of *A* on the rotation of *B* which causes *B* to move in a direction opposite to that of the translation. But there is also the effect of the rotation of *B* on the quasi-translation of *C*, which is moved up or down in the same direction as the end of *B* (at the joint *BC*), the translation (or quasi-translation) of *C* producing a rotation of *D*. As a result *D* experiences an inversion in the opposite sense to that of *B*, and we could compare this inversion of an inversion to the sign rule $(-) \times (-) = (+)$, except that it is more complicated because it is a result of the non-commutativity of rotations and translations. A quasi-translation acting on a rotation has a different effect from that of this rotation on the next quasi-translation (no inversion), whence the inversion of successive rotations (*B, D, F, H*, etc.: *B* and *F* in one direction and *D* and *H* in the other, etc.). What we have here is a special type of inversion: each rotation (or each screw) inverts the result of the previous one. This explains why success in situation VI does not entail success in situation VII, etc. unless there is a fresh step by step argument followed by the realization that the results differ from one rotation to the next.

Now this is precisely what our subjects fail to appreciate: their initial tendency is to apply to situation VII the generalizations they have applied to situation VI, or to start all over again as if they had learned nothing at all – some of them even insert screws in the vertical bars as well as the horizontal bars (CLA and JOS). Others nevertheless stated the rule that screws must only be inserted in the horizontal bars (ERI and DID) but failed to discover the alternation law, while yet others began with a step by step argument but generalized too early what they have observed in the simpler situations (CLA and DID at the beginning). In short, subjects at this level manage to co-ordinate the translations and rotations in situation VI (having grasped, as they do from level IB onwards, that the screw produces 'turns', and learning at stage IIA that this change of direction introduces a variable radius of action dependent on the position of the screw), but still fail to appreciate the non-commutativity of that process and hence the alternation law.

Stage III

Level IIIA brings the beginnings of a general solution based on step-by-step arguments and the gradual appreciation of the alternation law.

Examples (*level IIIA*)

CEL (10,5) passing from situations III and V to VI, begins by swivelling *A*, then inserts the screw in *B*: *When we pull, we make it circle round the screw.* In situation VII he pulls *A* to raise the sugar (as in VI) and says: *Because this one is like the other one: instead of two bars there are four but it's the same thing.* Then he pushes *A* and explains correctly: *That screw (B5) changes the direction: it's clamped down here so that this one (B) can't be pushed sideways. When we push this (A), that one (B) turns, which makes this (C) go down and turns that (D) which goes up on the side of the sugar.* Situation VIII (6 bars): *We have to do the opposite* (pull). *We'll have to see what happens in the end, whether it goes up or down* (he inserts screws in the three horizontal bars and gives a step-by-step explanation). Situation VIIIA (staircase): *Pull, because (F) has to go up on the right side.* And if we put in two more bars? *Pull; (F) ought to rise, so with 9 . . . oh, no, that won't work, (F) ought to rise, (G) ought to go up and (H) ought to go down on the right.* So what must we do? *Add some more* (he adds two bars to make a flight of five stairs): *(I) will go down if (H) goes down and (J) will go up on the right side.* Why? *Because they swivel, so if one goes down, the other one* (horizontal) *must go up.*

ARC (11,5). Situation V: *The bar will always turn because of that screw; if I go down* (i.e. push *B* down with the free end of *A*) *the bar goes down straightaway.* Situation VI: he inserts a screw in *B*3 and pushes *A* sideways: *I could do something else* (inserts a screw in *B*5 and pulls *A*). How did you think of that? *By chance; I saw that it can turn round there, so I knew that if I pull it will have to turn.* Situation VII: he inserts screws in the horizontals, pulls and gives a step by step explanation with the help of a three-bar model but using a false alternation law: *(A) goes down, (B) goes up, (C) goes down and (D) goes up.* Then he goes back to the articulated model: *That's wrong . . . it ought to go up.* Drawing: *(A) goes up, (B) has to go up; ah, no, it goes down here, (C) also goes down, and (D) goes up.* Why does *(D)* go up? *Because there is a small screw* (articulation): *(C) goes down, and (D) goes up.* Eight bars: he pulls *A* to lower the sugar with *H*, using a correct step by step argument, but generalizes from VI, then starts from scratch and concludes that *it's the other way round, there are less bars, there's an odd number of them.* Really? (He counts): *No, it's even.* But what he undoubtedly had in mind was the idea he expressed at the end: *With one screw you have to pull* (to raise the sugar), *with two you have to push.* And with six? *You have to push down* (= pull) *because there's an odd number of screws.*

UDE (12,1), similarly, having coped with situation VI and grasped why the bars lock when screws are inserted in the vertical as well as in the horizontal bars, uses trial and error for situation VII and then discovers the law: *That's it. I'd never have believed it,* and offers a good step-by-step explanation. How do we raise the sugar with two bars? *Pull.* And with four? *Push.* Why? *Because there are two screws.* And with five? *Pull, because it's odd. You push when it's even.* Why? *When I push (A) that makes (C) and (CD =* the joint of *C* and *D) go down and that makes (D) go up.*

Here for comparison are two level IIIB responses. These subjects insert the screws in the correct holes immediately and without any suggestion, and also have a clear grasp of the alternation law which they attribute to the fact that every screw reverses the direction of the bar.

Examples (level IIIB)

BEN (14,0) straightaway inserts screws in the horizontal bars for situations IV, V, VI, VII, etc. and immediately knows when to pull or to push: *There ought to be a law: when this joint (AB) moves, that one (CD) moves in the opposite direction.* Stairs: *if there is an even number* (of right angles) *it moves one way and if it's odd it moves a different way.* If there is a single step why must we pull? *This one (A) pulls that one (B) up because of the screw.*

CAT (15,0): *The screws swivel the bars.* If we have just one screw how can we raise the sugar? *Pull.* And five screws? *Pull.* Why? *With one you pull, with two you go up, with three you pull,* etc. And with 32? *You pull* (correct).

Clearly subjects at level IIIA have made two correlated discoveries: the need for a step-by-step argument to avoid precipitate generalizations of the type 'up, down, up', etc. (*cf.* CEL: *that won't work* or *We'll have to see how it finishes, whether it goes up or down*; or UDE: *I'd never have believed it*), and the non-commutativity of the relationship between rotation and translation (*cf.* ARC: *(B) goes down, (C) also goes down,* etc.), whence the distinction between an even and an odd number of bars and even and odd numbers of screws in the horizontals. At level IIIB, that law is partly deduced or reconstructed and no longer simply stated. In other words, the subject has finally come to argue about the whole system of possible transformations in terms of some of the transformation he has anticipated and noted and hence to effect operations on operations (a characteristic of formal operations) which enables him then, but only then, to conceptualize and hence to plan the entire action.

Conclusions

(1) This long process of development involves a gradual comprehension of the rotations and the co-ordination of the rotations with the translations. From the conceptualizations alone, it is clear that subjects at level IA do not consider the rotation: they fail to anticipate the movement of the horizontal bar (in situation IV) and, even when they make it swivel upon suggestion, they do not grasp what they have done and hence fail to appreciate that when they pushed or pulled one of the ends, their fingers moved in a direction opposite to that of the sugar: they believe that their fingers 'go down' when the sugar goes down, etc.

Level IB, by contrast, marks an incipient grasp of the rotation: the subject grants that the swivelling bar (IV) may *turn* (COR), *move crookedly* (MAR) or *circulate* (PIE). Moreover he recognizes that his finger and the sugar move in opposite directions. However, he does not yet treat the screw as a pivot and merely endows it with an auxiliary 'turning' power, similar to, and reinforcing, that of his own fingers. Nor does he understand that by shifting the screw he will alter the radius of action of the bar which explains why RIE inserted two screws in bar IV to increase its rotation without suspecting that the bar would lock, and why he thought that it would if the screw were inserted this side of H4. In situation V, these subjects move the free bar sideways and in situations VI and beyond, they make no generalizations and are therefore completely out of their depth.

Level IIA brings a better understanding of the swivelling effect: though the screw is still thought to have the kind of turning power with which it was endowed at level IB, the length of the bar between the pivot and the active end of the bar (moving the sugar) is treated as a radius of action. True it is not yet considered as the radius of a proper circle, but the subject has begun to think in the right way. By contrast, there is still a remarkable gulf between successes in situation V (loose bars) and failures in situation VI (articulated bars), because, in V, the free bar A is an instrument wielded directly by the subject whereas, in VI, bar A is linked firmly to bar B, so that the action of

117

the system must be broken down into a translation of *A* and a rotation of *B*, i.e. into two heterogeneous movements. In fact, it is the combined differentiation and co-ordination of rotations with translations that troubles subjects at level IIA, whence their tendency to fold *A* against *B* or to render the whole system rigid (with a third bar or by tightening the articulation screw, etc.), in an effort to effect either a global translation or else a global rotation.

With level IIB, by contrast, the problem of passing from V to VI is mastered more or less rapidly, and it is interesting to note that the nascent co-ordination of the rotations and translations goes hand in hand with the beginnings of a composition.[1] But, needless to say, when passing from VI to VII, these subjects do not even suspect that the co-ordination is non-commutative, i.e., that if one horizontal bar swivels one way the next one will swivel in the opposite direction. This alternation law is discovered gradually at level IIIA and partly explained in connection, let us note, with the (belated) grasp of the proper role of the screws, which none of these subjects insert in the vertical element, in contrast to what still happens at level IIA. Instead, they look on the screws as possible centres of complete rotations: *When we pull we make it circle round the screw* (CEL). Finally, at level IIIB (which UDE reached at the end of the examination), the reason why the alternations occur is grasped thanks largely to the correlation of the movements of the bars with the displacements of the joints: *when this joint (AB) moves, that one (CD) moves in the opposite direction* (BEN).

From the grasp of the semi-rotations which marks the transition from level IA to level IB, and a better interpretation of the swivelling effect at level IIA, the subject thus passes on to the co-ordination of these rotations with the translations (IIB) and the discovery of the non-commutativity of that co-ordination (the alternation law) at levels IIIA and IIIB. Hence, what we have here is indeed a continuous evolution towards the comprehension of the rotations and of the inversions to which they and the translations jointly give rise.

(2) As for the relationship between that comprehension and the action itself, there is a gradual reversal as the subject progresses through our six sub-stages, and this in a highly instructive manner: while action precedes thought at level IA, often by a long way, by

---

[1] *Cf.* Volume 28 of *Etudes d'épistémologie génétique, op. cit.*

the time the child has reached level IIIB, action is guided by inferential co-ordinations and this to the point that CAT was able to state that, to raise the sugar with the last of 32 (imaginary) steps, the first vertical bar must be lowered, because with 32 steps, the number of screws is even.

At stage IA, in effect, the subject does not generally know how to use the swivelling bar (IV) straightaway and must be shown that the sugar can be raised with one end if the other end is pulled down. True, JER immediately lowered the sugar by placing it near one end of the bar and pushing the other one up, but his description or conceptualization was a denial of what he had just done: he claimed that he had pulled his finger down, and all the other subjects at level IA produced distorted arguments of this type. The reason why comprehension lags so far behind practice in this situation is that the subject needs nothing but sensorimotor regulations to achieve success. Admittedly, inversions do not commonly occur on the sensorimotor plane, but sending a moving body in two opposite directions by placing it on two sides of the propelling body is not a difficult task, nor is the reversal of the direction of the thrust; indeed, it is the immediate nature of these compensating regulations which explains the failure to grasp the general process.

At level IB, by contrast, action and conceptualization seem to be on a par and hence to go hand in hand in negative as well as in positive respects: on the positive side there is the spontaneous utilization and relative comprehension of the swivelling of bar IV, while on the negative side, the effect of the displacement of the screws is not allowed for either in action or in thought. It is at level IIA that conceptualization begins to guide action, some subjects anticipating that the radius of action will be altered by the displacement of the screw, even before trying to test this assumption in practice: there is therefore a beginning of inferential co-ordination based on a partial representation of the swivelling process. But this slight progress in conceptualization goes no further, because subjects at level IIA cannot co-ordinate the rotations and translations when proceeding from situation IV to situation V without prior observations.

At level IIB, this co-ordination can be effected but often not until after many trials and errors, the importance of which increases as the subject proceeds to situations VII, etc. This type of experimental behaviour raises the problem of the precise relationship between action and conceptualization. The fact that the subject engages in a series of trials and errors shows clearly that he cannot make the requisite deductions and must therefore engage in further actions. However, every one of his actions is both the result of a hypothesis and also the stimulus for an interpretation that will guide the next sequence of actions. In these circumstances, one cannot argue that action precedes conceptualization; it merely precedes momentary interpretations, and is itself the result and simple verification of an inferential anticipation. What we have here, therefore, is an alternation of conceptualizations and of actions, quite unlike the initial trials and errors guided by prior sensorimotor schemata.

At level IIIA, these experimental trials and errors become an increasingly important part of conceptualizations in the form of inferential co-ordinations, and at level IIIB the latter suffice to provide a complete map of the action.

(3) We must still mention another, fairly important, conclusion. Almost every one of our subjects was seen during two sessions, the beginning of the second being devoted to a recall from memory of all the actions and facts observed at the first interrogation. We lack space to discuss the details of these memory tests and will therefore content ourselves with mentioning some of the more salient features, the more so as they have a bearing on our system of classifying successive stages. At levels IA and IB, the memory image is nothing but a schematization of what the subject has understood rather than of what he has perceived. This explains in particular why subjects at level IB forget about the screw (pivot) when describing situations IV or V. However, at level IIA, matters become more complex because, after numerous trials and errors, the subject succeeds in situation VI which, as we saw, he does not yet anticipate by a deduction based on situation V. Now, the child's memory shows us that this momentary empirical discovery is not stable: after a week, the same subjects have the utmost difficulty in recalling what they have done – clear proof that they are still uncertain. In general, whenever action is temporarily ahead of conceptualization, and particularly when it is the result of suggestions, apparent successes give rise to very unstable memories. This still happens in part at level IIB, where there is a common tendency to start off by pulling rather than pushing the free bar, by analogy with the elementary situation VI, when bar A is pulled down to push bar B and the sugar

120

up. Now this simplest of inversion schemata proves so powerful that even when these subjects discover in situations VII or IX that they ought, in fact, to have pushed the bar up, their memory recall is still based on their first anticipation. It even happens that this type of regress occurs when they are asked for a drawing at the end of the first session. It is only with the comprehension associated with stage III that the memory becomes a true reflection of the child's acquisitions.

This development of the memory thus fully confirms our system of classification (stages) and of our interpretation of the relationship between conceptualization and action.

Cars[1]

In this chapter we shall examine attempts to make various miniature cars describe a curved path by adjustments of the front or back axles or of the direction of the longitudinal axle carrying the other two, and firmly attached to the body of the car. The solutions offered help to assess practical progress in reaching a particular goal or in following a particular path and also to gauge the conscious grasp and comprehension of the actions performed.

The tests involve three cars without steering wheels, and a fixed longitudinal axis running along the whole body of the car. The first car has a fixed back axle and an adjustable front axle that can be set at right angles to the body (longitudinal axle), so that the car moves in a straight line, or rotated through 30° or 60° to the left or the right so that the car follows a curved path in one of these two directions. Car II has a fixed front axle and an adjustable back axle which can also be rotated through 30° or 60° to the right or left and send the car in the opposite direction. In Car III, finally, both axles are adjustable, and the car will only move if they are parallel.

The subject is shown Car I and asked to move it from *A* to *B* (across a table). Next, a building block is placed a few centimetres above the middle of *AB*, and the child is asked to round this obstacle, if possible along a set trajectory he can indicate beforehand. If he fails to set the steering mechanism by himself, he is shown how to do it. Next, the obstacle is placed in such a way that, to round it, the child must point the body of the car in a different direction, as well as adjust the front axle. Immediately afterwards, he is told to drive the car round an obstacle placed underneath instead of above *AB* (which means steering the car in the opposite direction). The child

---

[1] In collaboration with A. Moreau.

is asked, *inter alia*, what will happen if he continues to push the car with the wheels set at a fixed angle, i.e. along a circular path.

He is next presented with Car II and asked to predict the results of various settings of the rear wheels. He is also asked to tell the difference between the behaviour of Cars I and II, which are then placed side by side (several centimetres apart) with all the wheels facing straight ahead. A target is put down at some distance from and to the side of the cars and the child is asked what must be done to reach that target.

Finally the child is presented with Car III, with the front and rear axles set parallel to each other at about 40° and asked in what direction the car will go if it is pushed from behind.

Level IA

Subjects at this level guide the cars by hand and do not adjust the front or rear axles unless specifically asked to do so.

Examples

FIS (5,0) believes that the car must move along a straight path with a loop round the obstacle. He then pushes and turns the car with his palm. What did you do? (He points to the path.) But with the car? *I pushed it.* Try to push it with just one finger. (He does as before.) The steering mechanism is demonstrated and he makes various attempts to use it but fails, *because it turns.* Are these two the same (perpendicular and inclined axles)? *No. Here it goes sideways.* How will it go with that (inclined axle)? *It'll go straight ahead* (indicates a path perpendicular to the edge of the table). And with that (axle parallel to the edge of the table)? *It'll go sideways* (path parallel to the edge of the table, i.e. in the direction of the axle, not of the wheels).

CLO (5,2) moves the car by hand along *AB*. How did you hold your hand? *Like that* (above the car). And for this (slight curve round the obstacle)? (Same procedure.) How did the car move? *This way* (she points to the path). Is it easy to do it by hand? *Yes.* And do the wheels help? *Yes, they roll.* Start again and try to do it with the wheels. (Same procedure as before.) And like this (pronounced curve)? *I push it straight and then I lift it up to turn it.* Wouldn't the wheels help you to turn it? *Yes.* Show me. (Sets the axle at a slightly oblique angle.) Well? *If you put it like that, it'll turn.* And for this (greater curvature)? *Like that* (same setting of the axle, then corrections by turning the entire body). Clearly CLO not only fails to appreciate the significance of the various axle settings, but does not even notice over which part of the path she has steered the car and over which she has held it in her hand. However, after several trials, she eventually grasps what children at level IB take for granted from the outset. What do the wheels do? *They go round.* And if we moved the wheels (= turned the axle)? *When you move them it helps them to turn the car.*

CAR (5,0) pulls the car along the curved path: How did you make it go? *Like that* (points to the path). He is shown how the car can be steered. Would that help?... What good does it do if we turn the wheels? *It's hard* (to say). Try. (He turns the axle, pushes the car with both hands, then pulls.) And if you set it like that (demonstrator turns the axle)? *It'll turn.* He nevertheless guides the car by hand and when asked what path the car will follow with the front axle turned as far as it will go, he indicates a curve that evens out into a long straight line. After several attempts, he nevertheless manages to predict the correct path, but his only explanation is that *it goes there because of the wheels.* Same response with Car II.

One interesting feature of these subjects is their peculiar anticipation of the path the car must follow to round the obstacle: instead of imagining a large curve from *A* to *B*, they trace out a straight line with a bulge in the middle. In particular, they never think of placing the car at an angle to *AB*. There are no doubt two reasons for this reaction: the first (which characterizes the behaviour of a chicken in contrast to that of a dog or an adult ape) is that they find it hard to negotiate the obstacle and hence reduce their task to a minimal or purely local form. The second reason, which follows from the first, is that straight lines and shapes seem more pregnant than curved ones.

A second striking reaction is linked to the preceding one: we saw that there is a general tendency to believe that the wheels must, by their very nature, move in a straight line and hence cannot affect the direction of the car. This explains why subjects at this level do not attempt to steer the car but guide it by hand, even when the steering mechanism is demonstrated to them. Thus FIS believed that with its axle parallel to the edge of the table, the car itself would run parallel to the table. CLO and CAR did realize that by turning the axle, they could make the car describe a curve, but they made little use of that knowledge and also preferred to guide the car by hand. Nevertheless, unlike FIS, CAR anticipated the general direction the axle would impress upon the car, but failed to distinguish between the effects of different axle settings and later claimed that the car would describe a curved path and then finish in a straight line. CLO did not, at first, so much as suspect that it mattered whether the axle were turned to the right or to the left.

Their comprehension of their own actions is first of all centred on the results of the latter: asked to describe what they have done, these subjects simply point to the path the car has covered, and if they do go on to describe the course of their actions, they do so in global terms (*I pushed it*, said FIS), or else they try (unsuccessfully) to distinguish between those moments when they adjusted the path by hand and those when they relied on the axle settings.

Level IB

Subjects at this level begin to use the front axle as soon as their attention is drawn to it.

Examples

PAH (5,0) (intermediate case) pulls the car round the obstacle. What did you do? *I turned it.* How do you turn a real car? *By turning the steering wheel.* Does this bit (the axle) help you in any way? *It could help me to turn the car.* How? (He succeeds in rounding the obstacle by two or three successive adjustments of the axle.) What did you do? *I turned the wheels.* How many times? . . . If I set the wheels like that (parallel to the body) where will the car go? *Like that* (in straight line). And like this (slight inclination of the axle)? (He traces out a curve with a bulge round the obstacle, but with a somewhat greater inclination of the axle, he traces out a curve in the wrong direction.) *It turns because the wheels turn.*

SAR (6,0) first guides the car by hand: *You can see that the wheels move* (when the axle is rotated). Does that help? *Yes, it helps the car to turn.* Try it. (Same manipulation as before.) Did you use it? *No, because we can't turn it* (at will). (The demonstrator sets the axle.) (Success after several manual readjustments.) And like that (stronger inclination of the axle)? *It'll turn more because that* (the axle) *is twisted further back and the wheels have been turned more.* And to go this way (obstacle on the opposite side)? *We must turn the wheel to this side* (inclines the axle in the opposite direction). However, despite her correct predictions, SAR refuses to anticipate the overall path: Can you tell by looking at the car whether it will pass behind the cube? *No.* (Tries and corrects the path several times.) Total incomprehension when presented with Car II: *We shan't manage because it's at the back. It makes no difference* if the front or the back axle is used provided the setting is the same. Her practical attempts prove her wrong but she fails to act accordingly.

DIE (6,0) realizes straightaway that if the front axle is turned, the car itself will turn and indicates the correct direction. But to round the obstacle, he sets the axle for a concave course and not for the convex one he should have chosen. As the car approaches the obstacle, he readjusts the direction of the wheels. What did you do? *First I went straight, then I turned, turned back and turned back again and then I landed up here.* How many times did you turn the wheels? *Three times; here, there and there.* (What he points to are three positions round the obstacle, none of which corresponds to any of the points where he actually changed course.) His many other attempts are of the same kind: no attempt to steer the car, but several more or less correct segments with changes *en route* and failure to give an accurate account of the actions performed. When the demonstrator changes the setting of the front axle and also points the body of the car in a different direction, DIE believes that it is the latter which will determine the course of the vehicle. He also believes that it is only possible to predict the path of the car if the body is perpendicular or parallel to the edge of the table, so that the car *is dead straight and we can turn the wheels.* But even when the car is pointed that way, its path is uncertain *because one time it goes here and another time it goes there.* Moreover, if the nose is pointed obliquely *it's the car that turns, not the wheels.* Car II, after several attempts: *It's the other way round from the last one.* With the front axle set at a certain angle *the car turns this way,* and with the rear axle set at the same angle, *it turns that way.* This does not stop DIE from setting both axles at the same angle before eventually correcting his mistake.

ELA (6,8) at once sets the front axle to negotiate the obstacle: *I've started the car off with the wheels up to here* because in a real car you turn *the steering wheel and that turns the wheels and then the car turns.* All the same, she has to make several adjustments *en route,* all the while estimating the general direction more or less correctly and realizing that a change in the angle of the front axle changes the curvature of the path. Her only explanation is that the car *goes a different way, but I don't know why.* Above all, she cannot think of any setting that would enable the car to round the obstacle without further adjustment. As for pointing the body it is impossible to combine this effect with that of the front axle unless the car is perpendicular to the edge of a table *because else it* (the car) *is too skew.* The rear axle (Car II) *does the same* as the front axle: *The rear wheel goes like this* (↗) *and this one* (the front wheel) *as well. They both go to the same place but it's not the same wheel that's being turned.*

CAT (7,1): *We could start turning the car right away, for you can see straight off that it will turn this way.* She nevertheless has to re-align the car *en route,* and explains that *when the wheels don't lead the way you have to push because* (otherwise) *it takes too long.* In fact, she seems to expect the curvature to change (from concave to convex, or *vice versa*) and says: *Because the wheels turn, the car goes the right way when you push.*

It is interesting to discover that at this level when children, as we gathered from other studies, begin to predict that a small plate pushed at the centre will go *absolutely straight* while one that is pushed from the side *will turn,* they also begin to grasp that if the front axle of a car is turned, the car will turn as well. These are two instances of a nascent grasp of rotation, but in quite different dynamic and figurative situations.

Another, related, advance is the generally correct assessment of the path by which the obstacle can be rounded: a single curve and no longer two straight lines joined by a bulge.

Moreover the anticipation of the general direction in terms of the original setting gradually improves: the subject can tell whether the car will move off to the right or to the left and also knows which setting to those will take the car round obstacles above or below *AB.* However, he still makes many mistakes (e.g. SAR), and above all he fails to realize that the paths are regular of necessity: *One time it goes here, and another time it goes there* explained DIE at the age of 6,0.

On the practical plane, none of these subjects set the axle so that the car could travel without further adjustments, even though the general path was correctly anticipated. This general response clearly distinguishes subjects at level IB from those at level IIA.

Finally, their conscious grasp of their successive actions is no better than it was at level IA: DIE, for example, was mistaken in thinking that he had adjusted the wheel three times and pointed to three wrong spots, because he believed that the car had followed a path he felt it should have done, and not the one he had impressed upon it by his actions.

Level IIA

At this level, the subject either sets the front wheels correctly or else realizes where he went wrong and recalls what adjustments he had to make.

Examples

PIG (6,11): The front axle helps *to turn the car.* Try to make the car go round that block. (Success, with adjustments in the middle of the path.) Can you do it in one go? *I can push* (from the back) *and it'll turn* (after setting the wheels). For a sharper curve, he rightly starts the car off from a lower point, but fails to co-ordinate the direction of the body with the front axle and, after correction, simply says *I cheated a bit,* pointing to an adjustment he made along the path. He expects that he can achieve the same effect by setting the wheels of Car II in the same direction as those of Car I.

FRA (7,4) after discovering the front axle: *The wheels turn the car to one side.* He sets the axle fairly accurately and does not have to correct the path until the car is about to hit the obstacle. He rightly anticipates that, with the nose at right angles to the edge of the table, opposite settings of the front axle will have opposite effects, but is at a loss with a nose pointing obliquely and also with the adjustable back axle (Car II).

CIC (7,3) believes first of all that a single setting of the axle will not take the car all the way. Then after pushing the car with the axle turned as far as it will go, she correctly draws the paths of the two wheels. She fails to adjust the nose, but correctly anticipates the result of different axle settings: *Here* (small inclination) *it'll go more straight* (= longer arc) *and over there it'll turn a lot.* What is the difference? *It's different because.... And* if we kept pushing? (She draws a circle): *It'll come back to the same place.* The same circle for the two (settings)? *No, this one* (sharper turn of axle) *is a little straighter.* Which would make the larger circle? Is it this one (small inclination of the axle)? *No, that would make it smaller* (contradicting herself). And the other one? *Bigger.* Try it! *No, it's the other way round.* Why does this one (axle at the maximum inclination) make a smaller circle? *Because the wheel is against the wood* (the longitudinal axle). She believes that if the nose of the car is pointed in the same direction as the front axle, the curve will become sharper, but not necessarily so. She also thinks that Car II will behave differently but at first claims that it is impossible to tell just how, then makes correct predictions as she did for Car I.

MER (7,2) correctly anticipates the results of the front-axle setting. *It'll go round in a circle and come back to the same place. When you turn the car it turns and comes back to where it started.* Do these two (greater and smaller turns) make a difference? *Yes, with this one* (smaller turn of axle) *the car goes a bit straighter; it turns like an oval.* And like that? *The more the wheels turn the more they go to the side where we want to turn the car, and that makes a smaller circle.* And does this one (the direction of the longitudinal axle) matter at all? *No, it's enough just to turn the wheels.* With Car III, he at first anticipates that, if the front and back axles are parallel, the car will perform a double turn. *You can tell from the wheels.* From which? *From both* (pairs). But after testing his prediction he says: *In my opinion, it won't get there.* What are you looking at? *At the wheels and the body* (longitudinal axle). Do we only need the wheels to get there? *Yes, I think so, the body just follows the wheels.*

VIR (8,11) starts with Car II and after several trials manages to set the rear axle correctly. However, when he is next presented with Car I, he fails to set the front axle in the opposite direction. Where will it go to? *Forward.* Can the front wheels help? *Yes.* Well, have a go. (He sets the wheels in the wrong direction, then corrects his mistake.) *It's better to turn the back wheels.* Is it more practical? *Yes,* Why? ... Can you manage with that car (I)? *No, because ... it won't work. If I put it like this it goes straight* (upwards) *and if I put it on the other side it will hit the cube, so it can't be done.* He nevertheless succeeds in the end. When asked to set the axles of both cars, he sets them wrongly at first, then anticipates the path of Car I correctly but no longer knows to what side II will move.

The great practical achievement of subjects at this stage is that they have learned to round the obstacles with a single setting of the front axle, which involves a good directional sense. Hand in hand with this advance goes the realization that the car will ultimately return to its starting point, and though CIC was still mistaken about the two circles resulting from two distinct settings of the front axle, MER claimed that a smaller deflection would engender a larger circle (an oval) and a bigger deflection would make the car *turn less*.

It should also be noted that in the course of these attempts the subject comes to understand the reason for all the corrections he has had to make. This advance is coupled to greater accuracy in the determination of the path of the car (discrimination between various settings of the wheels). Now, the choice of the correct directions presupposes an active adjustment, which is the source of conscious understanding, while the regulations deployed at previous levels were of a more automatic type.

However, subjects at this stage are still at a loss when it comes to rounding an obstacle too distant to be reached with a single setting of the front axle; in that case, these subjects (e.g. CIC) simply move the starting point of the car back but fail to point the nose in a different direction. When questioned about this response, they, moreover, belittle the importance of the way in which the car is pointed: *It's enough just to turn the wheels*, said MER, because *the body* just follows the wheels.

This response also explains the failure of these subjects to realize that, with Car II, the setting of the back axle deflects the nose in the opposite direction: PIG and all the remaining subjects believed that like settings of the front and back axles would have like effects. Particularly striking was the response of VIR who was presented first with Car II, and made excellent adjustments in the course of his various trials, thus demonstrating clearly that practical successes precede cognitive successes. However, when confronted with Car I, he became confused and at first set the front axle the wrong way.

Level IIB and stage III

At level IIB the child begins to co-ordinate the actions of the longitudinal and front axles (Car I) and also to anticipate the effects of different settings of the rear axle (Car II) though, in contrast to subjects at stage III, he does not yet grasp the connection between these latter effects and the position of the longitudinal axle.

Examples (level IIB)

NIS (8,0) correctly anticipates the direction of the car for various settings of the front axle and quickly realizes that he will not be able to round a distant obstacle without repointing the nose of the car: *If I put it down differently it will knock against that cube.* And the wheels? *Like that* (maximum inclination of the front axle), *that'll turn a lot and do the job.* What are you looking at? *The wheel, how it's going to turn.* What's more important, the wheel or which way the car faces? *The wheel.* And the car? *Yes, that's as important.* Car II: *That'll turn at the back. To steer the car round, we have to turn that* (the back axle) *the other way.* Why? *Because if you put the wheels like this, the car will go in that* (the opposite) *direction.*

HAL (9,0) same reactions: What do we have to look out for? *The wheels.* And does it matter where the car is pointed? *Yes.* To which one must we pay more attention? *To both.* However, with Car II and front and rear axles parallel he anticipates a sharp rotation *because the two of them are turned round so much.* And why won't it go straight? *Because the wheels pull the body behind* (which is true of the front axle but not of the rear axle).

PEL (9,1) manages to negotiate the most distant obstacle. *I shall point the car like this* (at 45°) *and then turn the wheels up to there* (almost to the maximum). Explain what you did. *I started off like this* (he points to the angle of the car). Asked next to make for a different point (higher up to the left) with Cars I and II, he correctly sets the axle of I to the left and that of II to the right *because the wheels of this one* (II) *go this way, and those of that* (I) *go the other way.* (He draws the paths of the two wheels of II but says that they are of equal length.) How do you explain that? *I can't put it into words.* (He is shown a drawing of Cars I and II with the front axle of I to the left and the rear axle of II to the right.) Does this help you in any way? He now indicates that both cars will move in the same direction and is shown Car II again: Which way will it go? *That way* (correct direction and full circle).

131

BOU (9,2), like HAL, fails to solve the problem of Car III, even though she anticipates the directions of II correctly. For distant obstacles, she adjusts the nose which she refers to as *the direction of the car*, as well as the rear axle.

SEP (9,2) same reactions. For a distant obstacle, he changes the starting point of the car and sometimes re-points the nose, accurately predicting the effects of various settings of the transverse axles (and also the various circles the vehicles will describe).

TEL (9,6) same reactions. Immediately predicts the correct direction of Car II and adds: *It's as if the other one* (I) *were reversed*, which is an excellent formulation of the inversion but not a full explanation.

ALB (9,11) for a distant obstacle, repoints the nose of the car with immediate success. He correctly predicts the various directions and paths of the car when the maximum front axle setting is combined with different positions of the longitudinal axle: *Like this* (longitudinal axle at too small an angle) *it's going to travel further.* Why? *Because it goes like that* (small curve), *not like this* (large curve). With Car II, he indicates the correct directions straightaway and explains: *If they* (the front wheels) *were at the back and turned like this* (same direction), *the car would go like that* (opposite direction).

MIF (10,4). Car II: *It's the same at the back but the wheels must be turned the other way.* What do you look out for? *The position of the wheels and the position of the car as well.* With Car III (front and rear axles parallel), he eventually concludes: *It won't budge, unless it's set like this* (the two axles in opposite directions). This remark shows that he has advanced to stage III.

Examples (stage III)

GEA (12,7). Car II: *When the back wheels take over, the car ought to go in the opposite direction.* How can you explain that? *That's quite simple: the back wheels go the opposite way of the movement.* What does that mean? *Well, if you want to go to the right the front wheels will have to be turned inwards, to the right, and the others will go to the left: this* (the right back wheel) *will lead and that one* (the left back wheel) *will travel further because it's more to the outside.* (He draws the paths covered by the two wheels correctly.) So what matters most? *Pointing the nose in the right direction.* The nose or the

132

wheels? *If you pointed the nose to one side and there were no wheels the car would go absolutely straight, so I think it must be the wheels all the same.* And the nose? *Well, you can't point the one without the other. . . . You must use both.*

AED (12,3) Car III: Where will it go? *It can't go.* How do you know? *I've looked at the wheels* (points to the parallel settings). *The car won't turn, it'll be stuck.* Why? *Because these wheels point exactly the same way.*

Subjects at level IIB thus manage to co-ordinate the position of the longitudinal axle with that of the front axle in order to round even the most distant obstacle. Moreover, they have come to grasp that they must bear two factors in mind at once: the direction of the car is *as important* as the setting of the wheels, said NIS; *we have to think of both*, declared HAL (*cf.* MIF). However, they do not specify the composition of the vectors though they compose them in practice, and we know from other studies as well that such compositions first appear at this level.

It is therefore interesting to discover that they also anticipate that Car II will move in a direction opposite to that of the rear wheels, i.e. that the setting of the rear axle produces an effect opposite to that of the front axle. In fact, what we have here once again is a co-ordination of the transverse axles with the longitudinal axle, which is pulled in opposite directions by identical settings of the front and rear axles, an effect subjects at level IIB seem unable to explain. *I can't put into words*, said PEL and when TEL explained that the setting of the rear wheels had the same effect as reversing the car with the front wheels set in the same direction, he was merely trying to justify his prediction, not offering a causal explanation. PEL went further by drawing the paths of the back wheels, but as he made them of equal length, we cannot tell whether or not he considered the deflection of the longitudinal axle. As for the problem of Car III (front and rear axles parallel), its solution eluded all subjects at level IIB (except for MIF who came up with a stage III response), and hence provides a crucial test of progress: the anticipation that the car will move in a straight line calls for the composition of the traction and deflection effects that the two transverse axles impress on the longitudinal axle.

As for subjects at stage III, GEA's drawing of the paths of the rear wheels of Car II showed clearly that he had grasped not only the general direction of the car, but also the gradual rotation of a longitudinal axle, which, unlike Car I, is not pulled in the same direction as the wheels. AED, for his part, appreciated that, with Car III, the actions of the two parallel pairs of wheels cancel each other out, which meant that he, too, considered the longitudinal axle.

Conclusions

This long development leading from direct manipulations to axle settings based on the composition of their several effects throws a great deal of light on the way children come to combine distinct data (conceptualized or otherwise), on the nature of their inferential co-ordinations and hence on the links between practical successes and cognitive progress.

It should be noted, first of all, that though changes in the position of the longitudinal axle are not co-ordinated with the setting of the transverse axles until an advanced stage, the longitudinal axle constitutes the first of the data our subjects consider, because at level IA they guide the body of the car by hand, thinking that the wheels simply 'roll' but do not turn the car (CLO). Their implicit inference, therefore, is that, if they change the direction of the entire car and hence of its longitudinal axle, they automatically change the direction of the wheels. After several trials and after having been shown the effects of different axle settings, they discover a fresh effect at level IB: the fact that the car turns to the left or to the right if the transverse axle is not set at right angles to the direction of the car. In that case the longitudinal axle loses its importance and the implicit inference is now that the front wheels alone determine the direction of the car. Next, the subject discovers that though the path of the car from *A* to *B* round an obstacle can be anticipated, there is no way of setting the front axle to achieve this result without corrections *en route*. Whence the next discovery – characteristic of level IIA – that all changes, however slight, of the axle setting change the direction of the car, and that the setting must be closely co-ordinated with the proposed curvature. Quite apart from the active adjustments thus introduced and the greater comprehension they entail, this active co-ordination leads to a new inferential co-ordination: each of the curves corresponding to a particular setting of the front axle is part of a circle whose diameter is determined by that setting.

However, subjects at level IIA like those at level IB, still under-estimate the role of the longitudinal axle and hence fail to round distant obstacles without further adjustments or to grasp the effects of various settings of the rear axle (Car II). Further observations then lead to a new co-ordination, the moment the importance of the longitudinal axle, implicit in the manipulations of subjects at level IA but neglected at levels IB and IIA, is fully appreciated. That new advance, characteristic of level IIB, links the anticipated direction of the car as a function of the axle setting to the anticipated direction of the car as a function of the starting point (and hence of the longitudinal axle). However, this co-ordination is still semi-vectorial rather than causal, which explains why subjects at this level are still unable to cope with Car III. At stage III, finally, the co-ordination assumes a causal significance, that is, the role of the longitudinal axle is grasped as well as anticipated.

CHAPTER EIGHT

Boats[1]

A 50 cm sailing boat with a keel is floated in a large circular bowl. The boat has a rudder and a square sail, or more precisely a strip of Plexiglass fitted vertically into a slit in a round tin attached to the centre of the bridge, which allows the child to rotate the sail and also to slide it across. A hair dryer provides the 'wind' power, whose direction can, if necessary, be changed by the subject. In addition the bowl contains three buoys: one opposite the starting point of the boat, another to the right and a third to the left, the last two serving as targets.

The first questions bear on a boat that is fitted with a rudder but not with a sail and must therefore be propelled by hand. Unbeknown to the child, the rudder is set straight or at an angle and the demonstrator waits for the child to comment spontaneously on its action. If he fails to do so, his attention is drawn to it and he is asked to steer the boat towards the targets on the left or the right. His successes and failures are noted, and he is asked to describe his actions and to explain their results.

Next, the sail is fitted, with the rudder set straight, and the child's attention is drawn to the fact that the sail can be rotated or made to jut out over one side of the boat or the other. The demonstrator again observes his behaviour and the relations he establishes between the various positions of the sail and the direction of the boat (and also of the 'wind'). The child is again asked to describe his actions in detail and to explain their results.

Finally, he is asked to combine the effects of rudder and sail. The co-ordinations he has to effect are cognitive on the one hand – he must grasp that instead of turning the rudder in a particular

---

[1] In collaboration with S. Uzan.

direction, he can either rotate the sail until it lies in a parallel direction or make it jut out in the opposite direction – and active on the other: if the rudder is turned in one direction and the sail protrudes in the other direction, the directional effect of the former is increased; if both are pulled in the same direction. the effects cancel out: etc.

Stage I

At level IA, the rudder is thought to have no more directional significance than did the transverse axles of motor cars (chapter 7).

Examples (level IA)

DID (5,5) has no difficulty in sending the boat to *A* with the rudder set straight. And to get over there (*B*)? (He pushes the boat off six times in succession without bothering about the rudder: failure.) Can't we get it there (*B*)? *No.* (He pushes the boat sideways.) *It's turned.* Why?... What did you do?... A demonstration of the effects of the rudder apparently teaches him nothing.

URS (5,10) sends the boat to *A*. The demonstrator turns the rudder to the left and URS tries to reach *A* as before: *It's turned!* (New attempt.) *It's still turning.* Why? *Because this bit* (the rudder) *has been turned.* Can you make the boat go straight? *We'd have to put it* (the rudder) *straight. Perhaps we'd have to put it on the other side* (she tries). *It* (the boat) *goes back to the other side.* Why?... You managed before; do you know why? *No.* What does it (the rudder) do? *It's the motor.* What does it do? *It makes the boat go in the water* (i.e. it produces the motion, not the direction). How can we make sure it will go straight? *We must put the boat absolutely straight* (she does so, but with the rudder to one side). *It's turned.* Why? *I don't know.* (Demonstrator straightens the rudder.) Will it go straight now? *I don't know.* (Tries.) Why did it go straight? *Don't know.* URS then tries to send the boat off towards the lateral targets but ignores the rudder, even when the demonstrator sets it for her. However, when asked at the very end: Why did the boat go there (to the left)?, she replies: *Because you turned that bit.* Even so, she points at the keel, not at the rudder.

BAU (5,6) also thinks of nothing but the direction of the boat, and at first ignores the various settings of the rudder effected by the demonstrator. In the end, however, he sees the connection between the boat's advance towards *A* and the straight position of the rudder: What made it go straight? *That* (the rudder). What does it do? *Makes it go forward.* How? *It turns.* He points to the positions previously observed, but continues to change the direction of the boat by hand, not by means of the rudder.

We see that, naturally enough, these subjects start out by attributing the course of the boat to the way it originally points, and completely ignore the rudder, even when its setting is changed by the demonstrator (DID). Or else, discovering that the rudder does play some role, they think that it acts like a motor and *makes the boat travel on the water* (URS) or *makes it go forward* (BAU). This reaction is most interesting. It shows, first of all, that children at this level consider all motion as tending towards a particular objective. Hence, if the rudder helps the boat to move at all, it must encourage its progress in the 'right' direction. This explains why, to reach *A*, URS pushed the boat in that direction, and completely ignored the setting of the rudder. Subjects at this level, moreover, fail to distinguish between pressure against the sides of an object (whence its rotation) and against its centre (whence its translation), as if its ultimate direction depended solely on the direction in which it was sent off (hence on the subject). At level IIB, by contrast, the subject begins to realize that the rotations and translations depend on the point of application of the thrust and not only on the launching direction. As a result they begin to think that the rudder 'steers' the boat, though they still fail to appreciate its full effect. They also fail to grasp the function of the sail.

At level IB, by contrast, they begin to appreciate that the rotations and translations depend on the point of application of the thrust and not only on the launching direction. As a result they begin to think that the rudder 'steers' the boat, though they still fail to grasp its full effect. They also do not grasp the function of the sail.

Examples (level IB)

RIE (6,0) starts out (like subjects at level IA) by completely ignoring the rudder, although it has been turned to the left and the boat fails to reach *A*. The demonstrator straightens the rudder and the boat now makes straight for *A*. RIE is asked to make it go to the right;

138

he turns the rudder to the left but pushes the boat to the right, whence failure, followed by trial and error until he eventually succeeds. *Now for the left.* (He moves the rudder slightly to the left and launches the boat obliquely: semi-success.) What did you do? *I moved that red thing* (the rudder) *and pushed the boat sideways.* What's that red thing for? *To steer the boat.* How does it do that? *You turn it where you want to go.* And to go to the right? *You have to turn the red thing like this.* But in fact he straightens the rudder and pushes the boat off obliquely. Complete failure with the sail: to make the boat go straight, RIE turns the sail to the right, etc.

NET (6,4) also starts out by pushing the boat in the direction of the target and ignores the rudder, but eventually succeeds in steering a straight course: *It* (the rudder) *is big, and if it's turned, the boat has to turn as well.* And to go over there (completely straight)? *We have to put it straight, that'll make the boat go straight as well.* And if we put it like that (to the right)? *It won't go because the water is smooth and it cuts the water.* But what did you do before? *I put it straight and I pushed.* Could you go to the right like this (rudder to the right)? *Yes. We have to turn it a bit* (he moves the rudder slightly further to the right: semi-failure). *I turned it too much.* Why? *The water pushes against the boat.* And why does it go straight like this (rudder straight)? *It cuts the water and makes the boat go straight.* And to go over there (to the right)? *It's hard, I don't know how to make it turn.* And to make it go left? *It's hard to say.* And why does it go straight? *It cuts the water, and that makes it go straight.* And if I put the rudder like that (to the right)? *It'll cut the water, it's the same as with my hands* (general direction of the boat); *that'll turn it.* Sail: *If that is turned, it'll nearly turn the boat.* He pulls the sail to the right to make the boat go to the left, and *vice versa.* To make the boat sail perfectly straight, he sets the sail in various directions, and eventually concludes: *If it's in the middle* (at 90° to the bridge) *it won't turn because there is no push, so there is nothing to make it go straight.* He eventually manages to send the boat straight across the bowl and says: *It's because there is nothing on the side, and the push is from the side. If it's skew, that means it's being pushed over there* (on the right side); *the wind goes against the sail and pushes it.* Asked to compare the effects of sail and rudder he says: *I know, I know. That one* (the rudder) *works with the water: it's the water that makes it go the other way.* And with the sail? *It's the wind, because it's a sheet and when it's like that* (oblique) *it is pushed like this* (wrong direction) *because the sheet leans towards the water and that cuts it.*

STI (6,5) sets the rudder straight to go to *A*, then to the left to move the boat to the right: *I've turned it. Oh, no that's wrong.* (He turns the rudder too much to the right then, after observing the result, still turns it too much to the right.) To go to the left, he sets the rudder correctly, then straightens it again and pushes the boat to the left. Sail: sets it at right angles to the bridge and discovers nothing further.

RAY (6,6) tries to reach *A* with the rudder turned to the right, then, after four failures, moves the rudder to the left. After further failures, he straightens the rudder. To sail to the left, he leaves the rudder straight and pushes the boat off to the left: What did you do to make it go straight? *I put the rudder straight, otherwise the boat turns sideways.* Why? *Because that bit* (the rudder) *steers it.* How? *Because it's made of iron, and because the iron is curved, but not the wood.* And to go to the right? *I put the rudder straight and twisted the boat.* Could you have done it some other way? *No.*

GLAS (6,5) same initial reactions. Then says: *If we turn it, the boat will turn.* What about this way (rudder pointing to the right)? *It's going to go over there* (straight). Why? *No, I think it'll go over there* (to the left) *because it turns like this* (in an arc). What good does it (the rudder) do? *It makes the boat turn.* How? . . .

All these reactions show that, though the subjects have discovered that the rudder helps to *steer* the boat (RIE), they fail to anticipate the direction even after several observations. Thus when RIE, who seemed to have had a brief inkling of what was needed, went on to set the rudder *and* to push the boat off obliquely it was clear that he placed all his trust in the second method. NET arrived at much the same conclusion when he said that it was *hard* to steer by the rudder. STI who, after several mistakes, pointed the rudder to the left, changed it back to the right (wrong direction) and pushed the boat in the direction he wanted it to go. RAY realized that the rudder 'steers' the boat, but only if the boat goes straight ahead, since, otherwise, it is bound to veer from side to side. GLAS responded in much the same way.

If you compare these results with those discussed in the last chapter (on the steering of cars), we find that both sets of level IB responses have a common characteristic: the realization that a change in direction of a part of the moving body changes the

140

direction of the whole: the front axle of a car can be used to 'turn' the car in much the same way as the rudder can be used to 'steer' the boat. However, because the axle is at the front of the car and the rudder is at the back of the boat, the similarity stops there, the use of the first being much easier. By contrast, the role of the longitudinal axis is much more obvious with the boat than it is with the car, whence the tendency to push and let go. As for the sails, these subjects are at a complete loss, except for NET whose momentary intuition showed that he had reached the threshold of level IIA.

Level IIA

Subjects at level IIA still proceed by trial and error but begin to grasp the relationships involved.

Examples

AXE (7,3): What must we do to make the boat go straight? *Put the blade* (the rudder) *dead straight. If you put it like that* (to the left) *the boat will turn.* Why? *Because like that it will chase the water away.* And when it is dead straight? *It doesn't chase the water.* What must we do to go over there (to the right)? *Like this* (moves the rudder to the left). Why? *Because it's going to turn.* (Trial.) *Oh, I've moved the blade to the wrong side* (moves the rudder too far to the right so that the boat turns on its own axis). What happened? *We have to put it like that* (less to the right) *to get further.* Why? *Because the blade is less skew.* (The demonstrator moves the rudder to the left.) *It's going to turn over there* (to the left). And like this (rudder 90° to the right)? *If you push it off like that, it'll stop dead, because it'll block the water.* (Tries.) *I didn't think it would turn; it's as if the blade were like that* (45° to the right). Sail: How can we make the boat go straight? *By putting the sail straight* (perpendicular). And to the right? *I'd put it like that* (to the left). Why? *Otherwise it goes dead straight.* And to the left? (He moves the sail to the right.) *I turned it the other way.* Why? *Because the wind gets the sail down there* (on the protruding side). However, when he tries to rotate the sail, he pulls it in the wrong direction. Moreover to go to the right with the help of both sail and rudder, he pulls both to the left, and *vice versa.* After several trials: *We have to put the sail in one direction and the rudder in the other.*

CRI (7,11) begins, like AXE, by straightening the rudder so as to send the boat straight across the bowl, but turns the rudder to the left in order to send the boat to the right. After several trials and errors he moves the rudder to the right. *Oh!* To send the boat to the left he first points it straight that way and pushes, and then goes on to use the rudder. What have you done? *I put the rudder straight and then I gave it a little push.* And what else? *I put it a little to this* (the correct) *side. The boat had to be turned twice and then it got there.* And what did you do before that? *I made it go like . . . I don't remember.* He continues to make mistakes until, finally, he learns to set the rudder correctly from the outset: *I move the rudder where I want to go and the water lets the boat get there.* How does it do that? *It goes on the rudder and that makes it turn.* But isn't it already turned? *It hits against the rudder and that makes the boat turn.* And when the rudder is straight? *The two* (sides of the water; he points to either side of the rudder) *hit the rudder the same way.* Sail: centres it to go straight, but turns it to the wrong side to make the boat go to the right (*It's turned to the wrong side*) then to the left: *The wind comes in here and leaves that* (the left) *side,* which is correct as far as the angle of the wind is concerned but reflects an implicit belief that the wind pulls the boat towards the side to which it is deflected. When seen a week later, he sets the sail correctly: *I've turned it to this side because the wind makes the boat turn.* However, he fails to notice that the direction of the boat is reversed when the sail is slid from one side to the other: *We need the wind on this side of the sail.* (Tries it.) *Oh, no. On that side: to go to the right I have to put the wind on the left side.* And doesn't the rudder do anything? *Yes, it does something, but I don't know exactly what. . . . It helps to replace the sail when it isn't being turned.* No co-ordination between the rudder and the lateral translations (projections) of the sail: *We have to put the rudder and the sail on the same side.* Always? *Yes.*

JOH (8,2) begins by pushing the boat to the left and then to the right: *I aimed it over there,* etc. Is there some other way? *Yes, we can move the rudder a bit.* Can you make the boat go to the right like that? (He moves the rudder to the left, then, after testing the result, too far over to the right, hence semi-success.) Can you do better? (Corrects the setting slightly and almost reaches the target.) And to the left? (Puts the rudder too far over to the left, then adjusts it and succeeds.) How did you do that? *I turned the rudder and the boat turned.* Why? *The water makes little waves because the rudder has moved.* Sail: JOH leaves it centred, and steers the boat with the hair dryer. What is happening? *The foehn steers the boat. When I put it on the left side the boat went to the right, and when I put it on the right side, the boat went left.* Why? *No idea . . . the wind makes it go; it pushes the sail, which pushes the boat.* But he claims that the boat must be steered either with the sail or else with the rudder, but not with both.

KIB (8,5) states straightaway that to sail the boat to the right or to the left the rudder must be moved in the same direction, and her several trials are simply aimed at improving her course. With the sail, she begins by sliding the sail to the wrong side, but corrects her mistake after several trials. *To go to the right we have to move the sail so that the bigger side sticks out on the left. If you move it the other way, the boat will go to the left.* How do we go to the right with the rudder? *Move it to the right.* And with the sail? *With that it's the other way round, to go to the right we must put the big side on the left.* But she does not think of co-ordinating the effects.

VAL (9,9) sets the rudder straight to reach *A*. And to go to the right? *I move it like that* (to the left). *No, I was wrong.* (Moves it further to the left.) *I turned it too much* (keeps making adjustments and eventually succeeds). What happened? *It blocks the water, so it can't go this way* (to the right) *any more.* Lengthy trials and errors with the projecting sail and final success, but no co-ordination of sail and rudder.

Even older subjects (below the age of 11) still find the co-ordination of sail and rudder beyond their powers.

RUL (10,9) after attributing the directional effects first of the rudder and then of the sail to the action of the water and of the air (*I pushed the air on this side*, etc.) nevertheless concludes: *I've got it! Even with the sail we still need the rudder at the back. The sail is just for pushing the boat, so there has to be a rudder as well. We have to turn the rudder to one side, and put the sail straight. You don't steer the boat with the sail.*

RAN (10,9) similarly concludes that to go to the right one must either move the rudder to the right or let the sail jut out on the left, but *I don't think you can use both.* Hence if the sail is used for turning the boat *the rudder must be straight.*

The most striking advance of these subjects is that, after more or less prolonged trials and errors, they eventually arrive at a relatively stable correlation of the various positions of the rudder with the direction of the boat. CRI and several other subjects whom we have not quoted, also succeeded, after trial and error, to make the boat go to the required side with the help of the sail, clearly the more difficult task of the two. When it came to sliding the sail to the left or to the right (in a direction opposite to that of the rudder), there were several quick successes (AXE) no doubt due to the apparent similarity of this solution to the much simpler one of moving the hair dryer (in which case sensorimotor regulations facilitate the adaptation; *cf.* the case of JOH), or else the subjects (CRI, KIB, VAL, *et al.*) failed to notice the inversion (they move the sail to the side to which they intend to steer the boat and correct the error after observing the mistake).

What is so odd about all these subjects is that, having discovered the effects of rudder and sail on the direction of the boat, they should never think – and even reject the idea when it is suggested to them – of composing these two factors: the rudder, CRI claimed, *helps to replace the sail*. At most, they believe that the boat can be steered with the sail if the rudder is straight, i.e. if one of the two factors is neutralized (RAN).

There seem to be two reasons for this surprising reaction. The first is that, whenever the sail juts out, it has to be set in a direction opposite to that of the rudder. This is why CRI, even after discovering that *to go to the right I have to put the wind on the left side*, failed to correlate the effects of the sail with those of the rudder except to say that the two must always be on the same side (thus contradicting himself). The second reason is that even those subjects who have surmounted this difficulty are relatively incapable of composing two vectors or two forces in different directions. This was even true of several 10 year olds who ought to have moved on to level IIB (and who were able to compose more homogeneous forces). Thus RUL despite all his successes in steering with the sail nevertheless concluded that the sail is *just for pushing the boat*, and the rudder for *steering*.

Level IIB

Subjects at this level are able to co-ordinate rudder and sail, but fail to offer adequate explanations.

144

Examples

GUR (9,2) after immediate success with the rudder and several attempts with the sail, discovers the boat can be sent to the right if the hair dryer is played on the left side of the sail. She is asked for another solution: Do what you like. (To go to the right, she slides the sail over the left side of the boat and swings the rudder to the right): *Perhaps we ought to set the rudder and change the sail* (simultaneously). Why does the boat go to the left when the rudder is to the left? *The water pushes the boat if there is some current.* Is there any? *No.* So? *Because....* And the sail? *It's pushed by the wind.*

TOS (9,9) succeeds in sailing the boat to the left by moving the rudder to the left and sliding the sail over to the right *because the wind pushes it there* (on the right) *to make it go left and here* (on the left) *to make it go right.* Rudder: *It's like a hollow in the water for the boat to slide into.*

HUS (10,1) sets the rudder correctly and explains that *it cuts the water, it makes the water go up a bit,* and hence helps to turn the boat. He also discovers by trial and error that the sail must project over one side for the boat to go to the other. But when he tries (spontaneously) to add the effects and to steer the boat to the right, he moves both rudder and sail to the right: *It's like skiing, you put all the weight on one ski and that lets you go down in one direction. The boat's the same.* After discovering that he was wrong, he slides the sail to the left and moves the rudder to the right, but still hesitates: *I think it'll go to the right but I can't say for sure.* Then he observes and grasps the cumulative effect: *The wind swells the sails, they turn* (to the left), *and when this wood is turned to the left the boat goes to the left as well.*

PID (10,6) after almost immediate success, first with the rudder and then with the sail, thinks that they have separate effects, but then sees his mistake. If I move the sail over here, where will the boat go to? *The air hits the sail head on and slides across it, so the boat turns in the other direction.* And if we use the rudder as well? *There's no point.* Is there another way of getting there? *Yes, with the rudder. If the sail is straight* (centred) *you can steer with the rudder ... or by turning the sail.* What happens if we make the sail stick out on the right and use the rudder as well? (He slides the sail to the right and the rudder to the left): *It makes it go to the left.* And to go to the

145

right? He reverses both, but fails to explain their respective effects.

KAS (11,5) lets the sail project over the left side in order to steer the boat to the right. And how do we sail it to the left? *I'll put the rudder to the right and I'll blow on the sail on the right side so that it can turn easily.*

We see that at the age of 10 to 11 years, the normal age at which the easiest vector compositions emerge, subjects no longer have problems in composing the actions of sail and rudder. Only HUS and PID still hesitated, but PID because he thought there was no point in using both and HUS because of a mistaken analogy with skiing.

It should also be noted that these compositions of the directional effects are applied well before the subject manages to proffer the correct causal explanation. This means that the effects can be co-ordinated before their causes, which is only natural in our particular case: the effects are observable while the causes must be deduced. This explains why some subjects (e.g. PID) were at a complete loss, while others invoked weight, but in two distinct senses: either as being synonymous with the pressure of the water or the air, or else by shifting the balance of the boat to one side. GUR mentioned a current, then denied its existence, but could think of nothing better; TOS imagined a kind of furrow or *hollow* in the water which sucked the boat in. Most of these subjects referred to a link between the water and the rudder or between the air and the sail but in a global fashion, that is, without defining the details of the movements resulting from their contact. In other words, they described the observed effects rather than analysed the causes.

Stage III and conclusions

Subjects at stage III offer an adequate explanation of the respective effects of sail and rudder.

Examples

AMO (11,7): How did this happen (i.e. that the boat should have gone to the right when the sail projected on the left)? *The air did not push it dead in the middle, the sail hung right over the edge of the boat: it's as if we pushed it* (the sail) *to the left.* But why does it go in the opposite direction? *It's like the rudder, it is slapped over here;*

146

the water goes this way (↓) *but the air goes against the left like this* (↑) *and that sends it off to the right.*

DUN (12,0): What does the rudder do? *It steers the boat.* How? *It brakes one side . . . when the water gets there like this* (↓), *it hits the rudder which brakes the boat and then the boat turns.* With the sail on the left, by contrast, *the wind is sent back and that pushes the boat to the right. The wind leaves from here* (the left). How do you know that it leaves from there? *Because it pushes like that* (↑), *and can't get round to the back.* Can we use the rudder and the sail together? *We can put the sail like this* (projecting over the left side) *and the rudder to the right.*

WO (12,9). When the sail projects over the left side *the wind pushes* (↑) *more strongly there, and the boat goes to the right,* and when the rudder is turned to the right *it's not the same thing, the current* (↓) *is stronger there* (against the rudder); *it's not the same thing as if there was some wind* (↑).

PER (12,10). With the rudder turned to the left, *the water moves like this* (points along the axis of the boat) *and is pushed to the left.* Sail: *If the air hits the middle like this* (↑) *the boat goes to the right, so I must point the hair dryer at the right side if I want to make the boat go to the left.*

BUR (13,6) also explains why rudder and sail must be turned in opposite directions: *I think that it* (the rudder) *chases the water away; that stops the water from passing on the right side and makes it run more to the left – it slaps against the rudder like this* (↓) *and chases the water away.* With the sail, *the air passes diagonally, and puts more weight on this side than on the other.* When the sail is on the right side and the rudder is turned to the left *the wind passes more freely on the left than on the right and the water moves more easily on the right than on the left.*

BAU (13,10): *When I turn the rudder to the right the boat goes to the right because it holds the water back. The water hits it* (↓) *down here and the boat moves like this.* And when the rudder is straight? *Then it doesn't brake the water.* Sail: *To go to the right the wind must hit it* (↑) *on the left.*

STE (13,2) same reactions. *If I turn the sail to the same side as the rudder, the boat will go perfectly straight because the two cancel each other.*

All these explanations involve references to the vectors concerned, and hence represent a considerable advance: not only do these subjects realize that the wind pushes the boat forward (↑), which is obvious, but they also appreciate that the water, though immobile to all extents and purposes, is in relative motion (↓) with respect to the boat.[1] *The water comes this way* (↓) said AMO; *the water gets there like this* (↓) said DUN; *the current* (↓) *is stronger there* said WO; *it slaps against it like this* (↓) said BAU; etc. In other words, the rudder is believed to act like a brake on the force of the water (DUN, BAU and BER to some extent), whereas the sail is 'pushed' by the wind even though it deflects it to some extent because *it can't get round to the back* (DUN). Hence BUR's explanation: when the sail is on to the right and the rudder is turned to the left, *the wind passes more freely on the left than on the right and the water more freely on the right than on the left*, which comes back to saying that the water and the wind must 'slap' or 'press' on different sides of the boat and in opposite directions to produce the identical effect. If they 'press' on the same side then, as STE put it, *the boat will go perfectly straight because the two* cancel each other.

To sum up: at level IA neither the role of the rudder nor that of the sail is understood; at level IB the rudder and sometimes the sail are thought to 'steer' or to 'turn' the boat, but these subjects fail to establish the correct relations; at level IIA they learn to do so after numerous trials and errors but fail to grasp that the two factors can be co-ordinated; at level IIB they manage to compose them in practice but without understanding the causes, which they come to grasp at stage III.

If we compare these results with those described in chapter 7 we find that, with cars, subjects at level IA ignore the function of the front axle, and steer the car by hand, much as in the present case they steer the boat by hand; at level IB they come to appreciate that the axle helps to 'turn' the car and learn to tell in which direction more quickly than they do with the boat, because the axle is at the front, not at the back like the rudder; at level IIA they come to appreciate the precise effects of various settings of the front axle but fail to co-ordinate them with different settings of the rear or the longitudinal axles; at level IIB they learn to make such co-ordinations in practice

---

[1] The young Einstein is credited with joking during one of his frequent train journeys from Zürich to Bern: 'Can you tell me the name of the station that has just stopped outside the train?'

but fail to grasp the causes, which they begin to appreciate at stage III.

There is yet another similarity. With the cars, the causal co-ordination of the transverse and longitudinal axles involves the realization that the front axle pulls the body along, and that the back axle turns it in the opposite direction. With the boat, they establish similar relations between the actions of the wind and the sail on the one hand (from the rear to the front) and between the water and the rudder on the other hand (from the front to the rear). In both situations therefore, the subject has to effect one and the same vector composition and this is what he succeeds in doing at stage III.

These similarities suggest that the correlation of the data and even their interpretation depends on geometrical co-ordinations. At level IB, the latter are not advanced enough to link the positions of rudder and sail with the directions of the boat; at level IIA, operations in the form of correspondences enable the subject to grasp this link in respect of each of the two factors taken separately but not together. This is because their joint co-ordination demands a structuring of space (the beginning of co-ordinate systems) and this is not effected until level IIB, and even then without valid explanations, the child confessing his ignorance or invoking *currents* (GUR), or furrows and *hollows* (HUS), etc. At stage III, finally, the co-ordination of the positions of the rudder or the sail with the directions of the boat makes way for the vectorial composition of the direction of the water or the wind with that of the boat, coupled, moreover, to the idea of relative movements, and hence to a geometrical and dynamic (causal) interpretation of the system as a whole.

CHAPTER NINE

Winding up Chains[1]

Thin plates of various shapes (circles, squares, triangles) and with perimeters of two distinct values (we shall simply refer to them as large and small) are attached to an axle in such a way that they can be turned into a vertical position by couples. Their edges have grooves, and the children are asked to choose two chains (suspended from nails) that, when hooked up to two plates, will wind round them in such a way that their free ends will 'get to the top at the same time'.

This problem seems to be extremely simple: to solve it, the child has merely to select chains as long as the peripheries of the plates, i.e. two of the same length for two small or for two large plates and two unequal chains for two plates of different perimeter. (Occasionally, they are also asked to wind chains round three circles with different diameters.) In a preliminary experiment, we used different weights suspended from strings instead of the chains and asked questions about the simultaneous arrival of the weights, but we later decided to eliminate this irrelevant factor. In both methods, the subjects were asked, right at the end, for a brief account of their actions and for what advice they would give a comrade taking these tests, their answers providing an indication of their grasp of the processes involved.

But, as ever, the facts proved more complex than we anticipated, and the sequence of levels we were able to establish showed that, before they can produce the correct responses, our subjects must be able to allow for both the lengths of the chains and also for the size of the plates (which does not happen until level IB); to offset differences in the lengths of the chains (level IIA); to distinguish the

---

[1] In collaboration with T. Vergopoulo.

perimeter of the plates from their surface area (level IIB), and finally to deduce the solutions directly from the questions (stage III).

The slow pace of this development raises an interesting problem: if the subject fails to 'see' directly that two chains 'finishing' simultaneously must necessarily be of the same lengths as the perimeters of the plates, does not the discovery of this relation, inherent though it is in the spatial characteristics of the objects, presuppose the construction or the reconstruction of that very relation, but by means of geometrical operations? In other words, will not the solution of the problem demand, over and above 'empirical' or physical abstractions based on the objects themselves, the intervention of 'reflexive' abstractions based on the actions or operations of the subject? This is the central question we shall attempt to answer in this chapter.

Stage I

Examples (level IA)

MAR (4,8) with the string-and-weight method, concerns himself solely with the selection of equal weights (either one or two on each side) which he attaches to strings and plates chosen at random, including a small triangle and a large circle: What if you hang your weight up there (large circle) and I hang mine up here (medium circle)? *I'll win. Mine'll turn more quickly.* (Tries.) Why did you lose? *I don't know.* And why did these two arrive at the same time? *Because you pulled both of them . . . because they were turned.* (Two small plates): Who's going to win? *Me.* Why? *Because of the pull.*

BUR (5,3) hooks a long chain to a large circle and another large chain to a large triangle: *They'll get there at the same time.* Will one of them win? *Yes, that one* (the triangle). Why? *Because it's bigger* (Experiment.) *No, both.* But immediately afterwards, he places a long chain on a small triangle and a shorter chain on a large one. Which one will win? *That one* (the small triangle) *and the large round one will lose.* But I want them both to win (arrive at the same time). What must we do? *Use another chain as long as the first.* And with these (small square and large circle)? *They'll both win because the chains are the same length.* And so on for other plates despite repeated failures. Can we win with the same chains? *Yes.* Anywhere? *Yes.* And with the big ones and small shapes together?

151

Yes. And with only the small ones? *Yes, as long as the chains are the same* (lengths).

NIC (5,2) chooses plates of equal size but hooks up unequal chains: a long one to a small circle and a short one to a small triangle, then a long one to a small circle and a shorter one to another small circle, etc. At one point he hooks two small chains to two small circles and fails to see why they should reach the top simultaneously. Immediately afterwards, he hooks a long chain to a small circle and a short one to a small triangle. Then he seems to get the idea: *No, I was wrong. We must put a big one here as well.* But he simply changes the two chains round. At the end of the test, he is asked if there is some way of using two small plates so that the chains arrive at the same time, and he fits chains of equal length to them. But to explain his success, he merely says: *It's because both of them are small so both have won.* And why didn't it work with these two (large and small shapes)? *Because one was a triangle and the other one was round.*

Examples (level IB)

SEA (5,6) uses a large square and a large circle with long chains of unequal size and says: *They won't finish together. We have to use a very large one.* How do you know? *I don't know but it'll take a long time.* (Success.) *They finished at the same time!* Is there another way perhaps? *With a small triangle and a big one.* Will they finish at the same time? (He measures the length of the chains.) *No. . . . Yes. . . . No, because we haven't got two large triangles. We'd have to have two of the same because the small one is shorter and the big one is longer.* Even so, you can make them go round in the same time! (He selects two large circles and succeeds.) *I've finished. They're the same length.* And some other way? *I'd like two small ones* (succeeds with two small triangles). Any other way? (He selects two short chains of unequal lengths.) *I've taken two small chains. Oh no, one is larger* (chooses two equal chains and attaches them to two small squares). Will they finish together? *Yes, because I've made sure they're both twice the length* (of the chains). Any other way? *There isn't any.* A boy told me he could do it with a large triangle and a circle. *No, you need two large triangles, else it won't work.* Another boy told me that you could do it with a large circle and a small one but with different chains. *Well, let's see.* (He fits a double-length chain to the small circle and a single-length chain to the large circle.) *We need another bit.* But he said it was possible. *It won't work because that one* (the big plate) *takes up more chain and this one less, and so we need a small chain over here* (large circle) *and a big one over there* (small circle). But the boy said you could do it with two different chains. (He reflects.) *This one is bigger and that makes a bigger turn. Over here* (small circle) *we need less chain.* (Seems to give up.) But the boy used one chain for the small circle and another for the big one. *Well, then I'll take a small one for the small circle and a large one for the big circle.* (Success.) Can you also do it with a large circle and a large triangle? *Yes, but if we use different shapes we must use different chains.*

CHO (5,3) attaches two unequal chains to the two small circles: *No, it won't work because the chains have to be the same size.* (Correction and success.) *It works, because the chains are the same length. Idem* with two large circles. Isn't there some other way of doing it? (She places two chains of equal length on a large triangle and a small square.) Will they finish at the same time? *Yes, because they* (the chains) *are the same.* (Tries.) *No, because this triangle is too big.* (Takes a smaller one.) A boy told me it can be done with a small circle and a big one. *No, because if you use a large circle and a small one, the chain will be too big for one and too small for the other.* Try it. *No, they didn't finish together.* What can we do? (She points to two circles of equal size.) But that didn't work before. *Well, we need a smaller chain.* Why? *Because there isn't a bigger one.* But do we need a smaller one or a bigger one? *A bigger one.* Where are you going to put it? *On the small one* (circle). *If I use the same size it won't work.* Can we tell whether we need a smaller one or a bigger one? *A bigger one because otherwise it won't work* (she attaches a double-length chain to a small circle and a single-length chain to a big circle and tries). Did it work? *No, we need two small chains and two small shapes.* Try it. *They got there at the same time.* Why was the boy right? *Because we used a large chain with the large shape and a small one with the small.* But she rejects the suggestion that she should fit two large chains to a large triangle and a large circle: *That won't work, they have to be the same shape.*

MEL (6,8), after attaching a long string to a small triangle and a shorter one to a small circle and then a long string to a large triangle and a shorter one to a large circle, concludes: *We must have the same amount of string and the same size shapes.* The demonstrator ties a long string to a large triangle and a short one to a small triangle: Will that work? *No, because this one is big and that one is small, and the strings are different.*

PER (6,9) same reactions but also claims that when the plate *is bigger it'll turn more quickly.* He accordingly refuses to combine a large triangle with a big circle: *The first one is bigger; it sticks out so the string will be too short.*

SEG (6,8): *We need two chains as long as each other and two of the same shapes.* A boy told me that it will work with a small circle and a small triangle. *No, it won't, they aren't the same shape.* Try it. (He does so): *Oh yes, it works!* And with a large circle and a small shape? *Yes, it's possible.* (He uses the same chain.) *No, one is bigger.* So? (Further attempts with various pairs.) *No, it won't work. We need two big shapes or two small ones and the chains must be the same size.*

FOR (6,10) same reactions. And will it work with these two (a big and a small triangle)? *Yes, because they're the same* (shape). Try. (Failure): *No, this one is too small.* Does the size make a difference? *No, it doesn't.* So? *I don't know, we have to use the same chains.* A boy told me that it'll work with a long and a short chain and with different shapes. *Yes, with those* (large circle and large triangle). *We have to put the large chain here* (circle) *and the small one there.* (Failure.) The boy told me to use a big chain on the bigger shape and a smaller one on the smaller shape. *Yes* (success), *because the circle is bigger.*

MAR (6,6) succeeds with two small triangles. *Perhaps it works because the two are triangles.* (Square and circle): *It worked because the chains were the same size, they went round at the same speed.* Large triangle and large circle: Will that work? *Yes, because both of them are big.* But he also attaches two chains of the same length to a big and a small triangle: Will that work? *Perhaps, but you can't tell because the big one turns more quickly, so you'd have to turn the little one faster for its chain to get to the top.* Do these two shapes take up the same amount of chain? *Yes, because all of them turn quickly.* Does that mean they take up the same amount of chain? *Ah, no. The big one takes more and the small one less.* However, he goes on to attach a long chain to a small square and a short one on to a small circle and even hooks longer chains to smaller plates than to bigger ones, before finally compensating the effects.

No further examples are needed to show that the common tendency

154

of all these subjects is to attribute all their successes (to which they often refer as *both chains win*) to a single one of the two factors. With the string and weight method, MAR at first paid exclusive attention to the equalization of the weights and then, after repeated failures, to the speed of the rotation, with the (unexpressed) idea that a large circle revolves more quickly than a small one. However, after observing the result, he went on to ignore the size of the plates and no longer spoke of *pulling* or *turning*. With the chains, BUR ignored everything but their lengths, and claimed that the longer a chain, the greater the 'win' (over a shorter chain) regardless of the shapes and sizes of the plates. NIC, by contrast, relied solely on the size of the plates, and ignored their shape or the length of the chains. When he failed with two unequal chains on two small shapes, he simply changed the chains about and, to the end, completely ignored their length.

Subjects at level IB, by contrast, come fairly rapidly to pay attention to the length of the chain as well as to the size of the plates and to correlate these two factors. However, they still insist on using chains of equal length and often on using like shapes (*cf.* SCA and CHO at the end of the test, FOR and MAR at the beginning, and SEG's *We need two big shapes or two small ones*, etc.). In other words, what subjects at this level still lack is the ability to compensate the effects, and though most of them tend to ignore the shapes and dwell on the sizes, they do not realize that, in order to synchronize the winding of the chains on plates of unequal size they must attach a longer chain to the bigger plate and a shorter chain to the smaller plate.

Nor do these subjects try to compensate the effects without verbal suggestions by the demonstrator. Moreover, even when the demonstrator hooked a large chain to a large plate and a smaller one to a smaller plate, some of these subjects (e.g. MEL) contended that it would not work, because the shapes and (the length of) the strings *are different*. When the demonstrator went on to suggest the use of unequal chains with plates of different size, MEL admittedly changed his mind, but it is a remarkable fact that several others proposed compensations in the wrong sense: SCA wanted to add *a small bit* (of chain) to the big circle and a *big one* to the small circle. CHO, too, proposed attaching a *bigger* chain to the small circle, and MAR thought that the big circle turned more quickly and that the smaller one would have to be speeded up if two equal chains were to *get to the top* at the same time. Now it was this very idea (*cf.* PER) which doubtless explains the surprising initial errors of SCA and CHO: because the small plate is at a disadvantage (less speed or less power due to its smaller shape), it must be compensated with a longer chain.

Even so, some subjects did ultimately accept the demonstrator's suggestion and applied the correct method of compensation, but without any real understanding and simply relying on similarities in size.

Let us finally stress the fact that if, at the end of the test, these subjects are asked what advice they would give to others, they dwell exclusively on the selection of chains and plates of equal size and completely ignore the possible compensations.

Level IIA

Subjects at this level (from 7 to 8 years) spontaneously arrive at the idea of compensations when using plates of unequal size. However their approach is not as simple as it seems.

Examples

DID (7,5) attaches equal chains to a large circle and a large triangle. Can you think of something else to do? *I could take these two* (two small squares). How about the chains? *Yes, with a small square and a large circle.* Which chains would you use? *A small one here* (small square) *and a large one there* (large circle). Any other way? *We could put a long one on the large circle and a small one on the small circle.* How can you tell? *Because the long one worked on the big circle and the short one on the small circle.* Are you sure it will work? *Yes* (trial and success). Can you do it another way? *Perhaps a short one on the big circle and another short one on the small square* (!). Will that work? . . . Is there no way of telling? *No.* (He turns the plates halfway round.) *It won't work because one of the shapes is small, so it'll still be going when the big one is finished.*

FLO (6,11) first hooks two chains of equal length to a small square and a large circle, but, immediately after inspection, predicts that they won't finish together and substitutes one of the small triangles, then a large circle and a big triangle, etc. She selects various shapes and chains but always keeps them equal. She is handed shapes of unequal size and says: *The big one will get there first.* What must we do to let them finish together? *We'll have to change the chain because the big piece is not the same as the small* (she picks a long and a short chain). *They will finish together because the small triangle has a small chain and the big one has a big chain.* Asked to sum up, FLO states that equal chains must be placed on plates of equal size but that *if we use the big and the small piece, we must also take a big and a small chain.*

DOM (7,10) begins like DID by hooking chains of equal size to plates of equal shape and size, then tries a small and a large circle: *They didn't get there together because one is bigger than the other. If we take chains of the same size we have to put them on shapes of the same size.* But you are allowed to use different chains. (He hooks two long chains to a small and a large triangle): *You can tell straight off that it won't work* (substitutes a small chain for the small triangle). *Because this one* (the big chain) *will wind up more quickly because the shape is bigger.*

FIS (7,9) begins with plates of similar size but of various shapes. Why do they finish up at the same time? *Because the chains are the same length.* Wouldn't it work otherwise? *No, the shorter chain will finish first, the long one will come second.* And what if we put the same chains on these (circles of different sizes)? *The small circle will go more slowly and the big one more quickly.* I know a boy managed with these two, what do you think he did? *He put a long chain on the big one and a short chain on the little one.* (Experiment.) *There you are, both at the same time!* Can we do it like this (three unequal circles with three chains)? *Yes, we need a small chain for this one* (the big circle), *a medium one for that one and a big one for the little one.* Later: *No, we need a bigger chain for the big one.*

FLA (7,7). First uses chains of equal lengths and various plates of equal perimeter. Will it work with these two (unequal) chains? *No, they would have to be the same.* Are you sure? *You can't tell beforehand.* (Trial.) *No, one chain was a bit shorter than the other.* The demonstrator suggests two unequal triangles: *That one is smaller and takes up less chain. The other one is bigger, and needs more chain.*

CAR (7,11) starts out with one small and one large circle together with one short and one long chain *because that one is bigger.* However, she also selects two unequal chains for two small plates (square and triangle) fails and switches to chains of the same length. Then she goes back to plates of different size, hooks up the appropriate chains and explains: *I need a chain like that* (points to the small circle) *and a long one over here* (the large circle) *so that they'll finish together.*

MON (8,1), after several successes with pairs of large and small plates of different shape, explains: *You have to look at the shapes and the lengths of the chains, perhaps both have got to be the same.* Always? *Perhaps it will also work with a big chain and a small one. No, we need two big ones or else two small ones* (hooks them to a large and a small circle). Will that work? *I think so* (failure). *Perhaps it's because the chains are the same, we might need a larger one and a smaller one.* Would that work? *I don't know for sure but I think so.* Can't you guess? *No.* After several attempts: *It depends on the* (size of the) *plates and the chains. They must either be the same length or else they must be different.* When do you choose which? *We'll have to try and see.*

WYS (8,5) begins at random with plates and chains of equal or different sizes and concludes: *If we use two of the smaller chains, the big shape will still be winding up by the time the small one is finished.* Then, after further attempts: *You have to use the same chain each time.* And for those (large and small circles)? *No, for those we need a big one and a small one.* Three unequal circles: success with the two smaller ones after several trials and errors: *You can't tell without turning them.*

ARI (8,2) tries various combinations at random, then says *What bothers me is the length of the string. When it's shorter it should arrive first, shouldn't it?* She concludes that all the strings must be of equal length. And with these two (a large and a small triangle)? She hooks up unequal strings and says: *No, that one is too long.* But you haven't let them finish! *If I carried on the* (long) *one would come last.*

PAT (8,9) begins with equal chains and plates, then selects two unequal circles and two chains of different lengths: *I'm going to put the little one on the large circle and the big one on the small circle* (false compensation). (Trial.) *No, I was wrong about the sizes. . . . We need a smaller one here. This circle is bigger and so it goes up more quickly, that one takes up more chain so we need a bigger chain.*

VIV (8,7) uses trial and error before arriving at the correct compensation for a small square and a large circle. How long must the bigger chain be? *Fifty cm and the other one 20 cm because this one* (the square) *is half as much as that one* (the circle).

RYL (9,7) inspects the material. *It can't be done because some are bigger than the rest.* Then he arrives at compensations through trial and error but simply concludes that *the larger shape goes with the longer chain, and a smaller chain goes with the smaller shape.*

CEL (9,0) same reactions. *If the big circle would be bigger still it would use up more chain.*

JUD (9,0) same reactions. *This one is very big and so we need a very long chain.* How long? *I don't know* (attempt). *It's going to work: it's bigger so it makes fewer turns than that one* (the smaller circle).

We can see that all these subjects were able spontaneously to compensate difference in the sizes of the plates with a corresponding difference in the lengths of the chains or strings. However, we also find that their responses were far from uniform, so much so that we are entitled to wonder whether we are dealing with simple correspondences rather than with real compensations. The latter cannot be involved unless the subject, anticipating that the end of a chain will arrive earlier at the top of a large plate or later at the top of a small one, concludes that the chain must be lengthened in the first case and shortened in the second. As we saw, however, the responses of the subjects do not always reflect this conclusion.

The most elementary response was given by DID: the long chain *worked on the big circle and the short one on the small circle.* This subject clearly relied on simple correspondences. But even he must have employed a rudimentary form of compensation, because though he proceeded to an inverse correspondence (short chain on the large circle), he grasped that the long string on the small circle *will still be going, after the short wire on the large circle is finished.* The responses of the other subjects, too, showed every possible gradation from simple correspondences based on size to full comprehension of the temporal or kinematic differences in the winding up of the two chains.

However, none of these subjects was certain about the rightness of their predictions: *We'll have to try and see,* said MON (8,1) and *You can't tell without turning them,* said WYS (8,5), etc. The reason is that they simply compared the sizes, as VIV (8,7) stated explicitly when he claimed that a small square was *half as much* as a large circle. In short, these subjects, unlike those at level IIB, do not yet grasp the precise correspondence between the lengths of the chains and the perimeters of the plates. It is nevertheless interesting to observe the spontaneous emergence of compensations, i.e. the beginning of operational reversibility, at this level. It suggests that even though these subjects proceed empirically and do not arrive at the idea of compensations until after numerous observations have taught them that chains of equal length go with plates of equal size (except for CAR, who went wrong immediately afterwards), their compensations nevertheless involve inferential co-ordinations based on operational mechanisms (reciprocities). In other words, the correct interpretation of the physical data discovered by empirical abstraction presupposes a measure of reflexive abstraction, as the responses of subjects at the subsequent levels will make increasingly clear.

Levels IIB and stage III

Subjects at level IIB consider the perimeters and no longer the overall size of the plates, but only after several experiments, whereas subjects at stage III do so from the outset.

Examples (level IIB)

SNO (8,6) after several trials with shapes of equal size, selects a large and a small triangle: *No, it won't work because one of them has further to go.* So? *You have to look at the length of the chain and measure round* (the plate) *and once the chain gets to the top you have to cut it off.*

OLI (9,10) begins with equalities: *The chains are the same and so they arrive at the same time.* What does that mean? *It's the same number of turns* (he points to the perimeter). The same shapes? *No, not always. I think it's the same length round with these. . . . No, I'm wrong, the sides of the triangle are shorter* (than the circumference of the circle). And what about two of these small shapes? *They're equal, their edges are as long as each other.* And those (two unequal circles)? *Thirty cm for the small one and 40 cm for the big one.*

BOL (10,3) starts with a small square and a large circle and measures the chains. Why do you measure them? *Because I don't want them the same size.* Why not? *Because the square is smaller so it takes up the chain more quickly, the circle is bigger so I must take a larger chain.* However, he obtains the circumference of the circle by adding the lengths of two diameters at right angles to each other, and the perimeter of the square by the distance between the *sharp corners. The corners are in the way and take up more chain.* However, in the end, he does measure the perimeters of the *bits of cardboard.*

BOU (10,2) also begins with a large and a small plate and with unequal chains: *The big triangle takes a long chain and the small one a short chain because the big one takes up more room when you turn it, it has more space in there* (he points to the grooves). Is it wider? *No, longer.* Can you measure it? *Yes, with the chain* (he winds it round the perimeter). Then he measures the circumference of a circle and the perimeter of a triangle before attaching the chains to them.

RIC (10,5): *If the edge of this circle is longer it'll go more quickly, so it'll need a longer chain.*

CUR (11,2) also begins with inequalities and compensations. He measures the perimeters of a circle and a triangle and says: *If we go round this one and round that we ought to be able to tell if there's a difference.*

MAN (11,3): *They're not as long as each other when you go round them, so we need a big chain and a small chain.*

JEN (11,8). Chains of equal lengths can be used with different shapes, *because the circumferences are the same*; if they are not, the differences must be compensated.

Examples (stage III)

ABA (11,1) announces what he proposes to do: *I'll measure a circle and a triangle to see if there's a difference. If there isn't, it's easy, and if there is, I'll use a shorter string for the smaller one.* He measures the circumference of a circle and the perimeter of a triangle with strings and adjusts their lengths correctly.

HER (11,2): *Some* (chains) *will wind round more quickly than others depending on their length. We have to make some calculations* (measurements). With same chains *we must make sure that the periphery* (perimeter) *is the same, so we have to measure them first.* What if one is 40 cm and the other is 15 cm? *That's a difference of 25 cm: we should need a chain that is 25 cm shorter.*

PAR (12,1) for a square and a triangle: *We take* (measure) *one side of the triangle and multiply it by three and the square by four and*

161

see if it comes to the same. If it does, we can use the same chain, otherwise we must take one that is longer.

Although some subjects at level IA already succeed in correlating the lengths of the chains with the size of the shapes, they still treat the latter globally, that is, they consider their areas rather than their perimeters, whence the false conservations described by E. Lunzer and Vinh-Bang: these children believe that various rectangles with a constant perimeter must have a constant area, and *vice versa*. Subjects at level IIB, by contrast, distinguish between the two and hence grasp that, with shapes of different size (which BOL, BOU and others chose from the outset) the length of the chain must correspond to that of the perimeter and no longer to a global quantity. Some subjects came to appreciate this fact very quickly, while others needed more time. Thus BOL began by measuring two perpendicular diameters of the circle and by considering the *sharp corners* of the square as obstacles to the winding up of the chain, before he, too, took the perimeters of the *bits of cardboard* into account.

Finally, at stage III the solution is grasped as soon as the problem is stated. At level IIB and stage III therefore, reflexive abstraction has come to prevail over the simple and incomplete abstractions of stage I.

Conclusion. The roles of the two types of abstraction

Empirical abstraction proceeds from objects and allows the subject, *inter alia*, to retain from his perception of the chains and the plates only the length of the former and the size of the latter. Reflexive abstraction, by contrast, relates to the co-ordination of the subject's actions and enables him, for example, to deploy the transitive correlations involved in measurements, or the numerical correlations involved in the multiplication of the length of the side of a triangle or square by 3 or 4. But a material action, such as winding up a chain and even the mental recall of such an action constitutes a perceptible datum, on a par with the properties of an external object and hence gives rise to empirical abstractions. How then can we draw the boundary between these two types of abstraction? The question is complicated further by the fact that the same spatial relations make an isomorphous appearance in the geometry of the objects and in that of the subject. When HER, at stage III, compared two perimeters in his mind, and found that their difference was 25 cm, he decided to use two chains whose lengths differed by precisely that amount. Now, his actions clearly introduced relations into the objects that were in no way present before such compositions. To begin with, the perimeters and the chains had not yet been compared before the subject established their inequality. Next, establishing the inequality of the two chains A and B (or of the two perimeters) is tantamount to subjecting them to an action or operation of partition such that the longer chain B can be shown to have a length equal to A plus a length A' not present in A. Moreover, such measurements naturally imply numerous operations (units, partitions, and order of the displacements of the unit part) not contained in the object. In addition there is the correlation of the lengths of the perimeters with the lengths of the chains. Finally, the very concept of 'perimeter' implies that its variations are distinct from changes in area. In short, the objects were certainly comparable, equalizable, measurable, etc. before the action but only in relation to possible actions or operations not proceeding from them, even if the latter went no further than composing the data that, taken separately, constitute so many spatial properties of these objects.

What then is the geometry of the subject? First of all a set of compositions that impress an overriding form on a given content. Thus a displacement is a change in, or substitution of, positions such that, in the simplest case, AB is transformed into BA. But the positions of A and B are determined by one-dimensional relations once A and B alone are involved, but by two-dimensional relations if their reference points are defined, which presupposes a co-ordinate system (and hence co-ordinations in the true sense of the word). These compositions are isomorphous with those of logico-arithmetical systems, except that the criteria of correlation are 'neighbourhood' and 'continuum' and not merely similarities and differences (equivalences of various kinds). Now, even though they correspond to observable contents (but in a very inadequate way because the perceptive content can remain contradictory: B is indistinguishable from A, C from B, but not C from A), these compositions become forms in terms of relations or operational ordinations and colligations (embeddings). In other words, while the objects themselves involve a geometry (moreover a spatio-temporal one more or less bound up with a dynamic), that of the subject allows of its reconstruction and excels it in every way, whence the increasing importance of reflexive abstractions, whose function it is to provide the instruments of such reconstructions.

Seen in this light, the succession of our levels becomes much clearer. At level IA, the subject considers just one factor and his action is confined to dividing the objects presented to him into bigger, smaller and equal length. At level IB, he tries to correlate the size of the shapes with the length of the chains, which involves the correlation of relations: $(= x) \leftrightarrow (= y)$, or functions derived by reflexive abstraction from simple relations: $= x$ or $= y$. By contrast, the generalization in the form of compensations $(\pm x) \leftrightarrow (\pm y)$ is not made spontaneously before level IIA, because it presupposes a serial correspondence based on further reflexive abstractions. The distinction between the perimeter $+p$ and the area $+a$ of the shapes demands a new and more complex construction because it implies the non-correspondence (and hence the relative independence) of these two variables: whence a further advance in reflexive abstraction is needed. This is acquired at level IIB. Finally the deductions of stage III mark the beginning of the autonomy of the subject's geometry.

Naturally enough, these stages in the development of reflexive abstraction correspond to successive phases in cognitive development. One striking sign is the fact that, at level IB, the subject contents himself, when asked to sum up his findings at the end of the test, with references to the equality of shapes, sizes and lengths but not to the compensations he made when prompted by the demonstrator. At level IIA, he only remembers what inequalities he has grasped or anticipated, with the help of inferential co-ordinations and reflexive abstractions, but cannot conceptualize, after the event, what he has merely gathered with the help of empirical abstractions.

CHAPTER TEN

An Experiment in Reduction[1]

A string, free at A, is attached at D and can be made to slide round a nail B, when it is pressed down at C. When the string is pulled down at A, it covers a distance AA' twice the length of CX_1 (or CX_2, CX_3), CX being the distance the finger is moved from its original position (see Figure 10.1). This problem was examined in our

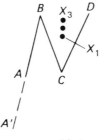

FIGURE 10.1

earlier studies of causality but we decided to resurrect it for the purpose of analysing the child's grasp of his own actions and observations. We discovered to our surprise that young subjects (level I) who are still unconversant with the conservation of lengths had no difficulty in recording the inequality of CX and AA', whereas subjects at level IIA, who have begun to accept the conservation of lengths are persuaded that $AA' = CX$ and hence refuse to bow to the data and instead resort to all sorts of subterfuge. Clearly, therefore, the problem we shall be examining is that of the role of the two types of abstraction, the 'reflexive' type intervening when inferential co-ordinations are added to the 'empirical' abstractions involved in the 'readings'. If this does not happen (as at level IIA),

---

[1] In collaboration with T. Vergopoulo.

there is a conflict between the two types of abstractions, unless (as happens from level IIB onwards) the nascent understanding of the mechanisms involved allows of a gradual reconciliation of observation with explanation.

At the beginning of the test, the children are shown a string with only two segments (ABC or $\wedge$), such that the rise of C is equal to the descent of A (on a table). However since we had reason to suspect that the readings of this simple arrangement would affect the interpretation of the more complex one, we began the tests with the set-up $ABCD$. Once he has anticipated the three points of arrival of C (X_1, X_2, X_3), the child is asked first of all what he must do to reach any one of them, and he generally replies that he must pull A. He is then asked to compare (or, if he is an advanced subject, to predict) the respective paths of the string from C to X and from A to A'. If he misjudges them badly (for instance by assuming that $AA' = CX$), he is asked to look more carefully or to check by measurement (rulers, strips of paper, etc.). It must be stressed that the child himself performs all these actions: he presses his finger[1] on C and pulls the string at A, and is thus provided with two sources of information, one visual and the other tactilo-kinesthetic. Next, part of the set-up is covered with a screen and the child is asked to predict the respective distances covered by A and C. Then, after a number of repetitions (with or without the screen) enabling him to determine the ratio (in fact simple or double) of CX to AA', the problem is reversed and the child is now asked how far A will rise when C is pulled down; the young subjects generally anticipate that A will cover a shorter distance than C because C is now being pulled instead of A. They are asked to check and then to explain. Finally, they are shown the arrangement ABC ($\wedge$) and asked the same question, before being brought back to $ABCD$ and asked to explain the difference between the two. The questions and answers we are about to quote represent just a small part of the actual test.

Stage I

Examples (level IA)

DID (5,3): If you had to get there (X_1), what would you do? *I'd*

---

[1] A ring is fitted to the string at C, and another at A which facilitates the reading of the data.

pull here (A) and that (C) will go up. Let's see if you're right. *This one (C) went up and that one (A) went down.* And if I hide this bit *(BCD)? I think it'll be like this ($X_1 \rightarrow X_2$). There you are* (he pulls the string at random). Can you measure it? (He takes a ruler and measures *CD* then pulls *A* at random.) Did this one (*A*) move the same distance as that (*C*)? *No.* More or less? *More.* How do you know? *Because . . .* (he tries to remember what he saw without the screen). Don't they always go the same distance? *Yes, over there (A), it's longer.* Why? *Because it pulls.* And this one (*C*)? *This one gives.* Which is longer, this or that? *This one (A).* And if we do it like this (pulling on *C* without the screen), will one be longer? *Yes, this one (C) because it pulls.* (The screen is brought back.) What must we do to get there (X_3)? *We must pull this one (C) up to the triangle (X_3).* Will this one (*A*) travel further or less far than that one (*C*)? *Further.* How do you know? *Because I played with it before.*

VIO (5,5) after the rise of *C* to X_1: Is the way up as long as the way down? *No, one of them is longer.* Which one? *That one (A).* If this one (*C*) takes two steps, how many steps does that one (*A*) take? *Three steps.* And if this one (*C*) takes five steps, how many steps here (*A*)? *Six steps.* Why? *Always one step more.* And if I hide them (screen)? *The same as just now.* With no reduction (a single nail at *B* and no *CD*), VIO denies the equality of the paths of *A* and *C*: *This one (A) is longer and that one (C) is shorter.* Back with *ABCD*: If we pull this one (*C*), will one travel further than the other? *Yes, the one we pull (C).*

BAR (5,6) also states that *CX* is shorter than *AA'*, *because I've pulled it.* Like VIO, she also thinks that, if one of the distances is three or five steps, the other will be four or six steps, thus treating the addition of the extra step as a kind of multiplication. If *C* is pulled, BAR claims at first that *A* will travel further, but she subsequently changes her mind and claims that *CC'* and *AA'* are *the same* because they finish up at the same level. Then she once again states correctly that *A* travels further *because I pulled it*, but ends up with the claim that *CC'* is longer *because I made it go down.* With the simple *ABC* arrangement, BAR also thinks that *AB* increases and *BC* decreases *because it's moved back* (when *A* is pulled), but cannot tell by how much.

PAD (6,8) same reactions. Screen: *I've thought about it. This one (AA') is bigger and that one (CX) is smaller. ABC*: same differences.

Subjects at level IB react in much the same way in situation *ABCD*, but show partial understanding of the equality in situation *ABC*.

Examples (level IB)

VER (5,8). *ABCD*: *AA'* is bigger than *CX*, and *vice versa*, when *C* is pulled down. How far has this one (*A*) travelled? *A fair bit*. And that one (*C*)? *A lot*. Look (the demonstrator places paper marks against *A* and *C* and against *A'* and *X*). Which has travelled further? *This one* (*A*). And less far? *That one* (*C*). Now I am going to hide them (under a screen) and you pull down (*C*). Which is longer? *This one* (*A*) *is shorter and that one* (*C*) *is bigger*. Why? *Because* (*C*) *has gone down and that one* (*A*) *went up*. Simple *ABC* situation: *A went further because it was pulled*. The demonstrator slides a ruler across and VER now states that, if one side moves *two steps* the other moves *two steps* as well. Hence she grants briefly that the displacements of *A* and *C* are *the same* in *ABC*, but immediately afterwards changes her mind and claims that a strip of paper tied to *C goes further because it moves up*.

JEA (6,7). *ABCD*: begins by thinking that the paths are equal (thus foreshadowing stage II) then discovers that *A* goes further. If this one (*C*) takes four steps how many will the other one take? *Six steps*. Under the screen: if *C* goes up six steps, *A* will go down *seven steps*. In the converse situation, i.e. when *C* is pulled down, JEA claims first that *C* will travel further, then changes his mind and says that *A* will *shift more when it's right on top*. If *A* and *C* reach the same level, they have travelled the same distance, if either is lower it has travelled further than the other. *ABC*: first inequality, but then *both of them are the same*.

GUI (6,7). *ABCD*: (*A*) *goes further*. By how much? *I can't say*. *ABC: They travel the same way, but if* (*A*) *is pulled out further it will go a longer way*. If (*A*) takes four steps how many will (*C*) take? *Four as well*. And if (*A*) takes six steps how many will (*C*) take? *Seven*. So sometimes it's the same and sometimes it isn't? *I don't know*.

Unlike subjects at level IIA (see below), these subjects have no difficulty in reading the data correctly after pulling *A* in situation *ABCD*. The explanation is not only that they are not yet bothered by the conservation of the overall length of the string but also that they believe that *AA'* is longer than *CX* because when they pull *A* they somehow 'stretch' it. In fact, before children in general adopt the conservation of lengths, they fail to distinguish between the act of stretching a moving body into a long thin shape from its displacement or simple change of position. This is borne out by their responses in the opposite situation (when they pull on *C*). Thus DID not only predicted, but even thought he had observed, that *CC'* was longer than *AA'* because *this one (C) pulls*. Similarly, VIO claimed that *the one we pull* travels further, and BAR took much the same view. The responses of subjects at level IB (VER and JEA with certain variations) were of much the same type.

In situation *ABC*, subjects at level IA fail to appreciate the equality of the displacements of *A* and *B* because they, too, think in terms of pulling and letting go, and hence fail to distinguish between elongations and displacements. By contrast, at level IB the reading of the data is slightly improved but only when the string is moved over short distances; else these subjects, too, believe that the leading string will be stretched and hence be the longer of the two segments (*cf.* VER and GUI).

In short, the reason why subjects at stage I give the correct answers, is not simply that they fail to appreciate the conservation of total lengths in situation *ABCD*, or that they have a rudimentary grasp of that conservation in situation *ABC*: the real explanation is their mistaken belief that by pulling a string they stretch it like an elastic band (*cf.* VER). Now, it is interesting to note that this confusion persists throughout the pre-operational level (4–7 years) and that it is gradually shed from about the age of 7 years onwards.

Level IIA

At this level, mistaken predictions and observations are due to the subjects' nascent grasp of conservation.

Examples

SUL (7,4). *ABCD: I pulled this one (A) until my finger went to there* (X_1). *How far did this one (A) go? A lot. And that one (C)? A little bit.* Let's do it without looking (screen). How far did your finger go? *From here (C) to there (X_2). And that one (A)? There.* Were the two distances the same or not? *The same.* If this one (*C*) takes four steps how many does that one (*A*) take? *Four steps as well.* (Measurement.)

How many steps did it take? *Many*. And (*C*)? *A few*. Why? *Because there are two strings*. And so? *One is fixed to the board*. And does one travel further like this (from *C* to *X*; visible)? *No, both are the same*. Why? *I started from here (A), pulled, and it went like this*. And now (*X₁*, visible)? *This one went further*.

FEO (7,4) notes that *A* travelled further than *C*. She is handed a ruler but does not use it. Screen: How do we know how far to pull? *By measuring it in our heads*. Measuring what? *That one* (*CX*). Why? *It helps you to see how far to pull. This one (A) will reach the same mark as that one (C)*. She takes the ruler and measures *CX*. How much? *Between 5 and 6* (correct). And did this one (*A*) travel the same distance? *Yes*. Next she observes that the path of *A* is longer *because it's the one we pulled*. *CX* is covered up, and FEO notes that *AA′* covers 7 units. And this one (*CX*)? *Between 6 and 7, no, between 4 and 5*. Why? *Oh, no. We have to make them the same, it's the same distance*.

KAL (7,7). *ABCD: They travel the same distance*. Would a ruler help you? *Yes, I think so*. (He measures *CX* and checks it against *AA′*.) *It's wrong. There's some trick here. When I pull this one (A) as far as here (A′) that one (C) ought to have gone as far as there (X)*. Which one is longer? (He measures with his fingers.) *It's all wrong, there's some trick to it*. And like that (pulling *C*)? *The two are the same*. Try again! *That one (A) is longer!* (New attempts.) *It's double!* Why? *Because here there are two strings. If there were just one it would be the same*.

EMA (7,8). *ABCD: I'm going to pull here (A) and that will make that end (C) of the string move up*. And will this ring (*A*), have gone as far as that one (*C*)? *Yes*. How do you know? *When you pull here (A) you start moving this one (C), and as soon as you stop, this ring (A) stops as well*. But how far do they move? *I'll have to measure the distance from here to there (C to X) and I'll try it against that (AA′)*. Well, go ahead. *I was wrong. I've measured it wrong*. What can you do about it? *Pull (A) a little bit further because I've measured it wrong*. So? (He measures again.) *ABC: Same distance because one goes up and the other one goes down*. And with that (*ABCD*)? *Also*. Zigzag with five nails but without reduction: *You pull and it's got to be the same distance because it's the same string. When you stop pulling one end the other end stops as well*.

JOR (7,4). *ABCD: They'll be the same distance*. Try. *This one (C) got shorter and that one (A) got longer*. The same amount? *Yes*.

170

(Checks.) Why weren't they the same? ... Are they the same distance?

LOU (8,1). *ABCD*: Several attempts. What is happening? *One gets shorter and the other one gets longer.* Have they moved the same distance? *If you don't pull they are equal but when you pull one is a little bit longer than the other.* Which one? *The one on the left.* And like that (pulling *C* instead of *A*)? *Ah! Then it's this one (C).* And the distances? *They're always the same because the string is the same length.* Would you like to measure? *All right. Here you are. No, they're not quite the same.* How can we tell exactly? *You'd have to know the dimensions. You take this one (CX), make a mark, and make the same mark over there.* (Fresh attempt.) *When (C) goes up, the other one has to come down the same distance.* Why? *Because it loses some string over there and gains it over here (A), because we didn't add any more string, so it has to be the same.* Aren't you going to measure it? (She does so.) *It's wrong, I didn't measure it properly.* Let's check. (Verification.) *It's wrong, we didn't pull it enough.* So? (She repeats the movements.) Did your two hands travel the same distance? *Not if you don't count the string.* What do you mean? *The string is always the same but one bit (A) is longer when you pull it down half-way* (at *C*). *It travels further on the one side but it's always the same string.* Try again. *Ah, that one (AA') is longer.* Why? *I can't say. . . . When you pull, one end always goes further.*

BUT (8,8). Same reactions. Did each of your hands travel the same distance? *Yes.* Try again. *If I bring this one (C) up, that bit (AA') is longer than this bit (CX).* By how much? *I don't know. It all depends. ABC:* Same distances *because there's just one nail. When there are two nails the string takes up more room.* Does that mean that over here (*ABCD*) this bit (*AA'*) is equal to that (*CX*)? *Yes.* So it's the same in both cases (*ABC* and *ABCD*)? *Yes. But when it goes down, there's more string and when it goes up there's less.* Why is that? *This one (CD) doesn't move but it gets smaller, and that one (BC) moves with this (AB).*

These reactions bear clear witness to a conflict between the reading of the data and the logical inferences based on the conservation of the length of the string. SUL and FEO who were still close to level IB read the data correctly at first, but just as soon as the screen was brought out they insisted that $AA' = CX$ without justification but obviously because of a nascent grasp of the conservation of lengths.

FEO, finding that her anticipation was false, reverted to the idea of 'stretching' (*it's the one we pull*), but when the screen was brought back reaffirmed her belief that the two distances must of necessity be equal. CAL, by contrast, doubted the evidence of his own eyes and spoke of some trick because *C ought to have gone as far as here*, that is, the same distance as AA'. In the converse situation, he first displayed the same obstinacy and it was not until after several attempts that he accepted the facts but failed to discover the explanation. EMA affirmed the equality $AA' = CX$ on the grounds that both sides of the string start and stop moving at the same time and blamed any inequalities on errors in his measurements: *I measured it wrong*. JOR was completely bewildered and, in the end, refused to comment on the data, let alone to proffer an explanation. LOU, after doubting her own measurements, took refuge in a subtle distinction: she argued that $AA' = CX$ *because the string is always the same*, but *when you pull, one end always goes further*. BUT used a similar explanation before finally coming up with the correct answer.

In short, all these subjects believe more in what they think is logical (namely the conservation of lengths, as in ABC) than in the facts, which they consider unreliable or rigged.

Level IIB and stage III

Nine to ten year olds accept the facts more or less quickly but cannot yet offer a stable explanation.

Examples (level IIB)

STI (8,11). Manipulation: *This finger (AA') went further*. By how much? *Twenty cm* (wild guess). If we call this distance (CX) four, how long would that one (AA') be? *Eight*. Why? *Because 4 and 4 is 8.* He is asked to pull C: *Now it's this one (AA') which will go less far*. Why? *The one that is being pulled has to go further*. (Checks but offers no explanation.) ABC (prediction): *They won't be the same*. (Checks.) *Oh, they are!* And why not here? ($ABCD$)? *The one that pulls covers more centimetres*. Over here ($ABCD$), one bit has two strings and the other bit just one string. So? *The one that pulls goes further*. And over there (repeated inversion)? *Oh! So that isn't the reason?*

RIO (9,6). *ABC: When you pull that one (A) down, the other one*

(C) *goes up the same amount.* And like that (pulling C with a screen over AB)? *I measure it in my head to get the scale.* How do you do that? *I . . . I can't really explain because it's all inside my head but I can't explain why. ABCD: If I measure the first bit (AA') I must divide the length I measured into two.* Are you sure? *I'm not really positive.*

BER (9,6). *ABC: When one goes up, the other goes down the same.* ABCD: He anticipates equality, but notes straightaway that he was wrong: *There are two strings and if I pull here (A), only that bit (BC) moves up.* (He measures CX): *We have to do it twice: that one (AA') is twice the distance of the double bit.*

FLO (9,11). *ABCD: That bit (AA') is longer.* Why? *Because it was pulled and when you pull, it gets longer.* However, if C is pulled, *this one (A) goes up a lot and that one (C) goes down a lot. The distances are the same.* (The demonstrator marks the levels.) *This one (A) is longer when it goes down.* And if that one (C) goes down? *Then it'll be longer.* Look! *Oh, no, it's this one (A) that went further, it's like before; it's just as if that bit (CD) wasn't there.* Look again! *If this one (A) goes down it's longer, and if that one (C) goes down it's shorter because over here (BCD) there's a loop and that shortens the string.* If this one (A) is 10 cm how long is that one (C)? *Five cm.* Is it always half? *Yes.*

SAN (9,2). *ABCD: They'll be the same, because I pull this one (A) and that will make that one (C) go up.* But how do you know that they will be the same? *When I stop this one that one stops as well.* (Experiment.) *No, it's shorter over here (C).* If (C) is pulled, the distances will be *the same.* When he discovers that A travels further, he says: *That one (C) has a loop which cuts off a bit of the string. The string makes a V, and my finger is over the middle.* However, when the demonstrator makes A very short and the 'loop' BCD very long, SAN reverts to his original anticipation of equality. Then, after several experiments, he says: *Well, I never!* And like that (ABC)? *It's the same because it's a single string. Here (BCD) it's two strings so it doesn't go so far.*

FAI (9,2). Notes straightaway that *this (AA') is half of that one (CX).* And if (C) travels 8 cm, how far will (A) travel? *Nine cm; it's a little bit longer.* And if we pull this one (C)? *It'll be longer over there (C).* Always? *No, not always. The two are the same, but when you pull that (C), it gets longer.* Experiment: *Oh, no it's twice as long over there (A).* (No explanation.)

LAU (9,1) same reactions, but when he discovers that *AA'* is always longer, even when *C* is pulled down, concludes that even with *ABC*, that one (*A*) *must be pulled twice as far.*

LUS (10,1) anticipates that the two ends will be equal, then, after verification, says: *We have to double the amount.* If there are bends, *A* must be pulled across a distance that is a multiple of *the bit of string that has been folded.*

ROB (10,6). *ABC: If you pull over here* (*A*) *you can be sure this end will be as long as the other side. ABCD: It won't be the same.* Why? *Because there are two strings and they're no longer the same length. The string has been divided in two, so you have to pull twice as far.*

CAT (10,5). *ABCD: My finger hasn't travelled as far as the other end.* And if you pull over here (*C*)? *The two are the same.* Then he corrects himself: because *AA'* is longer in *ABCD* he believes it must also be longer in *ABC*. Finally, he sees his mistake.

Subjects at stage III either anticipate the differences in *ABCD* straightaway, or else discover them in the course of the test and at once grasp the reason for them.

Examples (stage III)

DEB (10,8). *ABC*: equality. *ABCD*: expects equality, but then says: *Oh, no; wait, it won't be the same. That twine isn't straight, it's been bent double. I know: it's half as long on the one side, so I have to double it over here* (*AA'*).

REY (11,5). *ABC*: equality. *ABCD*, prediction: *We have to pull this one* (*A*). *That one* (*C*) *will move as far as this* (*A*). Try it. *Oh, it's longer over here* (*A*). *That one gets shorter because it* (*CD*) *has to take up the other end of the string* (*CBA*).

GRU (11,3). *ABCD: I'll pull* (*A*) *and this one* (*C*) *will come up.* (Pulls.) *This one* (*AA'*) *is longer than the other one.* Why is that one (*CX*) shorter? *Because it's held here* (*CD*); *that one* (*A*) *is longer because it must pull this* (*AB*) *and that* (*DC*) *but this* (*C*) *only pulls that* (*BC*). If (*C*) moves 10 cm how far will (*A*) move? *Twice as far* (without measurement). If we pull this (*C*), which will be longer? *This one* (*C*); *no that* (*A*).

COU (11,7). *ABCD*: predicts that the two distances will be the same, but after the first manipulation, says: *I've got it, it's double . . .*

because here (*C*) *there are two strings.* And if you pull this one (*C*)? *If you measure this bit* (descent of *C*), *that one* (*A*) *will be twice as much.* Why? *Because that end isn't bent double.* And like this (four strings)? *Four times as long.*

As far as their grasp of their own actions is concerned (the reader will recall that some of the tests were conducted with a screen, a fact we did not mention specifically on every occasion) and also when it comes to reading the data, the most remarkable thing about level IIB reactions is that, though these subjects are more at home with the conservation of lengths than subjects at level IIA, they do not seem in the least put out when they discover that the distance *CX* is shorter than the distance *AA′*. However, they do not anticipate the difference and do not fully grasp why it should occur. STI, for example, still believed that the end he pulled would travel over a longer distance than the other end (which did not prevent him from predicting correctly, for *ABCD*, that *AA′* would be twice as long as *CX*). RIO, who began with *ABC*, rightly anticipated the equality of the two branches even under the screen (but had difficulties in grasping the reason, whence this striking formulation: *It's all inside my head but I can't explain why*). Despite this difficulty, however, he immediately ventured the guess that in *ABCD* the ratio of *AA′* to *CX* would be as 1:2. BUR reacted in much the same way, and FLO claimed, like STI, that the element one pulls travelled a longer way, though when it came to pulling *C*, she first proposed a compromise (equal paths) before proffering the correct answer. SAN and FAI reacted similarly, and most of the subjects between the ages of 10 and 11 years came close to giving the characteristic stage III responses.

Their ability to read the data correctly poses a problem: at level IIA the reading was impeded by the nascent grasp of conservation (the reader will recall that the data did not present any difficulties at the pre-operational stage I), and we might have expected that, once this obstacle was overcome at level IIB, our subjects would have been able to come up with far better explanations than in fact they did. Must we therefore assume that the conservation of lengths (in the situation considered here) no longer constitutes a novelty, as it did at level IIA, and is taken for granted in all circumstances? It is difficult to justify this hypothesis. Far more plausible is the assumption that, being on the point of grasping the reason for the inequality in *ABCD*, these subjects are, by this very fact, prepared

175

for accepting the baffling evidence of their eyes, even when it runs counter to their predictions. In other words, though they were convinced that, if they pull one end of a single string, any part of that string must move through the same distance because, as SAN put it *when I stop this one (A) that one (C) stops as well*, as soon as they see the irregular arrangement of the string in *ABCD*, they are willing to accept the possibility of complications and this without having to regress in respect of the invariance of the total length of the string. This enables them to grant the existence of what, from the observer's point of view, might be called virtual perturbations or non-compensated 'virtual work', due to the intervention of additional factors. These call for additional arguments 'grafted' on to the old without necessarily contradicting them. In other words, these subjects feel that there may be a gap in, or a need for a complement to, their original assumptions, and this is why they are able to read the data correctly.

At stage III this gap is filled in the form of a valid explanation: the length of the string is conserved, but since it is fixed to *D* (*held*, said GRU; *bent double*, said DEB and COU) the rise of the ring from *C* to *X* involves the two segments *BC* and *CD*, whence *CX* must be one half as long as *AA'* if there are two strings in *C*, four times as long (COU) if there are four strings, etc. What we have here, therefore, are new operations effected on those ensuring the conservation of total length and applying this simple invariance to the more complex case of reduction. Subjects at level IIB, though they can read the data correctly, do not progress to this point, which explains why some of them even question the equality of the distances in *ABC* (*cf.* CAT at the age of 10,5). However, these subjects have started on the right path, and the great importance of their responses is that they provide a clear example of how children tackle new problems with the help of an earlier construction – in the event, the conservation of lengths.

CHAPTER ELEVEN

Equal Distances[1]

In the present study, the child is presented with two moving bodies (generally counters) in various positions and asked to make them travel over equal distances. This raises two special problems. In most of our other studies of this type, the child was asked quite simply to guide a moving body into a box, to reach a fixed objective, or to make use of various intermedia (for example a ball B which, when hit by a ball A, collides with a ball C). In the present case, by contrast, the child is forced not only to act but also to analyse his own actions because what is involved, in fact, is the construction of the concept of length.

The child is first handed a rectangular board with two holes

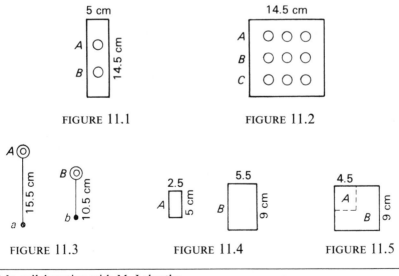

FIGURE 11.1   FIGURE 11.2

FIGURE 11.3   FIGURE 11.4   FIGURE 11.5

[1] In collaboration with M. Labarthe.

(Figure 11.1) containing two counters *A* and *B* of the same colour, then a square board (Figure 11.2) with nine holes and three counters arranged in various ways, and is asked to make them cover 'two equal distances' in any way he likes. Next he is handed two rings containing one counter each and asked to perform the same task. There follow two unequal rods or 'spoons' (Figure 11.3), each with a pearl on one side and a dish containing a counter on the other. Finally, the child is asked to move two cardboard rectangles with very unequal areas (Figure 11.4) or a square with a removable section (the irregular remainder carrying two counters; Figure 11.5). The subject is also handed several sticks to use for possible measurements.

Level IA

Examples

JAC (4,9) attaches no stable significance to 'equal distances'. In situation I, when the board is moved up and down, JAC says variously that the two counters *A* and *B* cover or do not cover the same path; in the second case, he thinks it is *A* that has moved further, though later he twice states that it is *B* (no doubt because it follows *A*). Presented with the two rings, JAC moves them along parallel curves, one of which is visibly shorter than the other. When asked to move them in straight lines, he brings *A* up to *B*, as if the 'same distance' were equivalent to finishing together. With the 'spoons', JAC variously moves the pearls or the counters to the same finishing line. When the demonstrator moves the 'spoons' along two parallel paths, JAC says that *B* has gone further *because it moved more quickly*.

COR (5,1). Rectangular board: The counter on top covers a longer distance because it was *in front*, but when the board is turned sideways, *B* moves further *because it was on the side*. Rings: the rings *go the same distance* regardless of their starting position, provided only that they finish up on the same line.

SAL (5,4). Rectangular board turned sideways: First claims that the counter on the right will travel further but then decides in favour of equality. In the upright position, *A* travels further, ostensibly *because it goes in front*, but in fact because SAL's finger pulls the top of the board *A*: when he pushes the bottom of the board he claims that *B* goes in front and hence travels further. When the board is pivoted round *A*, SAL claims either that *A* covers a shorter distance, *because its path is too small*, or else that *B*, which describes an arc of 180°, covers the shorter distance *because it's gone a very little way*. When asked to retrace the paths with his finger, he simply describes a recumbent figure 8. With the larger board and three counters, he claims the paths are the same *because they all went a very short way*, his method of saying that equal paths are those comprised in one qualitative category. With the rings, starting from the same line but with *B* travelling further, the distances are the same because *they finished up together*. With the 'spoons', the distances are variously judged to be equal because *they were together*, i.e. moved along parallel paths, or unequal because *one counter was in front*.

CIP (5,1) with the small and large boards, claims that the straight or circular paths are equal, etc., *because it's like the same car going for the same drive*. However, this is not yet the reaction of subjects at level IB, who also think the paths must be equal because the counters are in one and the same box, but rather reflects the view that the paths are equal because the counters took the same route. Thus when the rings are moved along parallel paths but from different starting lines, CIP also says *it's the same distance because they went the same way*. When the demonstrator insists that they did not start from the same line, CIP grudgingly admits that the paths could not have been equal, but twice points to the longer as being *the shorter*, which does not seem to be a slip of the tongue but a mistaken identification of 'shorter' with 'quicker'. To restore the equality CIP moves back the finishing line but fails to do anything about the unequal starting points. Are they as long as each other? *Yes*. Next he hits on the idea of making a detour with the counter nearest to the finishing line which brings him close to level IB.

These reactions make it clear that a distinction must be made between 'object-length' as a spatial property of solids in motion or at rest, or of their reference systems, and 'action-length' as the property of a movement with particular kinematic (space, time and velocity) and even praxiological (objective to be reached, etc.) characteristics. Now it is clear that the subjects we have just met do not distinguish between these two concepts and, instead of considering the distance traversed, focus all their attention on the praxiological characteristics of the movements they impress or see being impressed on objects considered as persons.

In addition, we must remember a general characteristic of level IA: the absence of all but ordinal quantifications. As a result, comparatives have no metrical significance but are treated as marks of rank: 'quicker', for instance, being treated as a synonym for 'ahead'. Accordingly, the length of a path is often evaluated in terms of qualitative categories: SAL, for example believed that all the counters in the big board had covered the same distance *because they all went a very short way*, and these subjects will often replace 'very small' with 'too small' without saying for what. In short, they treat magnitudes as absolute, not as relative, qualifications.

That being the case, it goes without saying that the criteria of distance they use are essentially polymorphous, and hence bound to be contradictory. Thus JAC began by applying ordinal criteria: he claimed that the first counter A (in the rectangular board) had either covered the same distance as the counter B because they had travelled the same way, or else that A had travelled further because B had to catch up with it. Next, he concluded that paths of equal shape (parallel lines or curves) or convergent paths must be of equal length regardless of their real dimensions. Finally he treated the length of a path as if it were a function of the speed of the moving body.

For COR the criterion of the longest path was, first, the position of the counters, (*in front* or *at the side*), and next the convergence of the finishing points. For SAL, too, the criterion was, first, the position of the leading counter (though he was, in fact, confused about which counter actually led the way). Subsequently he appealed to qualitative categories (*a very short way*), then to the simultaneous arrival of the counters at the finishing line (despite the spatial gap between them) and finally once again to the order of the positions. With CIP qualitative categorization went so far that he considered two moving bodies to have covered the same distance when they went *the same way*, regardless of the length of the journey. Next he equated the *shortest* path with the quickest.

In short, for children at level IA, the length of a path has a praxiological, not a quantitative, significance. Now, the equivalence of two paths can be evaluated by a multiplicity of criteria, and subjects at this level choose theirs at random, and make no attempt to co-ordinate them or to check their validity by spatial verifications.

Level IB

Examples

GIR (5,9) (intermediate case). Board with two counters: *the paths are equal because they are in a hole*. Why does that make them travel the same distance? *Because I turned them round*. Rings: GIR moves them in concentric circles of unequal radii. Do they travel as far as each other? *Yes, because I held them in my hands and made them go round together*. And if you move them in a straight line? (She makes them start from different points but finish on the same line): *The same distance because I made them go very straight*. Upon suggestion, she accepts that the distances could not have been equal because *one of them had that much more to do*. But then she reverts to her earlier opinion: *They've gone absolutely straight, so they must have come the same distance*. Same vacillation with the spoons: *It's this one* (the larger spoon) *because it's bigger. No, that's wrong, it's the same because they're on the same line*.

ALA (6,4). Board with two holes: the distances are equal even when the board is rotated, *because the counters are inside the board*. Rings: same distances *because I squeezed them together*. And like that (the demonstrator separates the counters)? (Parallel movements with gap on arrival): *It's the same distance because I made them all straight; neither of them went in a circle*. And like that (two equal but staggered paths)? *That one goes further because it's behind. No, they're the same because they followed each other*. And if we move them back? *Not the same; this one will have to go further than the other*. How can we make them equal? (He restores the staggered displacements.) *Like that. I made them go quickly so that both got there at the same time*. (Board with six counters, varied trajectories): *All of them finish together because they're on the same board*. And this one (at the back)? *It travels a longer way because it's behind*.

FUR (6,6). Board with two counters: same distance *because they all turned together* or *because they went straight with the board*. Board with six counters: same reaction at first; then *the red one will go furthest because it's right down* (at the back). Rings: to make them travel the same distance, FUR moves them along two symmetrical (but not parallel), curves and says: *The two of them start at the same time and finish at the same time*. And if they started like this (*A* lower than *B*)? (To offset the difference, FUR makes *A* travel further than *B*.) Why? *The red ought to go further than the blue.* And could we make them go the same distance like this (*A* touching the back of *B*)? *Yes* (she again makes them finish on the same line). Is that the same distance? *Yes.* And like that (departures from the same line but with staggered finishing points)? *The blue one* (shortest distance) *ought to have some fun on the way* (correct detour). Spoons with pearl *A'* lower down than pearl *B'*: FUR moves them in such a way that *A* finishes in front of *B*, making a false compensation as with the rings. Did you look carefully? *It's the same distance all the same.* Two cardboard rectangles with their bases on the same line: Same distance? *Yes, the big one is a bit bigger and the small one's a bit smaller. Now the small one is just as far ahead as the big one.*

BEA (6,9). Boards. Rotations, etc., with *A* leading: *Same distance because they're on the same board.* Rings: BEA moves them along various paths, but claims all are the same distance *because* (*B*) *follows behind* (*A*). Cardboard rectangles: false compensations like FUR.

KRE (6,10). Boards: Did they go the same distance? *Yes, because the counters are inside.* Rings: to equalize the distances, he moves *A* in a straight line and *B* obliquely, then brings them together towards the finishing line. When the demonstrator separates the rings and starts them separately, KRE makes them finish on to the same line. Did they travel as far as each other? *Yes.*

BUS (7,0). Perforated boards: *The two* (paths) *are the same because they travelled in the same boat.* (Rotation round *A*): The two are the same *because they're like two brothers.* Rings: he moves them in concentric arcs, but nevertheless claims they have covered the same distance because *they went at the same speed.* Large board: *This one* (*A*) *goes further because it's at the back.*

These subjects have made some progress inasmuch as, when the counters are in the same board, they make the positions of the latter their criterion of the distance traversed by the counters, whose own changes of position, however, they ignore, so much so that when the rectangular board is rotated round an (immobile) counter, they nevertheless think that both counters have travelled the same distance.

In fact, this bracketing together of bodies moving in unison is a clear sign not only that they have begun to differentiate the spatial characteristics of the displacement, but also that they attach growing importance to the ordinal criterion (order of succession of the positions), and hence come to appreciate that the displacements can be evaluated without actual measurement. In effect, assuming that two moving bodies cover the same path because they 'go together' is tantamount to assuming that they do not outrun one another (their relative positions with respect to the finishing line being ignored). Conversely, when two moving bodies advance without a 'vehicle', it is above all to the gap between them that these subjects appeal: they either squash the counters together to eliminate the gap (GIR, ALA, KRE), construct symmetrical or parallel paths (FUR, BUS), or else assess the distance covered by the relative positions of the counters (on the assumption that the one at the rear has to catch up with the one at the front: ALA, FUR at the beginning, BUS). The gaps between the counters are sometimes thought to play so important a role that FUR and BEA, for instance, corrected a gap at the start with a gap in the opposite sense at the finish, not realizing that they were in fact duplicating the difference.

However, though the ordinal criterion thus tends to prevail (to become systematic at level IIA), it does not yet, in these global forms, do away with a set of residual, contradictory criteria characteristic of level IA: GIR and ALA, for instance, judged distances by the straightness of the path; BEA by the general shape of the paths even though one counter went round the other; KRE by the finishing point of the counters regardless of the initial gap between them; BUS by their respective velocities, etc. Nevertheless there was clear progress, inasmuch as some of these subjects made one of the counters describe a detour in an attempt to equalize its path with that of another travelling along a short straight line.

Level IIA

At about the age of seven years there is a reversal of the method of evaluating the length of the path, the new criterion being the order in which the counters arrive at the end of their journey (longer path = travelling further). Here are some examples, beginning with three intermediate cases.

Examples

ZAN (6,9). Board with two counters moving upwards: Do they cover

183

the same distance? *No, one is at the back and the other is in front* (the first covering a greater distance). Can you make them equal? (He turns the board sideways): *Both of them are in front now, they're holding hands.* Show me how they went. (He indicates an arc for *A* and a to and fro movement for *B*.) Rings: he makes them go abreast. And like that (one behind the other covering the same distance)? *They didn't hold hands; one went in front of the other.* Equal paths with the same gap at the beginning and at the end: the one in front covered a greater distance *because it went longer.* Fix it so that they cover the same distance. (He makes them finish on the same line): *One catches up with the other, then they hold hands.* But did they go the same distance? *Yes. This one flies in a helicopter and it arrives at the same time.* Spoons: *This one goes further because the handle is longer.*

JAC (7,8). Board with two counters moving sideways: *The paths are the same because they move side by side.* And like that (upwards)? *It can't be done.* Try! (She pushes *B* from behind): This one (*A* in front) *has gone furthest, my hand* (behind) *has moved much less far, and this one* (*B*) *went halfway between them.* And if we take them back which will travel furthest? *Always that one* (*A*), *because it's at the back.* And if we move them forward? *The same one* (*A*) *because it came first.* However, when *A* and *B* are moved obliquely, JAC equalizes their paths by making them cross over. Are you sure it's the same distance? *Almost sure.* 'Spoons': claims that it is impossible to cover the same distances with the counters *A* and *B* and the pearls *a* and *b: We must make these* (*a*) *and* (*b*) *start from the same line, then they will go the same distance, but not the counters.* Try it like this (*A* and *B* on the same line, *a* behind *b*). *No, it can't be done. I must pull that one* (*b*) *back for it to go as far as the other, but then that's silly because that would make a longer path for B afterwards.*

DED (7,4). Two small beads threaded on two rods but at different heights: *I think it's the same distance because they go together.* And like that (same gap between the beads, but the two rods attached to a single hand)? *That one* (at the back) *is going to travel further.* And if we push (the two bars)? *They started at the same time but all the same it's the last one that went further.* By contrast, in the usual test of the conservation of lengths with two equal bars, first superposed, and then moved successively, she says that it is the one in front that *goes a longer way because it's come further.*

184

CIT (7,0). Two balls threaded on to a rod: *That one went furthest because it was in front.* Why? *When it's out in front it goes further like the locomotive of a train.* Double rod and irregular cardboard: same reactions.

PAT (7,1). Board with two counters: PAT is asked to make *A* and *B* cover the same distance: he starts off with *A* in front and finishes off with *A* at the back by way of compensation: *That one has turned the same way.* And like this (movement in a straight line)? *This one (B) hasn't gone as far because it is behind.* Why does that make it go less far? ... Can't you tell? *Because.... Unless we come back, (A) is in front one time and (B) is in front another time.* (Rotation round *B*?) *(A) has gone further; (B) didn't budge at all.* Rings: PAT constructs equal and symmetrical paths at the end of which he brings the rings back to their points of departure. He is then asked to construct equivalent distances starting from staggered positions, and does so by staggering the finishing points and then returning to the points of departure. And without going back? *No, that would make this one (B) go a longer way, because it's out in front.* Try it all the same. (He stops *A* and *B* on the same line, so that *A* travels further.) Did they travel the same distance? *Yes, (A) went a bit quicker; it caught up with (B) so they went the same distance.* But how do you explain this (staggering at the start but no staggering at the finish)? Are you sure they covered the same distance? *No, that one (B) didn't go as far, it was out in front.* But how can we make them go the same distance? (He again staggers the starting points but does not return the counters to them.) And like this (more pronounced staggering of the starting points)? (He makes the counters start together and hesitates between stopping them at the same finishing line and staggering them slightly.) Move each in turn! (Correct.) How can you make sure (he is handed measuring rods)? (He applies the same length to each of the two paths): *I did the same thing.* The board with the two counters is brought back: *That one went further because it was out in front.*

VER (7,7) moves the board with two counters in an arc and back again: *It's the same distance because I pushed both of them the same.* But when the board is moved in a straight line, *the white one (B) does not travel as far as the pink (A) because it's behind.* Three counters: same reaction. Spoons: *If you want the counters to do the same thing you must put them like that* (same finishing line), *but the spoons must leave like this* (same starting line). Rings with staggered starting and finishing points: *the same distance*. However, when the starting lines are staggered again, she moves the rings obliquely to the same finishing point, so that the distances are plainly unequal. What do you look for to see if it's the same distance? *We have to make a bit of a change* (she adjusts the meeting point of the rings so as to equalize the distance, then starts the rings off on paths equal to the initial segments).

AUB (7,9) twists the board with two counters round to compensate the effects. And like that (straight up)? *It's not the same distance. . . . Like that* (upwards) *it moves more slowly than like that* (sideways). Rods: *the two pearls cover the same distance. Oh, no there's a bit missing over here. The one in front goes further.* By contrast, with the rings staggered at the start but finishing on the same line, AUB realizes, after the event, that one has travelled further and thinks she can restore equality by returning both to their initial positions (which doubles the inequality).

ALB (8,1) thinks, like AUB, that if the board with the two counters is moved sideways, the counters will cover the same distance: *There's no need to twist them round, they can go absolutely straight.* But if the board is moved upwards, the bottom counter *will have gone further when I stop. This one* (the top counter) *has reached the end and the other one still has that bit to go.* However, if the board is rotated round *B*, *A* will go further *because the other one has done nothing but turn on the spot.* With the rings, he constructs equal paths by means of complicated straight or curved, but always parallel, trajectories, or else by crossing the rings over.

URS (8,1) begins by moving the board with the two counters sideways, twisting it first one way and then the other, so as to offset the difference. When the board is moved upwards in a straight line, the two counters will not cover the same distance *because this one is in front and the other one is behind and doesn't travel so far.* Rotation: correct solution. Rings: complicated but perfectly symmetrical curves. When the starting points are staggered, and he is asked to move the rings in a straight line, he begins by offsetting the gap between *A* and *B* (*A* at the rear) by adding it to the path of *A* (much as FUR did at level IB) and his own measurements fail to disabuse him at first. But then he corrects his mistake and finds the solution (same gap at the start and at the finish). However when the board is moved back to the starting point he is not convinced that *A* and *B* moving in a straight line have covered the same distance. Weren't the distances the same? *No, this one is in front and that one is at the back.* Spoons: They can't be made to cover the same distance *because that rod is shorter.*

CAT (8,8). Two beads on a wire: *I think the first one goes a longer way because it's further* (from the starting point), *so it had to go further.* Two wires: same reaction. Test of conservation (two rulers): *When you put one on top of the other, they are the same. When you push, one is longer than the other, but it's the same distance all the same.* And the ends that stick out? *The ends that stick out are the same.* Can you tell in advance which one will stick out? *No, you can't.*

GEN (8,2). Two rings starting from different points: GEN moves them to the same finishing line but then moves *A* back and *B* forward thus equalizing their paths. Can you do it in one go? (He moves *B* to a point as far in front of the finishing line as it was originally behind, which doubles the difference.) Why? *Because (B) was there and (A) was higher up and now (B) is on top of the other one.* And why does that make them travel the same distance? *Because one gets there first* (though it started last) *and the other came second.* Then he corrects his mistake and leaves the same gaps at the finish as he found at the start. Board with two counters: he turns it round so that the rear counter finishes up in front. Board with nine holes and three counters on a diagonal: *This one* (leading counter) *will go further.* Spoons: moves them sideways thus avoiding the problem. Small and large rectangles: starts with the small rectangle beneath the large and reverses the order when he reaches the finishing line.

PEL (9,0). Beads on one rod or on two parallel rods: *This one will go further, it moves first.* Test of conservation: *This one is longer, they are like a staircase.* And if we measure them? *They won't be the same.*

TRA (9,4). Rods, etc.: *This one has gone a bit further, it's up in front.* Conservation: *When you push them, they're not the same length; this one is longer.* And if we look at both sides? ... *We pushed them, so we can't tell which one is longer, so we have to say they're the same.* And if we measure them? *The same.* So it's the same distance? *No, not like this* (once one of them has been pulled).

ROS (9,5). Conservation: *This one is bigger* (after being pushed). And if we measured them? *The same, because they're the same length.* But you just said they weren't? *They're different if we measure them like that* (gap) *but before they were the same.*

187

NAD (9,0). Board with two counters: *No, it won't be the same; they'd have to be side by side.* Spoons: *No, it can't be done. One goes further than the other. The counters only go as far as each other if we move them forward together.*

Subjects at level IIA no longer apply the multiple and contradictory criteria of level IA, and instead concentrate on the ordinal evaluation of lengths by means of the gaps, but with a clear advance over level IB where that approach began to prevail: the subjects we have just examined consider the relative positions of the counters inside the moving board in terms of the movements of the latter with respect to the immobile reference system, i.e. the table. This advance is admittedly based on a fallacious generalization: instead of realizing that the counters in the board with two holes travel the same distance because they are displaced together even when the board travels upwards, these subjects argue that the leading counter must travel further because it outstrips the other one (instead of claiming, like subjects at level IB, that the rear counter travels further because it has to catch up with the first). But though they pay exaggerated importance to the original lead, their estimates are nevertheless more subtle, and this becomes particularly obvious when the board is rotated round one of the counters: in that case, they realize that the other counter alone is being displaced while the one serving as pivot stays in one place.

The two questions thrown up by these reactions concern the paradoxes to which the staggered positions of the counters give rise and the way in which these subjects manage in some respects to abandon the ordinal criterion and hence to acquire the correct notion of length as the interval between the starting and finishing points of a displacement.

As far as the first of these questions is concerned, the main problem is why these subjects centre their criterion of distance by the gap on the finishing point. At level IB, where the equivalence of the distances was still thought to depend on the common shape of the paths, the counters in one and the same board were thought to move 'together' and to cover the same distance, and so did bodies moving 'together' independently, except sometimes when one of them had apparently to catch up with the other. At level IIA, the notion of 'moving together', i.e. without a gap that has to be closed, becomes clearer, *inter alia* because the subject determines the positions of the moving bodies with respect to one another, with respect to the board and also with respect to the table. As a result, there is progress in dealing with the rotation of the board round one of the counters, but this advance goes hand in hand with the mistaken view that when one counter moving in a straight line reaches the finishing line before the second, it must have travelled further. The reason why these subjects neglect the starting points, is first of all that the co-ordination of several variables in space does not entail the immediate temporal correlation of the start and end points of the movement, and, above all, that the displacement is aimed at a goal, so that its end counts for more than its beginning. An additional factor, no doubt, as we saw elsewhere in connection with causality, is that it is not until level IIB that children begin to distinguish clearly between the displacement of an object and its elongation. It is unquestionably the combination of all these factors that presides over the choice of the final gap as the criterion of the distance run.

This explains both the artifices and also the paradoxical conduct of our subjects. The artifices consist of to and fro or circular movements, and even of twisting the board to offset the ordinal inequalities, the counter A arriving last because it started first (cf. PAT); the paradoxical conduct includes false compensations similar to those used at level IB and leads to a doubling of the gap (cf. AUB, GEN, et al.). But subjects at this level quickly correct their mistakes, except with the 'spoons' (counters and pearls at the two ends of two unequal rods): here they consider it impossible to equalize the distances (VER, NAB, et al.) because the counters and the pearls cannot be brought into coincidence. As for the reactions to the conservation test, they reflect a persistent distinction between object-length and action-length (CAT: *When you push, one is longer than the other*) and also a persistent failure to distinguish between elongations and displacements.

It nevertheless remains a fact that each of these subjects managed, after numerous trials and errors, to estimate the length of the path by the distance between the starting and finishing points. This is why JAC changed the positions of the counters A and B round ($\rightleftarrows$) and why ALB crossed them over ($\times$). In some rather unstable cases the subjects even managed to end up with the same gap with which they started, but failed to generalize this approach.

EQUAL DISTANCES

Level IIB

Examples

ATO (8,7) (intermediate case) pushes the board with two counters sideways: *When you push they are both on the same side, but if you turn them, this one will be more in front.* And like that (upwards)? *This one will go faster. At first it'll move nearer to the front but when you get to the end.* . . . (Hesitation.) *No, at the start there's a bit extra for one to go and when you get to the end there's a little bit left for the other one.* Are you sure? *The two paths are the same but the counters are not in the same place* (gap between equal trajectories). Despite this discovery, ATO goes on to move the two rings along two rectangular trajectories one of which is inside the other and plainly much shorter. He corrects his mistake by crossing their paths: *This one at the back always goes to the front.* Spoons: same gap at the finish as at the start. Which goes further? *They both go as far as each other.* Similar responses with the rectangles, etc.

ARI (9,1). Board with two counters: first claims that the leading counter travels further. Rotation: correct. With the rings, she starts off with a series of parallel or symmetrical paths without gaps, but when a gap is left at the start, she reproduces it at the end and affirms the equality of the distances: *I move them forward and then I can measure where the first one started, and then I do the same with the second.* But you said before that the one in front went further. *No it doesn't* (she measures the gaps with three small rods). Spoons: same distances. Oughtn't you to measure them? *No, I'm quite sure without. This one was out in front all the time, so it travelled the same distance.*

MIN (9,2) also begins with an ordinal evaluation, but for the rings she finishes off with the same gap she was asked to leave at the start, and says: *It's the same distance, they started off at the same time but not in the same place and they finished at the same time.* Spoons: *Same distance; one just happens to be longer than the other.* Board with removable sectors: *It's the same distance; this part has simply moved ahead. All the bits are the same* (i.e. part of a single whole).

BRO (9,0). Board with two counters: *It's the same distance even though the red one leads all the time. We ought to go back to the start else they won't travel the same way, because the black counter has not been as far as the red.* However, with the rings he conserves the original gap at the finish and affirms the equality of the distances:

190

They must be as far apart as at the beginning. Spoons: same reaction. Board with removable sector: *The whole lot moves forward at the same time. If we measure the distance it'll be the same.* And if you measure the path of the little square separately? *There's no point, we know it's all together.*

RIL (9,3) shows no hesitation with the boards (two or six counters): *They travel as far as each other because they're all together,* etc. However, when the boards are rotated *they may perhaps turn differently.* Rings: she conserves the original gap and affirms the equality, *because both have shifted over the same distance.* Spoons: same reaction but *they must go straight.*

The decisive advance of subjects at this level is their evaluation of distances, no longer in terms of the order of arrival but of the interval between the starting and finishing points. Two types of factors contribute to this final success. The first are logico-mathematical and are due to the development of metrical and co-ordinate systems which enable the child to compare the initial and final gaps. The other are of a physical type and involve the distinction between dynamics and kinematics, and hence between elongations and simple displacements. But the essential feature is the practical progress of these subjects: they have started to de-centre the action from the goal to be reached and no longer treat the whole of the trajectory in the static manner characteristic of stage I, but as something in continuous movement: the fact that most of these subjects, from ATO to BRO, began by relying exclusively on the ordinal criterion (end of the run), then hesitated and recalled the original gap, the better to evaluate the movement as a whole, shows clearly what great cognitive progress they have made. As a result they are able to co-ordinate the 'action-length' with the 'object-length' (and hence to endow the latter with stable characteristics).

Conclusions

The fact that the subjects examined in this study were expected to construct two equivalent paths rather than reach a particular target along a particular path, faced them with a special cognitive problem: whereas a single movement usually leads to results the child has come to expect without further ado, the equalization of two movements calls for a prior conceptualization, because what is involved

191

(see the introduction of this chapter) is the choice of a criterion of equivalence, and also because the performance of this complicated task, no less than the requisite adjustments, depends on the choice of this criterion. The gradual development of the equalization of distances thus brings us face to face with complex interactions between the conscious grasp of the action of displacing an object (already involved in single displacements) and the conceptualization of the equivalence of two corresponding paths.

We saw that subjects at level IA do not yet distinguish the object-length from the action-length. As for the latter, the subject's conscious grasp of it is characterized by the fact that predominantly qualitative (intensive) categories take precedence over extensive or metric quantifications (*a very short path*, *too small a path*, etc.), the child relying on shapes and ignoring their dimensions (straight lines *vs* curves) or even on the familiarity of the path (customary itinerary *vs* unusual detours). When it comes to determining the equivalence of two paths, even if the demonstrator specifically states that they are 'the same length', subjects at level IA never go beyond such primitive conceptualizations as equalizing paths of the same category (very small, etc.), of the same shape (parallel straight lines or similar curves) or 'going the same way'. In addition, however, these children have begun to apply special criteria of equalization, foreshadowing the ordinal criteria of later stages: two paths are thought to be equal if they lead to the same end, especially when the moving bodies 'go together', and unequal when they are separate and one has to 'catch up' with the other, or when one of the moving bodies, but not the other, is pushed directly by the subject.

These qualitative criteria still persist at level IB but with an advance whenever the moving bodies travel in or on the same conveyor: in that situation the fact that they describe paths of the same category, of the same shape, in the same direction and aimed at the same goal combine to impose the idea that they go 'together'. This relation thus becomes the chief criterion at level IB, and it may be called ordinal inasmuch as 'going together' means that neither of the two moving bodies outdistances the other (at least in global terms). In addition, subjects at this level try to impress parallel or symmetrical paths on counters moving independently so as to keep them 'together'. By contrast, if a gap is left between the two moving bodies, the most common reaction of these subjects is to invoke, not the lead of the body in front, but the need of the other to catch up and hence to restore the 'togetherness', and hence to travel further than the first. In short, there is a tendency at this level to subordinate the grasp or conceptualization of the length of the path to the equalization of the action-lengths.

The reactions of subjects at level IIA involve a subtler analysis of the relative positions of the moving bodies and of the reference systems, whence their refusal to grant the 'togetherness', or the equality of the paths, of the counters in the board with two holes when the latter is rotated round one of the counters, which is correct, but also when one of them moves ahead of the other in an upward direction, which is mistaken. The new fundamental criterion is the finishing order, and its choice represents an analytic advance coupled to more or less intentional neglect of possible perturbations caused by the inequality of the starting points, whence the correct or illusory compensations involving the reversal of the order of succession of the counters during the journey, etc., and also the refusal to accept that the paths of the counters in the spoons can possibly be equalized.

But it is also at level IIA that our subjects begin to pay heed to the gaps between the starting and finishing points when the paths of the two moving bodies are not identical (over part of the course) or parallel. This approach, reflecting an advance in the conscious grasp of all the variables and of metric co-ordination, is generalized at level IIB and hence leads the subject to the correct solution of the equivalence problems posed to him, and to the conservation of the object-length at long last clearly distinguished from the action-length whose privileged position still imposed the primacy of the finishing points at level IIA.

193

CHAPTER TWELVE

Mirrors[1]

We have previously had occasion to look at mirror problems in connection with our study of causality, but in the present analysis we shall be concerned with a different aspect of the subject. In particular, we shall be trying to determine whether the gradual advances made by our subjects are the result of simple feedback regulations or whether they involve causal inferences based either on earlier experiences or else constructed in the course of the present series of experiments. In other words, we shall try to determine if these advances are true co-ordinations of the data with certain products of the subject's own logic or geometry. Moreover, if they are, we shall also try to find out whether the subjects realize that, over and above reading the data, they are also, if not making inferences, at least acting in accordance with certain intentions, i.e. presupposing what ought to happen. Clearly, the results will tell us a great deal about our subject's conscious or unconscious conduct, much as the earlier studies told us a great deal about their conception of causality.

We use a long pocket torch with a fairly narrow beam, play it on a paper or cardboard screen and ask our subjects what 'path' the light has followed. Though we know that young subjects do not think light moves continuously through space but believe that it proceeds by jumps or actions at a distance, we nevertheless considered 'path' a convenient term to use, the more so as in this particular case the entire beam shows up clearly on the shining Formica table. Next, the light is projected to the side of the screen (at an angle of 45°) and the subject is handed a mirror measuring 15 cm by 25 cm and asked to use it in such a way that 'the light reaches the screen as it did just

---

[1] In collaboration with A. Henriques-Christophides.

now'. If he thinks this cannot be done (as, in fact, he does throughout stage I, i.e. from the age of 4 to 6 and sometimes even to 7 years), the demonstrator shows him how to produce the required effect (but with the mirror in one position only). Next, the torch is moved and the subject is invited to try again, which is done successfully by some subjects from the age of 4 years onwards. The subject is then asked to explain his procedure, and the demonstrator attempts to elicit the maximum number of possible definitions. Next, the experiment is repeated with the torch in various positions. For purposes of analysis, the subject is then shown a sketch on which the mirror is represented by a stroke parallel (mirror 'straight') or inclined to the table (mirror 'skew'), and which also shows the path of the light from the torch to the mirror, and asked to complete the sketch by simply drawing the path of the light from the mirror to the screen.

Next, the torch, the mirror and the screen are placed on the Formica table, which throws up a reflection in the shape of a V (referred to by that name). The demonstrator places a pencil on the branch of the V corresponding to the incident ray (pointing towards the mirror), and the child is asked to place another pencil on the second branch of the V (pointing towards the screen). Next, the demonstrator changes the position of the first pencil and asks the child to move the second pencil to an appropriate position. This raises much the same problems as the drawings but in a more graphic and direct manner, because the V is clearly discernible and, if he wanted to, the subject need do no more than rely on symmetry (which sometimes happens with young subjects, in whose case it is therefore most important to determine the precise degree of understanding).

Finally, the demonstrator brings out two mirrors, *A* and *B*, and asks the subject to make the light travel from the torch to *A*, from *A* to *B*, and from *B* to the screen. There is some advantage in presenting this more difficult test (which cannot be solved by sensori-motor regulations) in the middle and at the end of the interrogation to discover if the subjects have learned anything during the tests and especially from the pencil experiment.

Stage I

Subjects at this stage are unfamiliar with the process of reflection, and must first be given a demonstration of the actions they are

195

expected to perform. The demonstrator simply notes what conclusions they draw from the observed facts.

Examples

CRI (4,5). The light is thrown on to the screen, the beam being clearly visible on the Formica table: Can you trace out the path of the light with your finger? (He points to the light on the screen.) And like that (the mirror is set up in place of the screen)? *It leaves on the other side* (of the mirror). And like that (on the wall)? (Points to the light on the wall.) Here is a mirror (which is moved about to show the reflection of the light). Can you send the light over there (on to the screen) using the torch and the mirror? (He tries and succeeds.) Show me the path of the light. (Merely points to the screen.) Where did it start? (He points to the torch and the screen then, being reminded of the mirror, he indicates and then draws two distinct paths, one from the torch to the mirror and the other from the torch to the screen.) He is shown the V made up of the incident beam and its reflection and is asked to retrace this path with his finger: he traces out two lines converging on to the mirror then, after manipulating the torch, retraces the V correctly. And if we remove the mirror, will the light still go like that? *No, it'll go like this* (in a straight line). The pencils are brought out and he arranges them in various ways. The torch is switched off, set back from the screen but parallel to it, and he is asked how it can be used to light up the screen (which can be done by placing the mirror at an angle of 45° to the beam). He places the mirror at right angles to the beam, switches on the torch, and corrects the position of the mirror. By contrast, when the torch is placed on the other side but still parallel to the screen, he does not turn the face of the mirror towards it, thus demonstrating that the V-experiment has taught him nothing at all.

   MIR (4,11) also does not think that the light travels all the way from the torch to the screen, and merely points to its initial and final positions. He is at an even greater loss with the mirror, and it is only after a demonstration and numerous trials and errors that he manages to direct the light of the torch on to the screen. Where does the light from the lamp go? *There* (mirror). And afterwards? *There* (screen). Two mirrors: success with the first or the second but keeps forgetting the existence of the other.

VER (5,3) after watching the reflections from a mirror set in various positions, places the mirror parallel to the beam and moves it along the path of the latter. Having been shown the correct way, she places the mirror at a random angle to the beam but in its path *because the light is over here and the reflection* (on the screen) *is over there.* But she seems to think that it is enough to place the mirror close to the beam. At one point, she turns the mirror slightly and succeeds in reflecting the light on to the screen, but immediately afterwards she places the mirror too close to the torch and fails to repeat her earlier success.

FRA (5,2) begins by holding the mirror against the screen, then, after a demonstration, succeeds in lighting up the screen with the help of the mirror. How did you do it? *I put the mirror on that line.* On which line? *Of the light.* And if the light goes like that (other direction)? (Trial and error and success.) And like that (mirror perpendicular to the beam)? *Yes.* (The torch is lit.) *No.* Try to turn the mirror (despite this suggestive term, she merely moves the mirror to and fro at right angles to the beam). Look (the demonstrator holds her hand and turns the mirror for her). Could you do the same? *Yes* (she does so). What did you do? *I twisted the mirror.* And now (torch in a different position)? *Like that.* (She directs the beam at the unpolished side of the mirror.) (The torch is switched on.) *No.* (She adjusts the mirror until she achieves success.) How did you do that? *Like this* (points to the mirror.) And why not over here (to the side of the beam)? *Because there is no light.* (The torch is moved again and she places the mirror in the correct position.) What did you do? *Twisted it round.* And like that? (She places the mirror at right angles to the beam.) Is that what you told me just now? (Protracted trials and errors followed by success.) Can you show me the path of the light? (She points to the torch, then to the mirror and the screen, but jumps from one to the next as if there had been no continuous movement.) What did the light do when it touched here (mirror)? *It went away* (vague direction). The demonstrator produces two pencils and lays them on the V. When he picks one up and moves it to a different place FRA moves the other into a symmetrical position, but when he slides the first round, FRA slides hers in the same, instead of the opposite, direction.

ART (6,4) in order to direct the light of the torch on to the screen or on other objects places the mirror right in front of them. With the torch parallel to the screen, he inserts the mirror between them.

The demonstrator shows him how the mirror can be used to reflect the light, but ART merely engages in a series of pointless manoeuvres.

BER (6,6). Torch parallel to the screen: first places the mirror in front of the screen, then outside the range of the beam, and finally tries to rotate the torch. Reminded about his assignment, he rotates the mirror until it nearly faces the torch. He is shown the solution, and copies it almost immediately. For other positions of the torch, he again places the mirror facing the torch, rotates it and eventually corrects his mistake. Pencils: symmetrical arrangements but at too narrow angles. The torch is again set up in various positions and he again places the mirror at right angles to it or so that it deflects the light in the wrong direction, before achieving partial and, on occasion, complete success.

REN (7,7) places the mirror facing the torch and leaves it there. The demonstrator moves the mirror and produces various reflections, but REN merely reverts to his original procedure. The demonstrator then moves the mirror very slightly and encourages her to do likewise. In the end she succeeds. Show me the path of the light. *It's the mirror which makes it all light up.* Show me the path. *I don't know how to.* Where did it all start? *In the torch.* And then? *It turned* (points from the torch to the mirror then from the torch to the screen, rotating the torch very slightly). V: she continues to indicate that the light travels by discontinuous jumps from the torch to the mirror, from the torch to the screen, and from the mirror to the screen. The torch is placed in front of the mirror, and she constructs a Λ from the torch instead of a V.

The above responses show, first of all, that all these subjects are unable to use a mirror spontaneously as a reflector, but that once this possibility is brought home to them, they will often manage, from about the age of 4 to 5 years, to transmit the light of the torch on the screen. We shall see that subjects at stage IIB (9–10 years), by contrast, readily grant the possibility of reflecting the light of the torch with even two mirrors, though they still fail to do so in practice because the active co-ordination of two reflections must be guided by precise ideas about the relationship between the incident and reflected rays.

However, when he uses a single mirror and once he has discovered its relationship with the beam he can discern on the surface of the Formica table, the child need do no more than turn or move the mirror in various ways to achieve the same result in various situations, sensorimotor or quasi-automatic regulations sufficing to ensure his success with the help of feedbacks. But this raises two problems, namely the type of cognizance to which such regulations give rise, and whether the latter suffice to explain the overall success or whether a number of additional factors, in the form of relations established before the present experiments, must be taken into account as well. These two problems are moreover inseparable.

As far as their conscious grasp of their actions is concerned, our subjects know perfectly well that they have placed the mirror in a particular position (*I put the mirror on that line* said FRA) and moreover at an angle (*I twisted the mirror*), which indicates the use of active adjustments, i.e. of deliberate choices over and above the elementary motor regulations. Nor is that all. Our subjects behave as if the light moved from the torch to the mirror and on from the mirror to the screen, and as if these movements proceeded in well-defined directions, for they make detailed corrections as they go along. Does that mean that they are conscious of the actual path followed by the light? Now, the answer is clearly that they are not: whenever they are asked about the 'path' of the light (and that question is highly suggestive!), and though the path is plainly visible on the Formica table, they merely point to the torch and to the screen (*the light is over here and the reflection is over there* said VER) and fail to consider the movement of the light. Reflection, to them, is thus the result of an action at a distance,[1] and we shall see that subjects even at level IIA, still claim that light *cannot travel* (RAP). As for the directions of the light, they do intervene as global orientations, because the subject knows perfectly well that the light ought to reach the screen, but this is a far cry from the grasp of the precise directions followed by the incident and reflected rays which appears at stage III.

Moreover, while what few successes our subjects achieve are thus the result of insufficiently conscious regulations, the failures are due to preconceptions about the nature of mirrors. Now these preconceptions are incompatible with the idea of reflection and simply endow mirrors with the power of producing images regardless of the movement or direction of the light. That is why ART simply

---

[1] We have encountered the same approach in our study of causality (with de Lannoy).

placed the mirror, first right in front of the screen, then between the screen and the torch as if it behoved the mirror to arrange itself in such a way as to catch the image it was expected to project on to the screen. VER, for his part, placed the mirror parallel to the beam and simply moved it nearer to the screen in that position. Similarly, FRA placed it at right angles to the beam and contented himself with moving it to and fro. Other subjects held the mirror close to the torch, obviously assuming that if they moved it further away they would impede its powers of reflection. Yet others caught the beam in the mirror and then turned the mirror round. In short, all these subjects assumed that *it's the mirror which makes it light up*, thus treating it as a machine for sending images regardless of the angles of incidence and reflection. With the pencils or the drawing of the V, they allowed themselves to be swayed by the laws of perceptive symmetry, and whenever the pencil representing the incident ray was slid sideways, they simply slid the other pencil, intended to represent the reflected ray, in the same direction (*cf.* FRA).

Level IIA

Subjects at level IIA are able to use the mirror as a reflector spontaneously but without understanding the underlying mechanism.

Examples

JOE (7,0). With the torch set back from the screen but parallel to it, places the mirror in front of the torch and then rotates it in the right direction. Show me the path of the light. (Points to the lamp and then to the mirror.) And from there? *It goes on the cardboard* (screen). Different position: success, but claims that the light spreads across the entire surface of the mirror, then indicates the path torch-mirror-torch (by sudden jumps). V: indicates that the light is reflected to the same side as the incident beam then briefly corrects himself, but cannot be certain. Like other subjects at this level and also like FRA at stage I, he tends to come down in favour of reflection in the correct direction more often when the demonstrator picks up the pencil symbolizing the incident light and puts it in another position, than when he simply slides it about.

RAP (7,6) succeeds spontaneously from the start: *The torch gives off a small light which shines on the mirror.* What path does it take?

It goes like this (moves down) *and that one* (the screen) *lights up.* But where does the light come from? *From the torch, but it can't travel.* (The demonstrator moves the mirror up and down and produces oscillations on the screen.) Why does it do that? *Because you budged it with the mirror.* V: he is told that the first pencil marks the path of the light from the torch to the mirror and produces a symmetrical construction, correct in appearance, but when asked to send light back to a board at 90° from the screen he fumbles about until he finally succeeds, but obviously without having drawn any conclusions from the V.

AND (7,6) first of all places the mirror parallel to the screen, then looks at his own reflection, moves the mirror and finally succeeds. How did you manage that? *If it* (the light from the torch) *were over there, we would have to turn the mirror until it went here.* What was the path of the light? (Torch-mirror-screen.) And would it work like this (the demonstrator pulls back the torch without changing the directon of the beam)? *Maybe.* Aren't you sure? *No, because it's further away.* And so? . . . And like this (the demonstrator tilts the mirror very slightly)? *No, because it's going to end up behind the mirror.* He is asked to draw the incident and reflected rays with the mirror in various positions, and each time produces two almost parallel paths. Pencils: he produces divergent paths (of the type constructed by the demonstrator) but in several cases separated by a gap, as if the light travelled along the face of the mirror before being thrown back. Then he returns to paths very close to each other (angles between 5° and 10°).

RIE (7,7) first moves the torch, then the screen and gradually succeeds: *We have to do two things, first this* (places the mirror in the beam) *and then that* (turns the mirror and adjusts it until the beam reaches the screen). Which path did the light follow? *It lit up the mirror, and the mirror lit up the screen.* But when asked to reconstruct the paths on drawings or with the two pencils, she produces a random selection of responses: divergent incident and reflected rays with a gap between them, parallel rays with a big gap along the mirror, etc. With two mirrors: *I can't do it, they have to be two small ones* (because of the expected gaps between the incident and reflected rays). She tries all the same, but only succeeds in deflecting the ray to the screen from one of the mirrors.

TIA (8,2) first places the mirror in front of the screen, then succeeds after moving it sideways and tilting it round: *I tried it on both sides.* Can you show me the path of the light? (She points to a path running from the torch to one edge of the mirror, then to a second path running from the other edge of the mirror to the screen, as if the light could leave from any part of the mirror whatsoever.) Wouldn't it leave from here (common centre of the rays)? *That depends on the lamp.* She then agrees that, for certain very oblique positions of the mirror the rays will arrive and leave from a common centre, but when the inclination of the mirror is decreased she reverts to gaps between the rays and parallel paths starting from the two edges of the mirror.

AUT (8,6). Similar successes after trials and errors and paths in opposite directions but again draws gaps between the points of incidence and reflection when the mirror is very slightly inclined. Two mirrors: success with very simple arrangements.

NIQ (9,0) succeeds after trials and errors and correctly retraces the path from the torch to the screen. What if the light hit the mirror head on? *It stays on the mirror.* Does it actually stay there or does it go back to the lamp? (Long silence.) *It stays on the mirror.* When the mirror is more than 10 cm away from the lamp, she does not know how to place it in the beam. In her drawings, the reflected paths are shown to run close to the incident and then to diverge, though at highly irregular angles. NIQ grants that the angles of incidence and reflection are almost equal when the mirror is *quite straight* but not when it is *twisted*, a response we shall rediscover at level IIB. Two mirrors: confused reactions.

The greatest step forward taken by these subjects is their spontaneous success in transmitting the light of the torch to the screen with the help of the mirror. This advance is of a piece with the generalization of the idea of reflection we encountered in our study of causality with A. Munari: we found that 7–8 year olds considered polaroids as the centres of reflection of all surrounding coloured objects. Moreover, this advance is closely bound up with a nascent grasp of transitivity, as we shall see in the conclusion of this chapter.

However, though the spontaneous use of the mirror for transmitting the light is new, the sensorimotor regulation of the inclinations is no better than we found it to be at stage I, and above all the conceptualization of the action does not yet lead to a grasp of the movement of the light or of its direction.

202

As regards the movement, the light is admittedly considered to start at the torch and to travel to a goal, but it is still thought to proceed by jumps rather than by a continuous displacement, and this despite the fact that the reflection on the Formica table suggests the idea of a path, and that the demonstrator makes a point of using that very term. Thus RAP said plainly that light *can't travel* although it can be *budged* with the mirror; NIQ claimed that if the light hits the mirror head on, *it stays on the mirror*, etc.

As for the direction, TIA began by tilting the mirror to *both sides* but quite unsystematically, and the attempts of all the other subjects showed a similar lack of anticipation. But the most remarkable feature is the large proportion of subjects who did not think that the beam arrives on, and leaves from, the same point of the mirror. The reason is that these subjects still fail to appreciate that the incident and reflected rays are part and parcel of one and the same movement, so much so that AND and RIE even thought that the light travelled along parallel paths. Moreover, with the V, in which the two rays are graphically shown to have a common junction, these subjects, while generally anticipating paths in opposite directions (corresponding to the two branches of the V though, of course, without quantitative equality of the angles) often draw the two rays on the same side of the normal, especially when the mirror is inclined or when the demonstrator slides his pencil round, as if the reflected ray were pulled over to the side of the incident ray. This shows that they have an incipient grasp of the fact that the rays are inseparable, albeit without adequate understanding of their direction.

Level IIB

Subjects at this level at last attribute continuity and movement to the rays, even when the light is not reflected from the table and its course from torch to screen remains hidden from sight. Moreover, they invariably maintain that the incident and reflected rays diverge from a common point of a 'straight' mirror, but that the light 'slides' along tilted mirrors.

Examples

PIE (8,7) immediately places the mirror on the path of the light and then tilts the mirror: *The light touches the mirror and then bounces*

203

back on to the screen. He is handed a second mirror which he tries to co-ordinate with the first in various ways, finally bringing them together like a book open at 135°. Can you show me the path? *It went from the torch to the first mirror, from there to the second mirror and from there to the screen.* (In fact, the first mirror played no part in the reflection.) And like that (torch facing a single mirror)? *When the light hits the mirror it goes back in the opposite direction; it bounces back to the torch and goes absolutely straight.* V: he correctly anticipates the reflected paths, except when the demonstrator changes the inclination of the mirror: *If the mirror is more at a slant, the light is more bent.* In other words, the angle of reflection is changed by the inclination of the mirror (*cf.* GAU, PHI, *et al.*).

MAR (9,10) succeeds rapidly with one mirror. With two mirrors, he follows a procedure that is correct in principle, but fails to allow fully for the inclinations of the mirrors. With the torch parallel to the screen, he projects the light on to the mirror *A* in a direction opposite to that of the screen and then tries to throw it on to the mirror *B* (between the torch and *A*) with the intention of sending it back to the screen. When he fails to do so, he explains that the light travels from the torch to *B*, then back to *A*, and from there to the screen, clearly because the proximity of the mirrors confuses him.

GAU (9,7) succeeds just once, after protracted trials and errors, in using the two mirrors. However, when asked to reconstruct the path of the rays with the torch switched off, he sets the mirrors at the wrong angles, and says: *The light slides across here* (= very small angle of reflection) *because the mirror is tilted too far over.* Again, with the mirror inclined and the torch at right angles to it, he feels certain that the light will not be reflected: *It arrives like this* (obliquely) *and continues* (along the slope); *it doesn't go back, it goes down all the time.* And like that (torch perpendicular to a mirror set at right angles to the table)? (He indicates that the light is sent back): *You see, if the mirror were tilted like that* (towards the right) *the light would go back there* (to the right); *if it were tilted like this* (towards the left) *it would go back here* (to the left), *but seeing that it's straight it must come back dead straight, because then it doesn't slide.* V: GAU makes the angle of reflection equal to the angle of incidence when the mirror is not inclined. Is this angle the same as that (the opposite) one? *It slides about a tiny bit over here and over there as well, but they ought to be the same.* However, when the mirror is inclined, the equivalence no longer holds.

PHI (10,10) has difficulties in adjusting the two mirrors because, though he sets B correctly to ensure the reflection of the ray from the torch, he places A as if he expected the light to slide right across its surface. He then corrects the arrangement in such a way that the light from A could be reflected to B, but not the light from the torch by A. He produces much the same reaction when drawing the path of the light and when arranging the pencils in the V: if the mirror is at right angles to the table, the reflected ray travels in a direction opposite to that of the incident ray, but if the mirror is tilted, the two rays are far too close together: *Over here* (no inclination) *it runs straight to the top, but over here it can't.* Are the two angles equal? *With that* (inclined mirrors), *one is bigger than the other.*

AIN (10,4) also has some difficulty in adjusting the two mirrors, placing A correctly with respect to the screen but arranging B as if the light travelled along its surface: *I can't see how the light can possibly pass from here* (A) *to there* (B). His drawings are almost correct for the non-inclined mirrors (angles almost equal), but when the mirrors are inclined, the angle of reflection is far too oblique: *When the mirror is tilted, the two* (rays) *almost touch, if it isn't tilted, they spread out* (symmetrically). *They are always skew when the mirror has a slope.*

JUD (10,7) after the same difficulties with the two mirrors, produces almost correct drawings (opposite directions but not perfectly equal angles) for mirrors that are not or only slightly inclined, but brings the rays together on the same side when the inclinations are increased.

DAN (11,1) fails with the two mirrors and continues to draw paths that are too close together when the single mirror is inclined, but more or less correct when the mirror is at right angles to the table.

VIL (11,6) produces residues of level IIA behaviour at the beginning of the test in that she is reluctant to grant that light follows a continuous path. With two mirrors, she maintains that *if the other one is to the rear* (further away than the first), *the light cannot reach it. It always stays put but it is reflected. It works with one mirror but not with two. With one mirror, the light touches the mirror and then it goes over there and touches the screen,* etc. She makes the reflected ray go back in the same direction as the incident ray even when the mirror is not inclined, but subsequently corrects her mistake. With inclined mirrors the reflected ray follows the slope of the mirror.

The greatest advance of these subjects is their appreciation that light is not simply the power of illuminating objects at a distance, but that it travels continuously through space. *It bounces back; goes absolutely straight;* or *goes back*, said PIE; *it slides across* or *goes back* said GAU; *it runs straight to the top* said PHI; it *touches the mirror and then it goes over there* said VIL, and in the next section we shall see that even BEL (intermediate between this level and the next) still claims that *the stronger the light the more it slides along the mirror*, thus subordinating his nascent grasp of kinematics to dynamics.

This first advance entails a second: if light travels through space, the reflected ray must be in contact with the incident ray, that is, there can be no gap of the kind subjects at level IIA believed to exist between them.

Moreover, these subjects realize (a third advance) that, if light can be displaced like a body moving in a straight line, its reflection by the mirror must constitute a sort of deviation but reduced to a *minimum*. In other words, the reflected ray must be an extension of the incident ray in a symmetrically opposite direction. It follows that, when the mirror is 'straight', i.e parallel to the edge of the table or perpendicular to the child's line of vision, it will impress on the V, that is, on the arrangement of the incident and reflected rays, a qualitatively equivalent form with approximately equal angles. We discovered much the same reaction by subjects at this level when dealing with the reflection of a ball from a wall and in our studies with B. Inhelder of the induction of the laws of billiards.

However the child pays a price for all these advances: if light can indeed be displaced like a moving body, it must obey the general laws of motion and behave differently on different slopes. This explains the common belief of subjects at level IIB that, on an inclined mirror, *the light is more bent* (PIE) or that *it slides* because *it doesn't go back; it goes down all the time* (GAU); *cf.* PHI, AIN, JUD, DAN, *et al.* As a result, the reflected ray is thought to run back in the same direction as the incident ray, or as AIN put it, *they are always skew when the mirror has a slope*.

This 'sliding' effect of the light thus introduces a serious distortion in the child's anticipation of the direction of the reflected ray.

Hence we should not be astonished to find that the two-mirror experiment is so unsuccessful at this level. As we said earlier, it is too difficult to be solved by trial and error and sensorimotor regulations, because what is called for is the active adjustment of the first mirror with respect to the torch and to the second mirror (considered as a provisional screen), and the simultaneous adjustment of the angle of the second mirror with respect to the screen, and all this calls for careful anticipations and deductive compositions. Now since the grasp of directions at this level is strongly affected by mistaken ideas about the 'sliding' of the light, this inferential composition cannot be effected.

Intermediate cases between level IIB and stage III

Between subjects at level IIB, who think that the incident and reflected rays run in opposite directions if the mirror is 'straight' but that the angle of the reflection is influenced by the inclination of the mirror, and subjects at stage III who realize that the angles of incidence and reflection are equal in all circumstances, there are some intermediate cases, between the ages of 11 and 12 years, whose responses we shall now examine.

Examples

TIN (11,6) succeeds with the two-mirror test after numerous trials and errors: *I put one mirror in front of the lamp and the other in front of the cardboard for the light that goes to the first mirror to be reflected into the other and from there to the cardboard.* V: she starts out with the two rays making an angle of 90°. Will it make a difference if I move the torch? *No.* What do we have to do to change the direction of the (reflected) light? *Change the direction of the mirror.* She does so and after several observations succeeds in making the reflected ray run in a direction opposite to that of the incident rays: *When the light comes in this direction it can't be turned back any more.* Finally: Will the angles be equal? *Yes, almost completely equal.*

GAR (11,6) succeeds straight away with the two-mirror test after success with the single mirror. Can you draw the path? (He makes some drawings, all with the rays at 90°.) The light leaves the mirror at a right angle. Why? *Because when you look at a mirror, it shows you everything dead straight.* But when he examines the actual path of the light with the two mirrors, he exclaims: *It's no longer reflected at right angles*. What happens instead? *It's reflected at the same angle. If it's 40° here, it'll be 40° over there.* Does it always happen like that? *Yes, if we turn the mirror.... No, that's impossible because the light can't change itself.*

BEL (12,1) succeeds gradually with two mirrors. In her drawings, she begins with reflections in the wrong direction and explains: *I put the first mirror at a slight angle so that the light can move on to the second.* What about the direction of the light? *The stronger the light the more it slides along the mirror.* But then: *The glass doesn't change* (the direction of the light), *it always sends the light back vertically* (= at right angles). *I can't see any other way.* In the end, she nevertheless produces the correct drawing. What happens if the light arrives like this (roughly at 30°)? *Then it'll go back like this* (30°). Is it always the same angle? *I think it is, perhaps not exactly but almost so.* Drawing of the two mirrors: *I'd say that the angles are equal with the first mirror but not with the second.* Finally she makes the correct adjustment.

SAV (12,1) occasionally still makes the reflected ray run in the same direction as the incident ray because *when you move the mirror you change the angle.* Then he realizes that the angles are equal, no matter what the inclination of the mirror. Are they always equal? *Always, because the mirror reflects the light.*

And here finally are three clear stage III responses.

CAR (10,11) succeeds with the two mirrors and also produces correct drawings: *The light has to hit both mirrors.* Why like that? *Because we need almost the same angle.* Almost? *No, exactly the same.*

GEV (11,6): immediate success with the two mirrors. Did you get there by chance? *No, you can almost see that it's reflected at 45°. The two angles have to be the same.*

PAT (12,6) also succeeds immediately. How did you do it? *By tilting the mirrors more or less.... You always have to measure the angle over here* (incidence) *and the one over there* (reflection). For what reason? *They have to be equal.* Who taught you that? *I've often tried with the sun in a mirror.* And here? *When the light hits the first mirror we have to make sure that it keeps following the same direction on the other side.*

Thanks to the progress they have made, our intermediate subjects from TIN to SAV were able to solve the two-mirror test, though only after a number of trials. However, these trials were based on prior inferences and experimental verifications of the latter, and no longer on purely sensorimotor regulations. This suggests that these subjects had learned to anticipate the directions of the beam and hence to deduce, more and more surely, that the angles of incidence and reflection are equal. But, interestingly enough, before they reached that conclusion, they had to pass through an inter-mediate stage between mistaken solutions based on the alleged 'sliding' of the light along inclined mirrors, and the correct solution, the intermediate stage being characterized by the assumption that the light is invariably turned through an angle of 90° by the mirror. There seems to be a very simple explanation for this mistaken belief: the subject has begun to doubt his false hypotheses about the role of the angle of the mirror because they contradict the generally accepted notion that 'straight' mirrors help the light to pursue its course in a forward direction: *It can't be turned back*, said TIN; *the light can't change itself*, said GAR. In other words, these children have realized that the transmission of light is governed by a single law. This is what BEL meant when he said that, if the mirror is tilted it cannot change the relative direction of the rays, or why SAV after claiming that, *when you move the mirror you change the angle* (of reflection), finally pronounced in favour of constant angles. Now, since it is difficult to imagine the idea of relative constancy during continual changes of the reference system (= the plane of reflection constituted by the mirror) the simplest solution is, of course, to postulate an absolute constant: whence the idea of a deflection of the ray through 90°, the perpendicular being the simplest direction to grasp intuitively when the reference system changes.[1] Mention should also be made of the argument used by GAR: *When you look at a mirror, it shows you everything dead straight*, though it was more of a bad rationalization after the event than a true explanation.

However, just as soon as experience belies the 90° hypothesis, the simplest alternative is to assume relative constancy, which eventually leads to the realization that the angles of incidence and reflection

---

[1] It is worth pointing out that B. Inhelder discovered the same intermediate stage in billiard-ball experiments, deflections of 90° being postulated by subjects between levels IIB (search for co-variations) and stage III (equality of angles). Here, too, the reason was the search for constancy.

must be equal. It is truly amazing to see with what speed these intermediate subjects pass from perpendicularity to equality, GAR, for example, leaping straight from 90° to 40°, and BEL or SAV being almost as prompt in changing their opinions. As for subjects at stage III, from CAR to PAT, they assume the equality of the angles from the start and it does not seem that they had learned it at school, since they began with such cautious formulations as *almost*, *that depends*, etc.

Conclusions

We shall now look more closely at the development from stage I to stage III and at the respective roles of the child's actions and conceptualizations considered as the organization of the observable effects of his actions.

At stage I, during which the subject is unable to use mirrors as reflectors unaided, but often proves capable of copying the demonstrator or of adapting the lesson to new situations, we said earlier that, though the sensorimotor regulations intervening in such actions presuppose an ability to handle directions and hence implicit movements, the child fails to take cognizance of these factors and looks upon the mirror as a machine for producing images which need merely be brought into contact, in one way or another, with a torch and a screen for the light to jump from the former to the latter.

The first question raised by level IIA responses is therefore how the child comes to use the mirror as a reflector. Now, this advance is easily correlated with all we know about conduct relating to the transmission of movements, etc.: it involves the attribution of logical transitivity, constructed at about the age of 7–8 years, to the objects themselves in the form of a 'mediate transmission', which assumes a semi-internal character when the intermedia remain immobile. Hence when our subjects discover that the light of the torch can be reflected by a mirror and also that the mirror sends back their own image, we might expect them to conclude, with the help of transitivity, that the mirror is also capable of reflecting the light of the torch and to throw it on to a screen. However, since we are trying to correlate the child's conceptualization with his actions we cannot possibly invoke logical transitivity as arising independently of the causal conditions of these actions; we must therefore assume that, in this particular case, it was their manipulation of mirrors before the present experiments, which suggested to the subjects (S) the possibility of bringing objects (X) hidden from sight into view by appropriate orientation of the mirror (M), whence $X \rightarrow M \rightarrow S$, and hence $X \rightarrow S$, even if X and S are not in a straight line. This does not mean that transitivity in general has an empirical origin, because the interpretation of the above sequence of events in this form involves the use of endogenous operations. However, the construction of the latter is naturally encouraged by the correspondence of certain contents with such forms, and at level IIA such correspondences are discovered more and more frequently in all fields.

The second question raised by level IIA responses is therefore why, if nascent transitivity makes possible the spontaneous utilization of mirrors as intermedia, the subject does not take better cognizance of the conditions in which light is displaced and of the direction of the rays necessitating adjustment of these reflectors. Now, if it is indeed transitivity rather than a series of detailed experiments, which helps the subject to discover the use of mirrors, then he has merely to interpret his action to invoke the global connexion torch $\rightarrow$ mirror $\rightarrow$ screen by way of an inferential co-ordination; he does not need to specify all the details of the observable displacements and directions. Since the inferential co-ordination leads sooner or later to the analysis of these data (but does not presuppose them), all the subject has to assume is that, as a result of his own actions, the light of the torch is reflected by some part of the mirror towards the screen, without having to ask himself whether he is dealing with actions at a distance or continuous displacements in space, or whether there is a kinematic and spatial concurrence (angles, etc.) of the incident and reflected rays, whence the noticeable failure to take cognizance of the adjustments, however successfully performed in practice.

By contrast, it goes without saying that as active adjustments multiply under the influence of this co-ordination, they must gradually lead to an analysis of the data: whence, in the first place, the idea that light moves through space (level IIB), no doubt suggested by the discovery that the slightest modification of the position of the mirror tends to shift the beam of light. But this introduces new inferential co-ordinations, some of which are valid (the continuity of movement attributed to the light suggests the idea that the incident and reflected rays must have a common meeting point, or the idea

211

that they must travel in opposite and symmetrical directions if the mirror is 'straight'), and some of which are false (the idea that the light 'slides' along inclined mirrors). The inferences produced in this way do not, therefore, suffice to provide the anticipations needed for the solution of the two-mirror problem.

Finally, after the intermediate stage (constant deflection at right angles) there follows the complete geometrization of the relations between the incident and reflected rays (stage III). At long last, action is subordinated to comprehension which alone can ensure its complete success.

CHAPTER THIRTEEN

General Conclusions

Because the situations analysed in this work involve the resistance of objects, the subject must learn to cope with them by stages or by successive co-ordinations and not in the precocious manner described in our study of the grasp of consciousness.[1] In what follows, we shall therefore try to establish whether or not the new results we have obtained confirm our earlier views about the initial autonomy of action and of the process of conscious conceptualization as it progresses from the periphery to the central mechanism. Next, we shall examine what fresh light the new data cast on the reverse effect of conceptualizations on actions and on the respective roles or significance of practical success and notional comprehension. This will lead us to an examination of the explicative and implicative process of comprehension and finally to the relationship between affirmations and denials.

I *The grasp of consciousness and the effects of conceptualization on action*

The two main hypotheses advanced in our earlier work were that action constitutes an autonomous form of knowledge ('know-how') which is conceptualized by later, conscious assimilations, and that the latter proceed systematically from the periphery to the centre, that is, from accommodation zones to the object, ending up as internal co-ordinations of actions. Now we have found that these hypotheses, so easy to verify in the case of precociously successful actions, also hold in the present situations, in which success is achieved much more gradually. It must, however, be added that,

[1] *The Grasp of Consciousness*, Routledge & Kegan Paul, London, 1977.

from a certain level onwards, there is a reverse effect of conceptualization on action.

As far as the lag of consciousness is concerned, we saw, in chapter 1, that though subjects at level IA were successful in constructing roofs (two cards), houses of four cards, etc., they did not take account of the role of the inclinations in their conceptualizations, i.e., that the two cards support each other in the roof structures or that one card props up the second in the figure T. We also saw in chapter 4 that subjects at the same level were able to keep projecting boards in equilibrium by regulating the length of the overhang but that they did not take cognizance of that condition. As for the reflection of light by a mirror (chapter 12), young subjects were able to deflect a beam but did not suspect that the light must traverse a path, etc. In brief, we discovered that, in all these elementary successes, conceptualization lags behind action – clear proof that the latter is autonomous. Cognizance, for its part, was found in each case to start from the external results of the action, later to engage in the analysis of the means employed and finally to bear on the general co-ordinates (reciprocity, transitivity, etc.), that is, on the central but at first unconscious, mechanisms of the action.

But whereas these early successes corroborate the findings set out in our *The Grasp of Consciousness*, the situation changes markedly at subsequent levels, when conceptualization and action begin to have reciprocal effects upon each other. It is this essential process which we shall now examine. A particularly instructive example is that of the transmission of movement (chapter 3), in which it seems that, at the level where conceptualization attains transitivity, and where interpretation is based on a semi-internal mediate transmission (the impetus supplied by the active ball is thought to 'traverse' the passive balls while setting them in motion), action becomes changed in the wake of the rapid and systematic use of the mediators. This might suggest that the change is wrought purely by the subject's own logic and the physical explanations he draws from it. The first point to note, however, is that this transitivity does not drop out of the sky but that it is engendered by the actions themselves before it becomes a generalized operational instrument. As we saw in chapter 3, it is the product of two combined factors: the gradual substitution of material and moving objects for the subject's own body, that is, for his hands, which until then provided

214

the connections, and a constant order of succession subordinating the connections to an overall serial system. These are thus two advances due to the regulation of the action as such. By virtue of this very fact, the two advances lend new dimensions to the action and to its regulation: a certain capacity for anticipation and a more active regulation, that is, the possibility of choosing between different means in the place of automatic regulations by simple, compensating corrections. Moreover, these two factors favour the grasp of consciousness, since anticipations and choices pass easily from the level of material behaviour to that of representation. As a result, these various modifications constitute a source of new co-ordinations of the action and of the conceptualization, which do not, however, during these phases of transformation, constitute two independent realities: the material and causal co-ordinations of movements and the logical or implicative connections are but two faces of one and the same organization. By contrast, whenever cognizance lags behind precociously successful and rapidly organized actions, the result is a less directly dependent reconstruction.

We can now appreciate the nature of the reverse influence of conceptualization on action from which it derives its substance. It is not a mental transposition of the interpretations of the observable data or of the action for the purpose of constructing a detailed programme modelled on causal explanations, etc.; in other words it is not because subjects at level IIA interpret the transmission of movement by the passage of an 'impetus' 'across' the passive or mediating balls, that they go on to organize their actions so as to tap this impetus and to facilitate its circulation inside the balls (in the way that an engineer familiar with the principles of electromagnetism constructs instruments on the basis of Maxwell's equations). What conceptualization supplies to action is a reinforcement of its powers of anticipation and the possibility, in a given situation, of devising a plan for immediate implementation. In other words, its contribution is to increase the power of co-ordination already immanent in action, and this without the subject's establishing the frontiers between his practice ('What must I do to succeed?') and his conceptual system ('Why do things happen this way?'). Moreover, even in situations where the problems are distinct and where the point is to understand rather than to succeed, the subject who has become capable, thanks to his actions, of structuring reality by operations,

215

nevertheless remains unconscious of his own cognitive structures for a long time: even if he applies them for his personal use and even if he attributes them to objects and events for the purpose of explaining them causally, he does not turn these structures into themes of reflection until he reaches a much higher level of abstraction.

To take another example, when children discover or imitate the use of a pivoting bar to displace an object (chapter 6), their cognizance is markedly deformed: they do not, for instance, grasp that their finger must turn the bar at one end in a direction opposite to that in which the other end will move. Here we have a typical case of cognizance lagging behind action and a clear illustration of conceptualization progressing, in the usual way, from the periphery to the centre: it does not, at first, focus on anything but the results of the action and does not, until level IB, seize the idea that a rotation has taken place. At level IB, conceptualization and action begin to draw together, inasmuch as there is both anticipation and utilization of the swivelling of the bar considered as the movement of its two ends in opposite directions. But the comprehension of that rotation, in other words its conceptual interpretation, still lags behind the action inasmuch as the pivot is not conceived as a simple instrument of fixation allowing of circular movement without displacement of the centre of the bar, but is invested with turning powers of its own. On the other hand, neither in his actions nor in his conceptualizations can the subject account for what will happen if the radius of action of the bar is changed, that is if the pivot is moved from the centre towards either end of the bar. At level IIA, by contrast, there is correct anticipation of the effects of this change, and there is once again a levelling of conceptualization and action: this anticipation is, in fact, both the product of the motor co-ordinations of the action (foreseeing the end of the path of the part of the bar comprised between the pivot and the free end) and also of an inferential co-ordination of the conceptualization (representation of the pivoting process in the new situation). Similarly, the subject is able to solve Problem V (see the figures in chapter 6) by substituting the bar *A* for his finger, which is once again a simultaneous advance in action and in conceptualization with its powers of inference. By contrast, the passage from Problem V to Problem VI and the solution of Problems VII and VIII have to wait until level IIB, when the co-ordinations of the translations and the rotations are gradually

216

acquired thanks to constant exchanges between active trials and errors and conceptual inferences. Finally, at stage III we witness a gradual reversal of the relations between conceptualization and action: at level IIIA (11–12 years), Problems VII and VIII (two or three pivots on horizontal bars joined by vertical bars without pivots) are solved by successive attempts, and the subject discovers, on the conceptual plane, the non-commutativity of the relations between translations and rotations. At level IIIB (14–15 years) this law is finally deduced and not merely observed: reflexive abstraction is succeeded by 'reflected abstraction', in which the product of the former has itself become the object of reflection and of conscious formulation. As a result, the subject can plan the entire action, starting from the conceptualization (especially when the pivots are not fixed and the subject himself is asked to place them in position so as to obtain a particular result), and the situation prevailing at level IA is totally reversed. Let us recall that in order to verify this gradual liberation, culminating in the complete autonomy of conceptualization with its power to make inferential co-ordinations, we examined the subjects' recall of the experiments one or two weeks later. Now it was not until stage III that the memory proved true to the conceptualizations or the successful actions, even when these involved long hesitations and many trials and errors. Here we have one more indication of the instability of the exchanges between actions and conceptualizations, even when they begin to be effective, as they do at stage II.

All in all, it is thus clear that while the present findings corroborate the conclusions of our earlier study, namely that the grasp of consciousness lags behind precocious successes in the field of action and that it progresses from the periphery to the central regions of that action, they also face us with the new situation of practical success attained by stages with gradual co-ordinations at distinct levels: in these cases, there is, first of all, a more or less long phase (and chiefly at stage II) when the action and its conceptualization are almost on the same level and when there are constant exchanges between them. Then, at stage III, we find a complete reversal of the initial situation: conceptualization no longer provides action with limited and provisional plans that have to be revised and adjusted, but with an overall programme, much as happens at intermediate stages of technology, when practice is guided by theory.

This raises the problem of whether or not these superior forms of conceptualization follow the general progression from the periphery to the centre. But before we examine that problem, we must first look at the successive co-ordinations of the action and of the conceptual co-ordinations.

II *Success and understanding*

The answer to the problem raised by the title of this work seems at first glance to be perfectly straightforward: success means having enough understanding of a situation to attain the requisite ends in action, and understanding is successful mastery in thought of the same situation to the point of being able to solve the problem of the 'how' and the 'why' of the connections observed and applied in action. But if that were all, we should not have had to go to the trouble of amassing so much material. In fact, this common-sense solution does not explain anything at all – neither the considerable head start of practical success over conceptual comprehension with the subsequent reversal of the situation, nor the epistemological process of 'comprehending in action' or 'succeeding in thought'. In fact, the problems are much more profound, and they come back to determining the nature of the co-ordinations of the action in terms of its own schemata, and of the conceptual, logico-mathematical or causal co-ordinations in which thought, from the most elementary grasp of consciousness to the highest conceptualization, culminates.

(1) To take just the perceptual data, there is, in fact, a very appreciable difference between the two types of co-ordination, the first having a material and causal character because it involves a co-ordination of movements, and the second being implicative (it establishes connections between significations and not merely between propositions). It follows that the anteriority and autonomy of the co-ordinations of the action, and also their limitations (since, from a certain level onwards, they have to be first completed, then directed and finally replaced by the co-ordinations of thoughts) are due to the fact that being material they must proceed by systematic steps, thus ensuring continual accommodation to the present and the conservation of the past, but impeding inferences as to the future, distant space and possible developments. By contrast, mental co-ordinations succeed in combining all the multifarious data and successive data into an overall, simultaneous picture, which vastly

multiplies their powers of spatio-temporal extension, and of deducing possible developments. But they do so at a price, for when thought does not submit to strict rules of composition, it readily falls prey to distortions, false reconstructions of the past, false readings or interpretations of the present, and to mistaken speculations about the future.

This contrast between step-by-step material co-ordinations and co-instantaneous mental co-ordinations, on which we have dwelled in our studies of the sensorimotor intelligence, was also reflected in all the experiments discussed in this book. Thus, if we take the case of the dominoes (chapter 2), it is clear that all the initial con- nections were of a physical nature and established step by step. A domino is a material object. Dropping it on a second so as to drop the second on a third, involves a movement of the hand and pressure of one domino on the next – so many physical sequences learned from previous experiences and preserved by motor schemata so that there is no need for mnemonic recall. That the first domino must be close to the second, since too great a gap between them will prevent their contact, is once again a physical condition imposed by experi- ence, etc. The fact, moreover, that these material co-ordinations are effected step by step is perfectly clear: before stage II, our subjects do not even anticipate that if the first domino causes the second to fall over and that if the second has the same effect on the third, then the fall of the first must necessarily have an effect on the fourth – the latter is 'too far away'. Even at the beginning of level IIA we still find intermediate subjects (e.g. CRI, ARI and TIE), who cannot anticipate what will happen to elements beyond the fifth or sixth, unless they are asked about each successive element in turn, when they assume the transitivity or the recurrence of the falls without hesitation.

That being the case, our first problem is to discover how a material and causal co-ordination can lead to knowledge that, although limited to 'know-how' and not attaining to representation or comprehension, nevertheless elaborates structures foreshadowing operational structurations, which are the most general co-ordinations of actions (order, colligations, correspondences, etc.) and isomor- phous with certain logical co-ordinations. The reason for these cognitive powers inherent in action is, of course, that its causality is not just any causality, but an organic or biological and hence a cybernetic causality, deriving its powers of organization and even of self-organization from 'loops'. In other words, the movements constituting actions do not follow one another in a straight line but are joined together into the relatively closed cycles of schemata, and the latter are teleonomic (goal-directed). These schemata are conserved by their very deployment; they fit the objects they use into these cycles, and this is a process of cognitive assimilation. The latter has remote biological antecedents, and J. Monod has described the stereospecific discrimination[1] which enables proteins to distinguish macromolecules by their shape, and hence to exercise an order-creating function. The fact that these schemata and their assimilatory functions must be guided by perceptive signs naturally poses the question of the elementary consciousness accompanying sensorimotor activity, but though that question has a bearing on the eventual emergence of cognizance, it remains secondary in any discussion of the material functioning of schemata because of the large number of intermedia between the biological releasers and conscious perception. As for the anticipations of the sensorimotor intelligence, they do not involve the constructive deductions needed for the conceptual anticipation of new effects, but are based on prior information and experience: because assimilatory schemata can be changed by accommodation to the objects and are therefore open to various corrections, they are capable of applying to similar situations what has been registered on previous occasions.

In short, inasmuch as action can play a considerable and indeed an essential part in the formation of subsequent knowledge, even while remaining essentially material and causal, it poses a problem bearing on the relations between biology and cognitive activity. But this is not the place for returning to complex questions which we have discussed elsewhere[2]. Our present task is rather to discover if conceptualization and understanding have specific features, even though both proceed from a conscious grasp of mechanisms as different from them as are the co-ordinations proper to the material action.

(2) It is our hypothesis that the most general characteristic of conscious states, from the most elementary grasp of consciousness bound up with the goals and results of actions, to the conceptualizations of the higher levels, is that they express significations and

---

[1] J. Monod, *Chance and Necessity*, Collins Fontana, 1974, pp. 52ff.

[2] See J. Piaget, *Biologie et connaissance*, Gallimard, 1967.

connect them by what, for lack of a better term, we shall term 'signifying implications'.[1] In that case, everything concerning action and its context can be translated into significative representations by means of the usual semiotic instruments (language, images, etc.), though the functional nucleus of the co-ordinations, which is the root of the matter and remains causal on the plane of action, then finds its equivalent on the plane of thought in what is the most direct heir of action: the system of operational co-ordinations that transforms objects of thought in the same way as action transforms material objects. In that respect, an operation is not a representation of an act – strictly speaking, it is still an action since it produces new constructions, but it is a 'signifying' not a physical action in that the connections it uses are implicative not causal. Now at this point, where the union of action and of thought is most intimate, we find a most remarkable isomorphism between physiology and consciousness: the isomorphism of causality and implication,[2] such that, in this particular case, the specific compound of production and conservation characterizing the operation corresponds to a parallel composition on the causal plane. It is in this profoundly unitary sense that we can describe an operation as an internalized action.

Let us now return to the problem of the relations between success and understanding. If the passage from action to conceptualization is a kind of translation of causality into implication, we want to know what progress there is in this second system of expression. Now implication being a connection between significations, this progress takes the following form: whereas the causal co-ordinations of actions help the latter to attain their material goals, which is an important but limited achievement, the system of signifying implications supplies an element not included in either the goals

---

[1] The term 'signifying' is not used here in its linguistic sense, but merely to mark the fact that the implication involved connects two significations and thus enriches them. The linguistic distinction between 'signifier' and 'signified', by contrast, involves two planes that, according to Hjelmslev, must not be *conformal* (= no correspondence of the functions of the derivates of two functives). In this precise sense it is illegitimate to treat logic in general (or our 'signifying implications') as a language. (Louis Hjelmslev, *Prolegomena to a Theory of Language*, Indiana University Press, Baltimore, 1953, p. 72.)

[2] In Vol. I of our *Traité de psychologie expérimentale* (with P. Fraise) we tried to show that the famous principle of psycho-physiological parallelism comes back to this isomorphism.

or in the means, namely the determination of the reasons without which successes remain mere facts without signification. In short, understanding brings out the reason of things, while success is simply their effective utilization, which is admittedly a prerequisite of understanding, but which the latter transcends because it goes on to knowledge that can dispense with action.

This final period of transcendence nevertheless raises a problem. For, if the causal structures are isomorphous with actions and their objects on the one hand, and the implicative structure of thought on the other, the second being confined to supplying reasons for the former, how can we explain the fact that these reasons become autonomous to the point of dispensing with all actual objects? There are two complementary answers to this question. The first is that in seeking reasons for a physical phenomenon (by a causal explanation which the subject constructs with the help of conceptualizations and which is aimed at the effective or objective causality of the phenomenon but remains separate from it), the subject must needs fit the relations he actually observes into a world of possible relations: even in such simple situations as the recurrent fall of dominoes (chapter 2) or the translations and rotations of a series of bars (chapter 6), the subject must, in order to understand the process, be able to construct in thought indefinite series involving recurrence, transitivity or regular alterations, etc., and hence to treat the series he has actually observed as just one sector of this unlimited range of possibilities. Now to extend the research for reasons to the infinite world of possibilities, unquestionably calls for the transcendence of action. In the second place, though, at the level on which concrete operations are elaborated by a continuous exchange between the action from which they proceed and the conceptualization which renders them implicative, conceptualization does not yet transcend action. However, the operational power thus acquired by the subject is extended indefinitely by the construction of new operations on the preceding ones, and these operations of the second and ultimately of the nth degree are extended, for their part, to a world of possibilities that necessarily transcends the bounds of action. In brief, the comprehension of, or the search for, reasons cannot but transcend practical successes and enrich thought to the extent that the world of 'reason' spills over into the world of possibilities and thus surpasses the given reality.

III *From the periphery to the centre and the role of the future*

(1) Given this gradual emancipation of conceptualization, we shall now examine if it, too, proceeds from the periphery to the centre, that is, from the outermost and immediate zones of the interaction *P* between the subject and the object, towards the central mechanism *C* of the co-ordinations proper to the subject and towards the centres *C'* of the inner causality of the object. Now it is clear that the transcendence of action by conceptualization which we have noted throughout this work in no way changes the relations between the periphery and the two centres *C* and *C'*, or the equilibrium between progress towards logico-mathematical internalization and progress towards the externalization of the causal explanation which we have described in our *The Grasp of Consciousness*.

Two comments are called for. The first is that, if the transcendence of action by conceptualization (or let us say it now, of the realm of successes by the realm of reason), can be explained by the subject's acquired ability to construct new operations indefinitely on the preceding operations, this does not mean that what we have here are pure constructions without reference to a retrospective movement from the periphery to the centres of the operational structurations: clearly, each new construction is based on elements derived from previous levels by reflexive abstractions. We have dwelled on these processes in the conclusions to chapters 9 and 10, and there is no need to return to them. Now, even before it can proceed by conscious reflections towards 'reflected abstractions', reflexive abstraction already probes into the formative mechanisms, thus drawing closer to the more 'central' regions, and this is true *a fortiori* of reflected abstraction. To take just one example from contemporary mathematics, the concept of 'category' (a class of elements with all its structures) has not been derived from the concept of 'structure' (in Bourbaki's sense) but from the 'applications' or isomorphisms that allowed Bourbaki to determine the existence of their structures: abstraction, in this case, therefore proceeds from the formative mechanisms of the previous system and not from their results. In our terminology, this is a movement from a more peripheral state towards the central region (*C*) of the co-ordinations.

The second comment concerns the process of causal explanation, that is, of externalization. Clearly, proceeding as it does from the most obvious phenomena, explanation, even at the higher levels of scientific thought, never does more than shift the problem, or rather it raises new problems: starting with a model A which elucidates the peripheral phenomenon P it proceeds to a search of the 'why' or the 'how' of a particular transformation of the model A, whence the need for a new model B concerned with one of the aspects of A, and so on by an infinite alternation of whys and hows. We do not have to dwell too long on this point to realize that this series of 'reasons' approaches the central regions C' of the object by successive approximations.

Now it is remarkable that even in regions where conceptualization overspills into action, as in the experimental work of the physicist (and not merely in the trials and errors of subjects at levels IA–II examined in this work), there is a constant correlation between progress in interiorization (towards C) and progress in externalization (towards C'): sometimes it is the structures and the operators constructed by the autonomous thought of the mathematician which serve, *a posteriori*, as explicative instruments in physics (as happened in relativity theory and in several branches of microphysics): at other times it is the discovery of new experimental facts which poses fresh problems and demands the construction (by reconstruction, and not by imitation or reflection) of new mathematical instruments (as happened with spins, with Dirac's delta function and with Schwarz's theory of distributions). Viewed from the psychological point of view, what we have here is a spectacular extension of that constant equilibrium between the movements of interiorization and externalization which can be discerned from its modest beginnings in operational structures and causal explanation based on the experimental actions of the children.[1]

(2) This form of equilibrium being one aspect of the general process

---

[1] It might be objected that, in the history of western science, deductive mathematics was born among the Greeks, while experimental physics did not develop until the seventeenth century. But while this is indeed a considerable time lag, its full significance seems to bear less than one might think on the fundamental processes of interiorization and externalization in the sphere of non-axiomatized structures. In fact, in the sphere of axiomization and even of 'reflexive abstraction', the Greeks at no time arrived at mathematical structures of any generality whatsoever: no systems of co-ordinates; no algebra (except, in part, for Diophantine analysis), no fundamental groups, etc. One can even go so far as to say that the Greeks did not grasp the cognitive role of operations. In physics, accordingly, their understanding did not go beyond common sense, except for astronomy, Pythagorean harmonics, atomism, and Archimedean statics. In the seventeenth century, by contrast, the decisive advances of the operational approach

of equilibration[1] characterisitic of the development of the cognitive function, it may be useful to devote a few lines to a problem that arises whenever the relationship between understanding and success is examined. The stages in the development of effective action are invariably functions of goal-directed relations, that is of long- or short-term projects, while understanding or finding reasons, though it may also be said to aim at a permanent and global end, is much more strongly influenced by general processes of equilibrium than by clearly differentiated goals. What then is the relationship between finality and equilibration?

In his posthumous *Marxisme et sciences humaines*, L. Goldman maintains that 'the future is an essential dimension of all generalized forms of genetic structuralism' (p. 25), in which it appears 'as a determinant of the present'. He speaks of the necessary intervention of finalism in the classical sense but, in another passage, he also grants the existence of 'forces of dynamic equilibration directed towards the future' (p. 25). Now here we have a series of problems: it is not the future itself which determines the present but the desire to attain in the future a result anticipated in the present. On the other hand, it is clear that neither this conscious desire nor these anticipations suffice to explain the process of equilibration, which alone renders possible the gradual realization of these projects. One of the problems raised by the complex expressions of cognizance and conceptualization characterizing our successive stages, is therefore the relationship between conscious finality and the equilibratory regulations open to

in mathematics, marked by the emergence of algebra, analytic geometry, and infinitesimal calculus, prepared the way for experimental and theoretical physics and ultimately for the development of a methodical approach based on mathematics. Before that happened, physical experimentation consisted exclusively, as it does for our subjects at stages II and III, of more or less highly refined qualitative observations or manipulations (of the kind Aristotle was content to employ), except for Pythagoras and Archimedes who did use a quantitative approach but were unable to generalize it into a kinematics or a dynamics. The beginnings of modern physics, by contrast, were marked by a form of experimentation both systematic and metrical (and being systematic because it was metrical even in the case of the mental experiments performed by Galileo), extended to the problems of motion and dynamics and, in this respect, forming no exception to the reciprocity of interiorization and externalization. In particular, though the logico-mathematical construction of the instruments of quantitative co-ordination have thus presided over the rise of modern physics, at these higher levels of reflexive abstraction, we must not neglect the reciprocal role of physical preoccupations in the construction of analytic geometry and of infinitesimal calculus.

[1] First of sub-systems, and then of differentiation with integration.

the future during the passage from any one level to the next, but in a form that is today considered to be 'teleonomic' and causal rather than 'teleologic' or 'final' in the old sense.

To begin with action, a first and essential factor in the succession of stages is the pursuance by the subject at each level and in each particular situation of a more or less conscious aim (what is generally referred to as 'the motivation' of the action), be it only to fulfil his assignment. However, a series of derived aims is added as the subject proceeds: first of all the discovery of the means needed to correct the action in case of failure, and then the search for the reasons of the failures and (though perhaps with a time lag) of the successes. Yet three types of fact show that what we have here is not 'finality' in the classical sense of the term, that is, no effect of the future on the present.

In the first place it is not the future as such which plays a part in these goals, but the representation of what is to be attained in the future, which is quite a different matter: that representation admittedly constitutes an anticipation, but one that reduces to an inferential or implicative process in the present, always founded on prior, not on ulterior, information. In the second place, contrary to the finalist concept of 'final causes', according to which the end determines the means, all of the goals we have mentioned merely give rise to a search for, and not to the discovery or deliberate invention of, the appropriate means. In the third place, no matter whether the initial aim of the subject's actions is guided by the assignment or by a spontaneous intention, the secondary or 'derived' ends do not stem from this initial goal but are thrown up by the subject's trials and errors and hence by the very process of equilibration.

What then is this process, considered from the point of view of finality? Let us recall, first of all, that in human behaviour a goal corresponds to a need, and that this need is the expression of a want, in other words of a state of disequilibrium, and that the satisfaction of that need constitutes a re-equilibration. Let us also recall that, though gradual progress towards equilibrium involves a direction, it never involves finality, much as, in thermodynamics, the increase in entropy, though admittedly directed, is not finalized, whatever Duhem may have to say about it. True, in cognitive equilibration there are two aspects that seem to evoke finality: the increasingly anticipatory nature of the regulations (of correction or co-ordination) and the fact that every stage prepares the way for the next. But an anticipation, as we have just stressed, is simply an inference based on previous information, and hence does not imply finality. As for one stage preparing the way for the next, what is involved is, on the one hand, the persistence of gaps and, on the other hand, the new possibilities opened up by new acquisitions. The result is a new equilibrium in a direction determined both by the gaps and also by these recent achievements. As for the regulations ensuring this new equilibrium, which J. Monod has rightly or wrongly compared to Maxwell's demon (whose energy balance has been drawn up by L. Szilard and L. Brillouin), it admittedly introduces a 'teleonomy' into the co-ordination of the anticipations and retroactions but only in the sense that cybernetics speaks of a 'mechanical equivalent of finality', that is, in accordance with circular (feedbacks), not linear, causal relations.

All in all, this future-directedness which Goldman rightly describes as a necessary dimension of any explanation in genetic structuralism, in no way implies that the future acts on the present, or finalism in the classical sense, but rather a (partly or wholly) directed development, in other words the intervention of a direction in the vectorial and not in the anthopomorphic sense.

Now, if this is true of action, it is *a fortiori* the case with conceptualization: the search for the reasons to justify an assertion or to explain a phenomenon leads to solutions that raise new problems demanding new solutions, and so on. This succession admittedly involves a direction, but one that can only be identified after the event (especially the direction leading from P to C and C'), and certainly no finalism in the sense that future solutions determine present solutions. In other words, this direction oscillates between determination by the past and openness to unpredictable innovations: this happens at every successive stage of development because it is only by means of deductive instruments constructed at that stage that the new and unforeseen construction can be shown to be necessary in retrospect. This is particularly true of mathematical creations which are neither discoveries, because the entities thus constructed did not exist beforehand, nor inventions because their creator is not free to modify them at will – they are constructions with the particular property of imposing themselves of necessity just as soon as they are completed and closed on themselves, but never during their elaboration. In respect of teleonomy, they thus

227

provide a typical example of a direction without finalism, which is precisely the characteristic of an equilibration.

IV *Affirmations and negations*

In the construction of equilibrium, and also in the various stages and conceptualization of an action we have examined, we came up time and again against a problem discussed in detail by B. Inhelder, H. Sinclair and M. Bovet in their work on learning,[1] and of which I myself intend to make an epistemological study: the role of conflicts and contradictions whose elimination is an essential factor of development: it involves disequilibria and the re-establishment of equilibrium.

In this connection we might draw attention, among the results discussed in the present work, to a remarkable reaction which plays a role in these contradictions but which, above all, throws light on the existence of the initial disequilibria: the general primacy, during the early stages, of affirmations or of the positive aspects of the actions to be performed.

Now it is clear that, though an action is always directed towards an aim (inasmuch as it is an active anticipation and not a causal effect of the future on the present), and though this aim is essentially positive (because a negative aim is nothing but a means of reaching another positive aim), it is nevertheless a fact that every action tends to change or negate an initial state in favour of a new one. The same is true of operations: to join an element A to an element B means first of all removing A from its initial position in such a way that, at the level of concrete operations, where an addition is effected by displacement, an additive operation presupposes a subtraction. Moreover, every operation involves an inverse operation, etc. In short, there is no cognitive activity, be it a material action or a mental operation, in which the positive elements are not fully compensated, as a logical necessity, by negative elements corresponding to each in turn. Now the systematic reaction of subjects at the more elementary levels is to discount or neglect these negative elements, and to focus attention on the positive, and hence more striking, properties.

---

[1] B. Inhelder, H. Sinclair and M. Bovet, *Apprentissage et structure de la connaissance*, P.U.F., 1974.

Let us look first of all at displacements. A typical example is the construction of equivalent paths (chapter 11): young subjects concern themselves exclusively with the end points and neglect the starting points. Precisely the same thing happens in all similar tests involving two parallel boards or rods, one of which projects beyond the other. Similarly, in the reduction tests (chapter 10), subjects at the corresponding levels believe that they lengthen one of the strings when they pull it up, and never so much as suspect that this effect is offset by the shortening of some other part of the system. There is a similar neglect of the starting point in the case of the dominoes (chapter 2), younger subjects believing that the first will topple the second regardless of the interval between them. In brief, whenever there is a displacement, the subject ignores the fact that reaching the end involves a removal from, or a change of, the initial situation.[1]

When we pass from translations to rotations, we find that subjects at level IA (chapter 6) do not realize that in order to raise one end of a pivoting bar they must pull down the other end. The problems of setting the rear wheels of a car or the rudder of a boat (chapters 7 and 8) give rise to similar difficulties.

With weights, which can be used variously to topple an object over or to support it, the initial reaction is to pay heed exclusively to one of these two aspects. Now this seems to have no bearing on negation and merely to reflect the difficulty of keeping two conditions or consequences in mind simultaneously. In fact this is a very simple thing to do whenever the two conditions are not related: to observe and recall that a flower is both pink and scented is not at all difficult since these two qualities involve no contradiction. It is therefore not the 'span' of attention, that is, the extension of its simultaneous field of application, which matters here, but the fact that, because the subject considers one of the characteristics to be positive, he also considers it a negation of the other: now the initial reactions to

---

[1] It is instructive to recall that the first of the laws of modern physics to be established both mathematically and experimentally, namely the law of falling bodies, raised a problem of this kind. Thus J. B. Benedetti, the immediate precursor of Galileo, criticized Aristotle's explanation of acceleration in terms of the proximity of the falling body to its final goal, when, in fact, its velocity increases 'the further it is from its starting point' (quoted by A. Koyre in *Etudes galiléennes*, II, p. 82). And, indeed, a body falling from a higher point travels more rapidly than another when they are at the same distance from the goal, and the qualitative explanation based on the arrival at the goal has no meaning except from a finalist and psychomorphic point of view (e.g. Hull's goal gradient).

weights and counterweights bear out this point precisely, since when the subjects think in terms of the toppling effect, they forget the retaining effect and *vice versa* (chapters 4 and 5). Similarly, with the cards (chapter 1): when young subjects discover that a card held in a vertical position does not lean to the right or to the left, they dwell on this positive aspect and ignore the fact that the card will fall to one side or the other just as soon as their hand is withdrawn. Again, when subjects at stage I discover that $A < C$ and that $B < C$ and fail to deduce that $A < C$, this does not mean that they have forgotten or repressed $A < B$, but merely that they dwell exclusively on the positive value in each of these relations, and hence fail to conclude that $A < B$ excludes $A > B$ or $A = B$, or that the term B in $B < C$ does not represent just any positive element, but an element already qualified by its exclusions no less than by its effective connections. We have always explained non-transitivity by the absence of reversibility in the form of conversions (turning $A < B < C$ into $C > B > A$), but this is not a sufficient explanation as long as the given relations are not qualified by their negative implications (exclusions) as well as by their positive implications.

In our *The Grasp of Consciousness* we listed many similar responses: in the case of the ping-pong balls with a reverse spin, young subjects do not notice that in throwing the ball they press their finger on its back; when building a road up a hill they do not see any need to move back the starting point in order to decrease the gradient, or to do the same with the ball in the catapult tests in order to send it over longer distances, etc.

It would thus seem that the initial primacy of the positive over the negative elements is the general rule and that this rule applies most particularly to the mechanisms of cognizance: quite obviously, affirmations without the complementary negations logically attached to them must lie on the periphery of the subject's activities, because all the observable features are perceived in their positive aspects before giving rise to negations: we perceive that an object is red, or square, or on top of another, etc. well before we register the fact that it is not blue, not round, not placed on the same table, etc., the negative qualities having no significance except in relation to other objects used for comparison, to predictions that do not come true, or to momentary needs that are not satisfied. Moreover, and by virtue of this very fact, the negations lie closer to the more central regions: they involve correlations, co-ordinations and often increasingly complex inferences. We are therefore dealing with a particularly important example of the general progress of cognizance from the periphery to the centre.

In the second place, when the negation is connected to the conditions preceding an action, as in the case of displacements, where the position assigned as the goal of a movement implies a departure from the initial position, this negative element often impedes precocious successes in action, giving rise to more or less persistent failures and necessitating subsequent co-ordinations, as happened, for instance, with the construction of paths of equal length (chapter 11).

In the third place, and especially in the case of gradual successes, the neglect of the negative element introduces all sorts of disequilibria and contradictions, which explains why we started this series of studies with causality, went on to the conscious grasp of the actions performed and their successive co-ordinations, to end up with an analysis of the contradictions and the way they are surmounted.

Finally, both this analysis of general co-ordinations and also the specific question of negations throw up the problem of reflexive abstraction, because the latter is both a constructor of novelties and a restrospective process bearing, as it does, on anterior mechanisms that lend themselves to generalization. As far as the elaboration of negations in particular is concerned, we must ask ourselves just how far they can proceed from empirical abstractions, seeing that they do not spring from immediate observations, and from what point and why they involve reflexive abstractions.

Clearly, though the modest facts assembled in this work may have permitted us to answer a few minor outstanding questions, they continue to pose a host of problems. This may well perturb even the most patient of readers, but does not daunt the research worker to whom new problems are often more important than the accepted solutions.

Index

abstraction, 216; empirical, 151,
160, 162–4, 165–6, 231;
reflected, 217, 223; reflexive,
39, 71, 96, 97, 151, 160, 162–4,
165–6, 217, 223, 224–5n, 231
action, relationship with
conceptualization, 119–21,
210–12, 213–18, 221, 224
additivity, 64, 92, 97
affirmations and negations, viii,
213, 228–31
aid concept, 69
alternation, 101, 110, 111–12,
113–14, 115, 116, 118, 217
Amman, M., 81n
analogy, 146
analysis, 193, 211, 214
Archimedes, 225n
Aristotle, 225n, 229n
assimilation, 213, 220
attribution, 40, 216
autonomy: of action, 213, 214, 218;
of conceptualization, 217, 222

Benedetti, J. B., 229n
Biologie et connaissance, 220n
Bonnet, C. L., 27n
Bourbaki, 223

causality, 27, 33, 38, 39, 40, 49
52, 57, 68, 89, 97, 98, 106,
111–12, 133, 135, 146, 165, 189,
194, 199, 202, 210, 215, 216,
219, 221–2, 223–4, 231;

co-ordination, 148–9, 215, 218,
219, 221; final causes, 226;
inference, 194; transmission,
94, 95
chain reactions, 33, 36, 46, 47,
48, 69
cognitive powers, viii, 1, 11, 80,
103, 130, 134, 164, 191, 199,
210, 211, 216, 219, 225, 226,
228; cognitive assimilation, 220
compensation, 65, 68, 92, 97, 154,
155–6, 158–60, 161, 164, 185,
186, 193, 228; false, 182, 189,
193; non-compensation, 176;
quantitative, 64
composition, 97, 118, 133, 134,
144, 146, 148–9, 163, 219;
deductive, 207; quantitative, 65
comprehension, *see* conscious
understanding
concatenation, *see* chain reactions
conceptualization, viii, 1, 10, 11,
16, 24, 30, 32–3, 40, 41, 51, 52,
56, 57, 58, 63–5, 70–2, 81, 94,
97, 98, 100, 113, 117, 119, 134,
164, 191–3, 202, 218, 220, 225,
227, 228; anticipation, 220;
autonomy, 217, 222;
co-ordination, 218; distortion,
103; emancipation, 223;
relational, 59, 66, 71–2;
relationship with action, 119–21,
210–12, 213–18, 221, 224;
systems, 215

232